12-2000
THOMAS M. COOLEY
LAW SCHOOL BOOKSTORE
$26.95

Wills, Trusts, and Estates

D1279235

Editorial Advisory Board

Aspen Law & Business

A Division of

Aspen Publishers, Inc.

Richard A. Epstein
James Parker Hall Distinguished Service Professor of Law
University of Chicago

E. Allan Farnsworth
Alfred McCormack Professor of Law
Columbia University

Ronald J. Gilson
Charles J. Meyers Professor of Law and Business
Stanford University
Marc and Eva Stern Professor of Law and Business
Columbia University

Geoffrey C. Hazard, Jr.
Trustee Professor of Law
University of Pennsylvania

James E. Krier
Earl Warren DeLano Professor of Law
University of Michigan

Elizabeth Warren
Leo Gottlieb Professor of Law
Harvard University

Bernard Wolfman
Fessenden Professor of Law
Harvard University

Wills, Trusts, and Estates
Essential Terms and Concepts
Second Edition

Mark Reutlinger
Professor of Law
Seattle University School of Law

formerly published by
Little, Brown and Company.

ASPEN LAW & BUSINESS
A Division of Aspen Publishers, Inc,

Copyright © 1998 by Mark Reutlinger

All rights reserved.
Printed in the United States of America
ISBN 1-56706-767-0

This publication is designed to provide accurate and authoritative information in regard to the subject matter covered. It is sold with the understanding that the publisher is not engaged in rendering legal, accounting, or other professional services. If legal advice or other professional assistance is required, the services of a competent professional person should be sought.

—From a *Declaration of Principles* jointly adopted by a Committee of the American Bar Association and Committee of Publishers and Associations

No part of this book may be reproduced or transmitted in any form or by any means, electronic or mechanical, including photocopy, recording, or any information storage and retrieval system, without permission in writing from the publisher. Requests for permission to make copies of any part of this publication should be mailed to:

Permissions
Aspen Law and Business
A Division of Aspen Publisher, Inc.,
1185 Avenue of the Americas
New York, NY 10036

1 2 3 4 5

Library of Congress Cataloging-in-Publication Data

Reutlinger, Mark.
    Wills, trusts, and estates : essential terms and concepts / Mark Reutlinger.— 2nd ed.
        p.   cm.— (Essentials for law students)
    ISBN 1-56706-767-0
    1. Inheritance and succession—United States—Terminology.
    2. Will—United States—Terminology.   3. Trusts and trustees—United States—Terminology.   I. Title.   II. Series.
    KF753.Z9R48   1998
    346.7305'2—dc21   97-50050
                                                                            CIP

About Aspen Law & Business, Law School Division

In 1996, Aspen Law & Business welcomed the Law School Division of Little, Brown and Company into its growing business—already established as a leading provider of practical information to legal practitioners.

Acquiring much more than a prestigious collection of educational publications by the country's foremost authors, Aspen Law & Business inherited the long-standing Little, Brown tradition of excellence—born over 150 years ago. As one of America's oldest and most venerable publishing houses, Little, Brown and Company commenced in a world of change and challenge, innovation and growth. Sharing that same spirit, Aspen Law & Business has dedicated itself to continuing and strengthening the integrity begun so many years ago.

ASPEN LAW & BUSINESS
A Division of Aspen Publishers, Inc.
A Wolters Kluwer Company

To my father and to Analee and Eliana; and in memory of my mother, Esther Reutlinger.

Summary of Contents

PART I:

ESTATES   1

PART II:

TRUSTS   141

Contents

PART I:

ESTATES   1

Contents

Contents

Contents

Contents

Contents

Contents

Contents

Preface

In considering changes in this book for its second edition, I sought comments and suggestions from those who market, use, or recommend it. The primary message I received was that the book worked very well as it was and I should not tamper with a good thing. In other words, "If it ain't broke, don't fix it." I decided to take that advice. On the other hand, there were things I could add to the existing text to enhance its usefulness and value. Therefore, there are two major changes in this edition, one in form and the other in substance. Both are intended to make the book more "user friendly" and even more adaptable to every course approach than it already is. On the formal side, I have italicized all definitions, the first sentences of each entry. This format, which I first used in my Evidence book for this series, has proved a useful way to set the short definition apart from its explanation and examples and to make use of the book as a quick reference even quicker.

Substantively, I have added references to the Uniform Probate Code and a separate table (following the Master Word List) showing where each reference can be found. I recognize that some Estates and Trusts courses put heavy emphasis on the UPC, and even those that do not may use it occasionally for purposes of comparison. All of the major casebooks contain extensive references to or set out substantial portions of the UPC. While the first edition mentioned the UPC in certain contexts where it provided an example of a particular way to approach an issue, most entries did not refer to it at all, much less cite the relevant UPC sections. The second edition does contain such references, as well as a means of working from a known UPC section to a discussion of its subject matter.

The Uniform Probate Code was first enacted in 1969, and in 1990 there was an extensive revision (followed by periodic amendments ever since). Although the 1990 version of the UPC is largely identical to the original 1969 Code in substance, there are areas in which there have been significant, and in some instances very controversial, changes. Many states that adopted the 1969 Code have not (at least to date) replaced it with the 1990 version or have changed only certain parts; and some states that have generally adopted the 1990 Code have rejected some of its more controversial provisions. Thus although most references to the UPC in this second edition are to the current, 1990 version as most recently amended, where I considered it important I have included references as well to the original 1969 Code. A designation "UPC(69)" indicates the pre-1990 version of the Code, that is (unless otherwise stated), the original version plus any amendments predating the 1990 revision. There is also a separate list of references for the 1969 Code.

In addition to UPC references, I have added many new terms and concepts, primarily those that have become more prominent in the standard estates and trusts course than they were a few years ago. Thus, for example, devices such as the "supplemental needs trust" and "durable power of attorney," which permit the estate planner to take disability or incompetency into account, have become important adjuncts to their more traditional cousins and are included in this updated edition.

I hope this "new and improved" version of *Wills, Trusts, and Estates: Essential Terms and Concepts* will prove to be even more helpful, and make life a little easier for even more students, than the first edition. As before, I would be pleased and grateful to receive your comments, positive or negative. They will be considered most seriously, and they probably will influence a future third edition of this book.

Mark Reutlinger
Tacoma, Washington
January 1998

Acknowledgments

I wish to thank Dean Jim Bond and the Seattle University School of Law for the support and encouragement that made possible the publication of this book. In addition, I appreciate the comments and suggestions of my colleagues William Oltman and John Weaver and the substantial assistance of my secretary, Nancy Ammons (who suffered through many drafts and more than one computer crisis), and the editors and staff at Little, Brown and Company and its successor, Aspen Law and Business with whom I worked on this and the previous edition. Finally, I thank my students—past, present, and future—for and because of whom, after all, I have written this book.

About This Book and How to Use It

1. Functions of This Book: When and Why to Use It

One of the most difficult aspects of a student's attempts to master a legal subject is the new, esoteric language that each subject employs. As a student you encounter not only unknown words but also unfamiliar concepts requiring more explanation than a dictionary definition can provide. Moreover, these terms and concepts are not necessarily encountered in the order in which they are taken up in class; they appear all along the way, since it is difficult or impossible to cover early materials (and edit early cases) without referring to concepts that will be more fully discussed later.

Even after you have studied a topic in class, there will be specific terms and concepts that you no longer recall (or fully understand) when they arise in a later context or when you are reviewing for exams. Resolving this problem may call for anything from a simple definition to a more detailed discussion complete with examples.

Of course, you can look up individual words in a law dictionary; there they are briefly defined and scattered throughout the book, with no immediate connection to one another. At the other extreme, you can turn to a full treatise, look for the term or concept in the index, and, if you are fortunate and the index contains what you are seeking, you can read a lengthy discussion that at some point and in some manner relates to the term or concept in question. Most often, however, the index either is insufficiently detailed and lacks the particular term in question or contains the term but leads to a much broader discussion than you want at this stage.

What you need for all these related purposes is a quick-reference text geared to specific terms and concepts. This is that book. It is neither a legal dictionary nor a treatise. It goes beyond mere definition of terms and concepts but does not purport to cover all their legal implications and permutations. It is, rather, intended to be used as a companion to your casebook or text. As such it has been organized for use in two principal ways:

(1) As a quick-reference glossary of definitions and explanations of individual terms or concepts in the law of estates and trusts. In this mode, it is a resource for the times when, in reading an assignment, you encounter a term or concept that has not yet been covered in the course or whose meaning you cannot immediately recall. Even if a term or concept is vaguely or generally recalled, reference to it in these pages will offer another definition that may solidify your understanding of it. Many entries include detailed examples that supplement those in your casebook or class notes.

(2) As a brief overview of a given area of the law of estates and trusts. While not intended as a comprehensive text (and containing none of the case or statute references of a research volume), this book is structured by topic so that it can be read as a unified discussion by moving through a chapter from one entry to the next. At the beginning of most topics and subtopics, a brief introduction sets out the general content and organization of the material that follows. This topical format can serve several related purposes: It can be used to survey briefly an area of the law prior to detailed treatment of that area in the course, familiarizing you with the meaning of the major terms and concepts before they are encountered, and puzzled over, in the assigned materials. This should make your subsequent reading of the cases and other materials easier and more productive. It can, of course, be used for exam review. And because related terms and concepts are placed together in logical order, you are encouraged to read beyond the initial entry that you looked up to learn about related concepts, thus putting the discussion into context and resulting in a better understanding of the relevant area of law.

2. Format of the Book: How to Use It

As indicated, terms and concepts in this book are set out in logical, not alphabetical, order. To find an item alphabetically, simply look it up in the Master Word List in the back of the book, where you will find the page on which it is principally discussed. To look up an item according to its topical placement, turn to the beginning of any chapter and review its table of contents, where each term or concept is listed in the order in which it is found in that chapter.

Principal terms and concepts are set out in **bold type** prior to their discussion. Within any entry, other terms or concepts that are primarily explained at that point are similarly set out in **bold type**. If a term or concept is primarily defined or discussed elsewhere in the book, it is in normal type. If you wish to find that discussion, simply look up the word in the Master Word List. By using cross-references you can obtain a more comprehensive understanding of the concept that you first looked up. However, each entry is intended to be self-contained and generally should not require reference to any other.

There are also frequent references to the Uniform Probate Code (UPC), as revised in 1990 and amended since, and a few references to the original, 1969 version of the UPC (as amended before 1990). References to the current Code are simply designated "UPC," while those to the original version are referred to as "UPC(69)." Both current and original references can be found in separate lists that follow the Master Word List.

3. Notes on Style

You will note the frequent use in this book of terms such as "general" and "usual." Because it is not the purpose of the book to set out "all of the law" in an area, but only to familiarize you with the general meaning and application of a term or concept, in most instances no attempt is made to account for all possible variations of a definition or doctrine that states might have developed. Thus reference is made to the "general" rule, what is "usually" done, or what "most" statutes provide. If you are concerned with the law or practice in a specific jurisdiction, you should be sure to seek this information in an appropriate text or statute, and you should not assume that the general statement set out here necessarily applies to your state. (The diversity of state probate law is discussed further in the entry under "Probate Code.")

The terms "state," "jurisdiction," and "statute" (as in "some states [jurisdictions] [statutes] require . . .") are usually used synonymously and interchangeably for stylistic variety, not to connote different concepts or legal entities.

The definition or explanation of a term or concept in this book relates specifically to the subjects of estates and trusts, although there may be other meanings or usages of the term outside these fields. The term "limitation," for example, is defined here according to its use in a will or trust; it has a much wider meaning in general usage and in other legal contexts.

In diagrams, where some parties are underlined and others are not, a party who is underlined is alive; others have predeceased. An equal sign (=) indicates marriage.

4. Topical Organization: An Overview

Because the organization of this book is similar to that of most casebooks in estates and trusts, you should be able to follow in it the progress of the course. The book is divided into two parts, the first covering estates and the second trusts. (Of course, much overlap exists between these two parts, and necessarily some entries are found in one part that could easily have been placed in the other.) Each part is divided into chapters representing the major topics in the course and in the law of estates and trusts. Within a chapter, terms and concepts are set out and discussed individually in a logical, unified order. Subheadings are used to indicate a logical breakdown of subtopics within a chapter, and each chapter and subheading begins with a brief overview of the material to follow.

Here is a synopsis of the topics covered. (You may want to look up any of the terms you do not recognize, as they are all explained in the chapters that follow.)

Part 1 begins with a general chapter explaining the various common-law and statutory sources of the modern law of estates and trusts. The subject of intestacy begins the first substantive chapter (Chapter 2), covering terms and concepts relating to persons dying without a valid will. Chapter 3 introduces wills and the formalities of their execution, while Chapters 4 and 5 discuss circumstances (such as incapacity or fraud) that give rise to will contests and the manner in which wills are revoked and revived again. Chapter 6 explores various changes in circumstances between the time of a will's execution and the testator's death (or beyond) that can affect the will's provisions, and Chapter 7 sets out the rules for construing those provisions, including the admissibility of extrinsic evidence of the testator's intent; a separate section is devoted to construction of future interests. Chapter 8 covers the special rules relating to the documents that make up the entire "will" of the testator, while Chapter 9 discusses a number of restrictions that might be imposed by the testator or by rule of law. Chapter 10 explains the many instruments, such as life insurance policies and joint tenancy agreements, that can serve as substitutes for a will in passing property at death. Part 1 concludes with Chapter 11 on the subject of probate and administration, the manner in which a will is validated and the property of the decedent is distributed to the estate's beneficiaries.

Part 2 begins in Chapter 12 with, as you would expect, the general components and characteristics of trusts, followed in Chapter 13 by the rules for altering or terminating an interest in a trust. Chapters 14 and 15 digress to discuss the unique concepts of powers of appointment and the much-maligned Rule Against Perpetuities. Chapter 16 then covers the special case of charitable trusts. Finally, Chapter 17 explains the rules governing the powers, duties, and liabilities of trustees and other fiduciaries who control and administer estates and trusts.

This is the logical order in which these topics generally arise. But the book is meant to be used in any order, topic by topic or term by term. Turn to it often and let it help you around and through both the basic and the more esoteric concepts in the law of estates and trusts.*

---

*This is the only footnote you will find in this book, and it is on a wholly extraneous subject. You might notice that while in some chapters the names used for examples of concepts are merely random or alphabetical (or occasionally historical), in others the names are literary allusions, in the very loosest sense of that phrase. You may choose, wisely, to ignore this feature, as it has no bearing on the substance of the material. If, however, you would like to match the names to the book, play, operetta, and so forth, from which they have been taken and are curious about any of the references, I invite you to write to me in care of my publisher, and I will be pleased to tell you from what source, if any, the names were appropriated.

Wills, Trusts, and Estates

PART I
ESTATES

1

In General: Sources of the Law

A.   INTRODUCTION AND OVERVIEW OF CHAPTER

The sources of the law of estates and trusts are ancient. While this is true of most areas of the law, none is more clearly indebted to, nor more currently dependent on, the law of past centuries. If you awoke a legal "Rip van Winkle" who had fallen asleep in eighteenth century England and slept until today, he would feel right at home with most of modern probate law, although he would feel somewhat less comfortable practicing modern trust law.

This chapter explains the sources of probate and trust law, dividing it into its common-law (nonstatutory) and statutory components. Following a brief explanation of the concept of common law (and the Common Law) are descriptions of the principal Acts of Parliament on which our present probate codes are based and the modern "uniform acts" that influence ongoing revision and reform of those codes. Given some of the directions in which these latter proposals are moving, within a few years it might be necessary for our friend Rip to go back to law school after all.

B. NONSTATUTORY SOURCES OF THE LAW

Common Law

*The general Anglo-American legal system (in contrast with, for example, the **civil law** system, based on Roman law, that prevails in most European countries, the state of Louisiana, and the Canadian province of Quebec); or the body of rules and principles developed by a jurisdiction's courts rather than set out in its statutes.* Much of a state's probate law may be a part of its common law, to the extent it has not been codified; and in every state (except Louisiana) it is derived from the law of wills and trusts that formed part of the English Common Law. On the other hand, as will be seen, the Common Law of England was based largely on a few sixteenth and seventeenth century Acts of Parliament. Often only the context of the phrase tells us whether it is being used to signify the Common Law system or merely the nonstatutory law of any legal system.

Another, more limited use of the term "common law" is in reference to a state (as a "common law state") that does not have a system of community property.

C. STATUTORY SOURCES OF THE LAW

Many statutes have contributed to the development of modern probate and trust law, and today most of that law is codified in state probate codes. This section first discusses these contemporary codifications. It then identifies the principal Acts of Parliament that form the basis for most of those codes.

Probate Code

A state's codification of its probate law. Some states have adopted all or part of a uniform set of probate laws, such as the Uniform Probate Code. Others have codified all or part of the common law of wills or trusts that had developed over time in that state or was borrowed from the English Common Law. The important thing to remember is that while many aspects of probate law are similar or even identical in most states, major differences exist in some areas and minor differences in most. Therefore it is inadvisable to assume that because one state, or several, may follow a given rule or practice, the state with which you are concerned does the same. And it is equally unsafe to assume that because two statutes appear to state the same rule or

practice, both perhaps derived from the same source, they are in fact identical; it is typical for a legislature to adopt a common or uniform rule of law
with the (intentional) addition or deletion of a particular word or phrase,
thus changing the rule in some crucial way. Only a careful reading of the
statute in question can confirm whether this has been done. In sum, the law
of wills and trusts in America (and, for that matter, in all Common Law
jurisdictions) is uniform and regular in its general principles but remarkably
diverse and unpredictable in its particular manifestations.

Statute of Uses, 1536

An English statute that provided the foundation for the modern law of trusts. A
use, the precursor to the modern trust, was a conveyance (by the "feoffor to
uses") to another (the "feoffee to uses") to be held by the latter as owner,
but for the benefit of a third person (the "cestui que use"). In modern terminology, these are the trustor (or settlor), the trustee, and the beneficiary
(or cestui que trust), respectively. The interest of the cestui que use was
equitable rather than legal, enforceable in the court of chancery.

Uses were employed to avoid, among other things, the legal prohibition
against devises of land by instructing the feoffee to transfer the land to a
designated cestui on the death of the feoffor. The Statute of Uses attempted
to abolish this circumvention by "executing" the use, that is, causing the
legal title to pass to the cestui immediately, thus converting equitable into
legal ownership. However, the statute did not apply to uses of personal
property, which continued to be "put into trust"; and it did not execute
"active" uses, in which the feoffee had actual duties to perform. (It also did
not execute a "use on a use," but that is a complication that needn't be
taken up here.) These exceptions became the basis of modern trusts of both
real and personal property. And the loss of the use as a device to pass realty
at death led to the passage of the Statute of Wills of 1540 and the modern
law of wills.

Statute of Wills, 1540

*A statute of England that forms the foundation of the modern Anglo-American
law of wills.* It permitted, for the first time, wills of most types of land. Such
wills had to be in writing, but they did not require a signature or attestation.

Statute of Frauds, 1677

*The English statute that first required (with a few exceptions) that all wills, of
either real or personal property, be in writing and that wills of realty be signed by
the testator and attested.* In many states the requirements for due execution
of wills are based on this statute.

Wills Act, 1837

The English statute that established the procedures for the formal execution of wills (such as signing at the end and in the presence of all witnesses) that still prevail, with modifications, in much of Anglo-American probate law.

D. UNIFORM ACTS AND REFORM PROPOSALS

This final section discusses the modern uniform acts, promulgated by bodies of scholars and practitioners, that would either restate, refine, or in some instances totally alter the traditional approach to estates and trusts. (Their specific proposals are referred to throughout the book, in the discussions to which they relate.)

Uniform Probate Code

A modern, comprehensive set of probate statutes promulgated by the National Conference of Commissioners on Uniform State Laws. The UPC covers almost all aspects of the subjects of wills and trusts. It has been adopted wholly or in substantial part in about one-third of the states, and individual sections have been adopted in almost every state. While the UPC does not have the force of law where it has not been enacted, courts often refer to its terms or commentary as persuasive authority in interpreting similar non-UPC statutes or in applying the state's common law.

The original UPC was promulgated in 1969. It was conceived as an extensive revision of an earlier uniform set of statutes, the Model Probate Code, which was much less comprehensive than the UPC and differed in both language and philosophy. The MPC is seldom cited today. The UPC itself has undergone extensive change. In 1990 substantial parts of the Code (and especially Part Two, dealing with wills, intestacy, and donative transfers) were revised, in some instances radically. Many of the Code's present provisions depart fundamentally from even the more modern current probate codes; it remains to be seen to what extent state legislatures will either adopt the latest proposals or enact local versions of similar effect. Many states that adopted all or parts of the original UPC still retain those provisions and many may continue to do so.

In this book, references to the current UPC, as revised in 1990 and amended since, are designated "UPC [section]"; those to the original version (as amended prior to 1990) use the form "UPC (69) [section]."

Restatements of the Law

A body of uniform laws promulgated by the American Law Institute. (The "ALI" is an organization of prominent lawyers, law professors, and judges.) Like the Uniform Probate Code, Restatements are not themselves law, but they can strongly influence the enactment and reform of state legislation. While the basic mission of the Restatements is to do just that — to "restate" the existing law on a given topic — in recent years the Restatements have often become proposals for change, recognizing but not necessarily restating the law as it currently exists. (The lead taken by the Second Restatement of Torts in the area of products liability is perhaps the most prominent example of this approach.)

The Restatements primarily concerned with the field of estates and trusts are (in their current versions) the **Restatement Second, Property (Donative Transfers), and the Restatement Third, Trusts.**

Before a proposed change in a Restatement is approved by the ALI, it goes through several "tentative drafts" (sometimes 10 or more, over several years) that are circulated to the members of the Institute and are debated at the Institute's annual meetings. As a result, at any given time many tentative drafts are extant, in various stages of finality. Therefore although drafts can be important and persuasive, it is important always to note whether the Restatement one is consulting or citing is a finally adopted "official" version or only a tentative draft.

2

Intestate Succession

A. INTRODUCTION AND OVERVIEW OF CHAPTER

This chapter covers the concept of intestacy, or the succession to property in the absence of a will. It first explains the general concept of intestate succession, after which it traces the familial relationships to the decedent that determine who takes intestate property, in what order of priority. Finally, various doctrines that might limit or change the order of succession are discussed and compared.

B. THE PROCESS

This section briefly discusses the concept of intestate succession and the terms that relate to it. No attempt is made at detailed explanation or examples of the process; these are left for the following section on the relevant relationships.

Intestate Succession

The passage at death of the property of a person who has died without a valid will.
Such a **decedent** (person who has died — not to be confused with the term

"descendant") has "died intestate" and is also referred to as "the intestate." If there was a valid will, the decedent died testate and is referred to as a testator. The rules of intestate succession (or **intestacy**) are set out in each state's probate code. Intestacy laws provide a statutory estate plan, generally intended to pass property as the average intestate would have wished.

Descent and Distribution

The intestate succession of real property (descent) and personal property (distribution, from the Statute of Distribution, 1670). Intestacy statutes thus are often referred to as "statutes of descent and distribution." While the distinction between types of property generally is ignored today, it still may have significance in some circumstances.

Partial Intestacy

Intestacy as to only a part of a person's estate. If a testator has left a valid will that serves to pass only part of the estate (perhaps because one of the gifts was invalid or the terms simply did not cover all the testator's property), the part of the estate that does not pass under the will passes by intestacy, just as if there had been no will as to that part.

Moiety

A part of the estate. The term (which rhymes with "soya tea") is outdated, but occasionally it still is employed to indicate a division of property, as in "the estate is divided into equal moieties."

C. RELATIONSHIP TO THE DECEDENT

If intestate succession is a procedure whereby the property of a decedent who has died without a will is distributed to the decedent's heirs, the key to the intestate succession process is the determination of those heirs and the pattern of distribution among them. This in turn depends on the relationship of surviving family members to the decedent and to one another. This section describes those relationships, sets out their priorities, and demonstrates with the aid of "family tree" diagrams how these concepts are applied.

As mentioned in the Introduction, in the diagrams that follow underlined persons are alive, and "=" indicates marriage.

Heir

A person who is entitled to another's real property by intestate succession. Those entitled to another's personal property are the intestate's **distributees** or **next-**

of kin. The distinction between real and personal property may no longer be significant, and many modern statutes use the term "heir" to designate the intestate takers of any type of property. See UPC 1-201 (21). Similarly, reference often is made (and generally is made in this book) to the "heirs" of a person who is still alive, although technically a living person has no heirs: A person who would inherit from another if the latter died intestate at that moment is called a "presumptive heir" (or **heir presumptive**, in the traditional form of the phrase); one who certainly will inherit when and if another dies intestate, needing only to survive the intestate, is called an **heir apparent**. (The difference is that the heir presumptive, although presently next in line to inherit, may lose that right if someone with a closer relationship or superior claim comes into the picture by birth, marriage, or the like, whereas the heir apparent has a claim that can be defeated only by failure to outlive the intestate.)

Although the technical meaning of "heir" is as indicated above, the term sometimes is used (or misused) to mean "children" or "issue." It also might refer to a person who is not an heir at the decedent's death but who *would* have been an heir had the decedent died at some other time. Generally if the testator's intent is clear, a court will give the term its intended meaning; however, this is a matter governed by the rules of construction and sometimes by statute. (See *"Heirs" (When Determined).*)

Issue

A *person's* **descendants** (*or* **lineal descendants**), consisting of one's children, grandchildren, and so forth down through later generations. (Thus the term is used in the sense of "issue forth," as children do from their parents, in a "descending" line.) See UPC 1-201 (25).

Example 2.1:   In the following diagram, the issue of **A**lbert and **B**etty are Eddy, their son, and Gertrude, their granddaughter. The issue of Conrad and Dora are Fannie, their daughter, and Gertrude, their granddaughter. Gertrude is issue of Eddy and Fannie (parents), Albert, Betty, Conrad, and Dora (grandparents), and all of Gertrude's other ancestors.

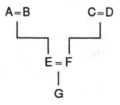

The term "issue" is found not only in intestacy statutes but also in wills, trusts, and other personal documents.

In drafting, "issue" should not be confused with "children," who comprise only one (the first) generation of a person's issue. However, in the construction of a will or other document, a court sometimes will find that the drafter meant one term but used the other, in which case the court must decide whether to reform the instrument in keeping with this intent. Issue never includes relations by marriage, although it may (and today usually does) include adopted and illegitimate descendants. A gift to "issue of the body" designates a fee tail, where that estate is still extant. "Lawful issue" usually, but not always, is construed to include only those born in wedlock.

Ancestors

A person's parents, grandparents, and so forth up through prior generations. Ancestors are sometimes called "lineal ascendants," ascending in a line up from one, as one's lineal descendants descend in a line down. (Put another way, one is always the issue of one's ancestors, and they are the ancestors of their issue.)

A person related to another only by marriage is not considered an ancestor. Two or more persons have a common ancestor when they descend — in the same or different lines — from the same person.

Example 2.2:   In the following family diagram, **Andre** and **Becky** are the parents of **Gary**, and Gary and **Harriet** are the parents of **Monica**. **Clark** and **Dena** are the parents of Harriet and **Ian**, and so forth. Monica's ancestors are Gary and Harriet (parents), Andre, Becky, Clark, and Dena (grandparents), and the parents and earlier ancestors of Andre, Becky, Clark, and Dena. Harriet and Ian are siblings, sharing Clark and Dena as parents (and, technically, common ancestors). Monica and **Nicky** are cousins because their parents Harriet and Ian are siblings. Moreover, Monica and Nicky share the common ancestors Clark and Dena, their grandparents on one parent's side. Each, of course, also has ancestors in the other parent's line (Andre and Becky, **Elton** and **Flora**), who are not common. **Olivia**, on the other hand, whose parents are **Kirk** and **Lena**, is related to the other family members only by affinity (marriage), and so (at least so far as this diagram indicates) shares no common ancestors with them.

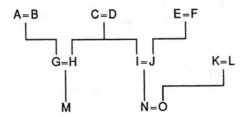

It should be clear that, because everyone (notwithstanding recent biotechnological anomalies) has two parents, four grandparents, eight great-grandparents, and so on, the higher (earlier) one goes in search of ancestors, the more rapidly their numbers increase. Yet if one proceeds far enough back, by Biblical reckoning we all share the same two common ancestors, Adam and Eve.

Collateral Relatives

A person's blood relations (relations by consanguinity, as opposed to affinity, or marriage) other than ancestors or issue. If two or more persons share a common ancestor but descend in different lines, they are collaterals. The clearest example is one's brothers and sisters, but also included are uncles, aunts, and cousins.

Example 2.3: In the following diagram, Lon's collateral relatives are Harry, his uncle, and Kate, his cousin. Harry's collaterals are Ida, his sister, and Lon, his nephew.

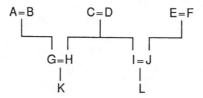

Those relatives descended from (issue of) one's parents (siblings, nephews, nieces) are called **first-line collaterals** because they are in the first line down after one's own issue; the issue of grandparents are "second-line collaterals." In the above diagram, any other issue of Ida and Jaime (Lon's parents) would be Lon's first-line collaterals, whereas issue of Ceasar and Dottie or Ephraim and Fay (Lon's grandparents) would be Lon's second-line collaterals, and so forth upward to great-grandparents' issue and beyond.

Consanguinity

Relationship by blood. Relationship by marriage is referred to as **affinity**. (The term **relatives** usually encompasses both categories.) Technically, one spouse is related by affinity to the other spouse's blood relatives (but, interestingly enough, not to the other spouse), and the blood relatives of each are related by "secondary affinity." The more common term for such relationships, of course, is **in-law**, which signifies that the only relationship between two persons is a result of the status "in law" of (someone's) marriage.

Example 2.4: In the following diagram, Franklin is related to James (son), Avery and Bobbie (parents), and Elwood (brother) by consanguinity, but to Candance and Delbert (parents-in-law) and Kami (daughter-in-law) by affinity and to Hiram and Iris (daughter-in law's parents) by secondary affinity.

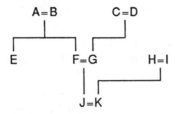

With a few exceptions, property passes to an intestate's spouse and/or blood relations; relations by affinity (in-laws) generally are not provided for under the laws of intestacy. See UPC 1-201(33).

Half-blood

A person who is related to another through only one common ancestor. The clearest example is one's half-brother or half-sister, the child of one's father but not of one's mother, or vice versa. ("Whole-blood" or full siblings share the same father and mother.) Since one's ancestors and issue are necessarily all related by full blood (one cannot have a "half-son" or a "half-grandmother"), we are generally speaking here of collateral relations. Half-blood relations are the result of second marriages, issue outside of marriage, and similar causes of sharing only one parent in common.

Example 2.5: In the following diagram, assume that **Dyan** is the daughter of **Abe** and **Bianca**; after Dyan's birth Bianca divorced Abe and married Conway, by whom she had another daughter, **Elise**. Elise and Dyan thus share the common ancestor (mother), Bianca, but have different fathers (Abe and Conway): Elise and Dyan therefore are half-sisters. (Of course, the same would be true if, for example, without the benefit of divorce Bianca had borne Elise as a result of adultery with Conway.)

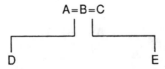

Half-bloods must be carefully distinguished from **steprelatives**, between whom there is no blood relationship. Step relations are created by the marriage of a person whose children are not otherwise related to the other spouse.

Example 2.6:   If, before her marriage to Conway, **B**ianca had daughter **D**yan by first husband **A**be, Dyan is the stepdaughter of Conway. If Conway had been previously married to **X**ena and had a son, **Y**ves, by that marriage, upon Conway's marriage to Bianca his son Yves would be the stepbrother of Bianca's daughter Dyan.

Note, however, that Yves and Elise, like Dyan and Elise, would be half-siblings, because they share the same father or mother, respectively.

Although historically one could not inherit from a half-blood relation, modern statutes generally make no distinction between half-and whole blood relations, both being equally eligible to take by intestate succession. See UPC 2-107. Some statutes, however, do distinguish for certain purposes, primarily (though not always) when there are both half-and whole-blood relations, in which case the whole-blood relations may be favored. In another common variation, whole-blood relations are favored only as to **ancestral property**, that which came to the intestate by gift or devise from an ancestor. If this doctrine is followed, the property descends only to those who are "of the blood of the ancestor" from whom it derived. The ancestral property doctrine is illustrated in Example 2.7.

Example 2.7:   If **E**lise died intestate and if she had a whole-blood sibling (**F**ern, another child of **B**ianca and **C**onway), then **D**yan, Elise's half-sister, might be barred from inheriting from Elise any of Elise's property that Elise had received from her father (ancestor), Conway. Dyan might, however, be permitted to inherit property Elise had acquired in any other manner, including from Bianca, since Dyan is "of the blood" of Bianca but not of Conway.

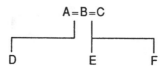

Fortunately, such complications are seldom encountered.

Adopted Child

A person who has become, for purposes of the law, the child of another person (the adoptive parent) by virtue of the adoptive parent's fulfillment of the statutory requirements for adoption. Although for purposes of intestate succession a lawfully adopted child is generally treated today the same as a child born to the adoptive parent, this was not always true. The English law did not even provide for adoption until 1926; some American statutes still draw distinctions between adopted and biological children or are unclear on certain aspects of the adoptive relationship.

Often a jurisdiction's probate statutes are not well coordinated with its general adoption statutes, making it necessary to consult both in order to ascertain what, if anything, they provide with respect to testate or intestate succession. While there are many different variations, typically a modern statutory scheme will deem the adopted child to be the child of the adoptive parents, and no longer the child of the biological (birth) parents (referred to by the UPC as **"natural" parents**), for all purposes. See UPC 2-114(b).

When a statute does draw a distinction, it is often between inheritance *from* the adopted child (or from more remote kindred "through" the predeceased child), and inheritance *by* that child from or through the parents. For example, an adopted child may be permitted to inherit from biological kindred but those kindred not be permitted to inherit from the child. When a gift is to a class like "children" or "issue," adopted children usually are included. See UPC 2-705(a). In some states, however, the **stranger to the adoption** rule may apply, determining inclusion on the basis of whether the donor or testator knew about the adoption (and so presumably had the adopted child in mind) at the time the language in the relevant instrument was drafted. Some states also distinguish between persons adopted as children and as adults, barring the inclusion of the latter unless specifically and expressly intended. See UPC 2-705(c) (to take from anyone but adopting parent, adoptee must have lived in parent's household as a minor). Obviously, it behooves the drafter to ascertain the donor's intention in this regard and to be specific if there is a clear intention either to include or not to include adopted children.

A **stepparent adoption** presents a special case, one that has become fairly common in modern society. For example, if a woman whose child was born out of wedlock (or who is a widow or divorcee) marries, her husband becomes the child's stepparent. If her husband then adopts the child, he generally becomes the child's legal parent for all purposes. Some statutes, however, which use language such as "an adopted child is no longer considered the child of the natural parents" do not take into account that the child's birth mother remains a custodial parent whose rights should not be affected by the child's adoption by her new husband. This can cause considerable confusion and necessitate some fancy interpretive footwork by a court. Modern statutes do take into account stepparent adoptions, although in different ways. They may preserve the child's relationship only with the custodial natural parent, or with both the custodial natural parent and the other natural parent. Compare, *e.g.*, UPC 2-114(b) (stepparent adoption has no effect on child's relationship with *either* natural parent) with the pre-1975 version of UPC(69) 2-109(1) (no effect on relationship with *custodial* natural parent).

A related doctrine is that of **equitable adoption**. A court may decide that the conduct of the intestate was such as to warrant treating a claimant as a lawfully adopted child for purposes of inheritance. The usual bases for such a decision are a failed, good-faith attempt by the intestate to adopt the child, or the intestate's breach of an agreement to do so. In either case, the child would be permitted to inherit from the adoptive "parents," but of course the parents, having no equitable claim on the child's estate, would not be permitted to inherit from the child.

Illegitimate Child

A child born out of wedlock. Historically, an illegitimate child (or, more technically, a **bastard**), often called a **nonmarital child** today, was given no inheritance rights; thus the appellation **filius nullius**, "the child of nobody." Largely because of United States Supreme Court decisions declaring discrimination against illegitimate children to be unconstitutional and the growing incidence of illegitimacy in the United States, such children today are generally accorded the same rights as those born in wedlock. Some legal discriminations, however, still exist in some states, often based on problems of proof: The fact of giving birth is obviously sufficient proof that an unmarried woman is the child's mother for purposes of inheritance, but some more specific proof of parentage (such as an express or implied **acknowledgment** of the child's status) may be required before a man will be recognized as the child's father.

Note that for policy reasons a child born to a woman then married to a man other than the biological father (that is, as a result of adultery) may be deemed the child of the mother's husband, regardless of available proof to the contrary.

When the construction of a will or trust is in question, a court will have to determine whether there was an intent to include nonmarital children in gifts to "children," "issue," or the like. Often a court will follow the state's rules for intestate succession in the absence of a contrary expression of intent. Here, as in the case of adopted children, the drafter should try to anticipate such ambiguities and include or exclude such persons expressly. The term **lawful issue** often is employed to designate those born in wedlock and as a shorthand way to exclude nonmarital children; but given the uncertain "legal" status of nonmarital children today, it bears the risk of mis-interpretation.

Posthumous Heir

A child conceived before but born after the death of the parent. The French term is **en ventre sa mere**, or "in the womb of the mother." For most purposes, a posthumous child will be considered to have been born to the parent as of the date of conception. See UPC 2-108.

The recent advances in the technology of freezing sperm for later in-semination, possibly decades after the death of the father, has led to speculation about inclusion of these "posthumous" children, and to such tongue-in-cheek appellations as "en ventre sa Frigidaire." The law relating to these matters is very much in its embryonic stage.

UPC 2-901(d) (the Uniform Statutory Rule Against Perpetuities — see Chapter 15) addresses the "sperm bank" problem with respect to the Rule Against Perpetuities by declaring that, for purposes of the Rule only, the possibility of a child being born after the parent's death should be dis-regarded.

Representation

The right of a person to take the share of an estate that a predeceased ancestor would have taken (to "represent" the ancestor). If there are two or more rep-resentatives, they divide their ancestor's share. All intestate succession stat-utes permit some form of representation, although they vary greatly in detail. See, *e.g.*, UPC 2-106.

A person can represent only an ancestor who has already died. It is said that one "stands in the shoes" of the ancestor represented, and one can do so only after those shoes have been vacated. By the same token, there can be no representation if the person to be represented has left no descendants to fill the empty shoes.

The technical term for representation is distribution "per stripes" ("by the stocks," or roots), as opposed to "per capita" ("by the heads," or number of individuals), although a scheme of representation may include elements of both types of distribution.

Per Stirpes

A scheme of representation whereby descendants of a deceased taker of a share of an estate receive their ancestor's share. Although the term "per stirpes" (pro-nounced to rhyme with "Murphey's"), which literally means "by the stocks," is sometimes used loosely to refer to any form of representation, a "pure" per stirpes ("stirpital") distribution, also called "classic" or "strict" per stirpes, initially divides property at the level of the original taker's children (the first generation) *even if no child survives*, allocating a share to each surviving child (if any) and each predeceased child who leaves living descendants. See UPC 2-709(c). (More modern schemes make their first division at the first generation with a surviving member. See, *e.g.*, *Per Capita with Representation; Per Capita at Each Generation.*) A pure stirpital distribution would be as follows:

Example 2.8: Iris, the intestate, has died a widow having had three children, Ari, Brigitte, and Camilla; only Brigitte survives her. Ari predeceased Iris, leaving a wife, Wendy, and a son, David; and Camilla predeceased Iris, leaving a husband, Hobart, a son, Eric, and a daughter, Fleur.

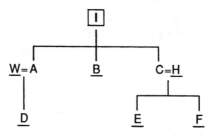

Assuming that the state's intestacy statute directs distribution of Iris's property to her issue by a strict per stirpes scheme, had Ari, Brigitte, and Camilla all survived they would have divided the estate equally. Since Ari and Camilla predeceased Iris, however, neither takes a part of Iris's estate (and so it cannot pass through their own estates to their surviving spouses), but instead they are "represented" by their children. David represents Ari and takes all of what Ari would have taken (one-third of the estate), while Eric and Fleur together represent Camilla and divide Camilla's share equally between them (one-sixth each). Brigitte, of course, takes her one-third. David, Eric, and Fleur have taken "by the stocks" because they took by virtue of being descended from Ari and Camilla, their respective "stocks" or "roots."

 Generally descendants take in their own right, what is now their own share, and not subject to the debts or other obligations of the ancestor they represent.

Example 2.9: In the same family as in Example 2.8, Eric has predeceased Iris, leaving issue. Eric's issue would take Eric's one-sixth share per stirpes:

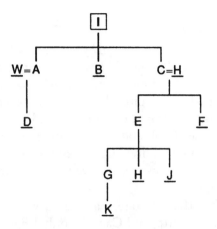

The "stirpes" or stock would be Eric, and his surviving children would take by representation his share (which of course he himself took by representation of his mother, Camilla). They would divide Eric's share equally unless one or more of them had predeceased Iris, leaving issue who would take per stirpes, and so forth through the generations. In the diagram, Eric's children Helena and Jerome have survived Eric, but Gracie has predeceased, leaving her son Kelly. Kelly's share is one-eighteenth.

Example 2.10: Assume now that none of Iris's children survived her; Brigitte predeceased, leaving no issue, but all of Ari's and Camilla's children have survived:

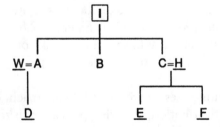

Under a pure per stirpes distribution, the estate would still be divided at the first generation, that of Iris's children. Brigitte (or, more accurately, her estate) would not take a share, since a per stirpes scheme still contemplates representation by a person's descendants, and persons leaving no descendants have left no one to represent them. But Ari and Camilla, having left living descendants, would each be represented by those descendants, who would be allocated the equal shares (one-half each) that Ari and Camilla would have taken had they survived Iris in person. As a result, David would take Ari's share of one-half, while Eric and Fleur would divide equally Camilla's share of one-half, taking one-fourth each.

Per Capita

A scheme of distribution of an estate whereby all individuals of the relevant status take equal shares. A per capita distribution of an intestate estate should be contrasted with one that is stirpital, under which shares of deceased takers are divided among their issue, often leaving some takers with larger individual shares than others. (See Per *Stirpes.*) Under a per capita scheme, persons take "by the heads," literally by counting the heads of those issue who survive the intestate and dividing the estate equally among them, regardless of what their ancestors would have taken had the latter survived.

Example 2.11:   Iris, the intestate, has died a widow having had three children, Ari, Brigitte, and Camilla; only Brigitte survives her. Ari predeceased Iris, leaving a wife, Wendy, and a son, David; and Camilla predeceased Iris, leaving a husband, Hobart, a son, Eric, and a daughter, Fleur. (These are the same facts as in Example 2.8 above.)

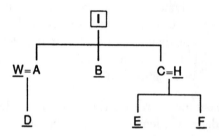

If all the surviving issue (Brigitte, David, Eric, and Fleur) were to take per capita, they would divide Iris's estate four ways, regardless of generation. (As explained in Example 2.8, if the four took per stirpes, Brigitte and David would each take one-third of the estate, and Eric and Fleur would each take one-sixth.)

No modern statute uses a pure per capita approach, but many combine the two systems of distribution, directing per capita distribution to the first generation having living members and representation thereafter. Usually these statutes are worded simply to state that the first generation having living members takes equally, one share for each living member and one for each deceased member who left surviving issue, those issue to take by representation. The equal distribution at the first level is, of course, a per capita scheme, and the representation thereafter is per stirpes; thus the scheme often is called **"per capita with representation."** It also may be called **modern per stirpes.** The original UPC adopted this approach (see UPC(69) 2-106), but the 1990 revision replaced it with "per capita at each generation."

To illustrate, in Example 2.11, Brigitte would be allocated one share because she survived Iris, while Ari and Camilla would be allocated one share each because, although they predeceased Iris, they left surviving issue. Thus the result would be the same as under "pure" per stirpes. However, the important difference between the theories occurs if Brigitte has not survived, leaving a first generation with no living members:

Example 2.12: Assume the only survivors of Iris are Ari and Camilla's spouses and children.

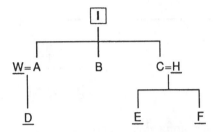

The first generation (of Iris's children) would be skipped over entirely, and the estate would be divided equally (per capita) at the level of grandchildren (David, Eric, and Fleur), they now being the first generation with living members.

This result is quite different from that under a pure per stirpes scheme, as it gives one-third each to David, Eric, and Fleur rather than the uneven distribution of one-half to David (representing Ari) and one-fourth each to Eric and Fleur (representing Camilla). Note that if Eric had predeceased Iris, leaving issue, the generation of grandchildren still would be the first with living members, so initial division still would be in thirds; but Eric's issue would take Eric's third by representation, and so forth through the generations until everyone's "shoes are filled."

Per Capita at Each Generation

A scheme of representation whereby all takers of an estate in a generation are treated equally, regardless from whom they are descended or how many siblings they have. This formula, which has recently been adopted as the primary or an alternative method of distribution by some states and the Uniform Probate Code (UPC 2-106, 2-709(b)), is thought to adhere more closely to what the average person would desire.

According to this theory, distribution is still initially to the first generation having living members, as for "per capita with representation"; but if any deceased members of that generation left living issue, their successors in the next generation do not take their parents' shares by representation, but per capita. Thus:

Example 2.13: Iris, the intestate, has died a widow having had three children, Ari, Brigitte, and Camilla; only Brigitte survives her. Ari predeceased Iris, leaving a wife, Wendy, and a son, David; and Camilla predeceased Iris, leaving a husband, Hobart, a son, Eric, and a daughter, Fleur. (These are the same facts as in Examples 2.8 and 2.11 above.)

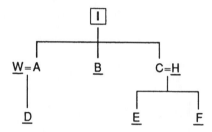

Under per capita at each generation, Brigitte would receive one-third of Iris's estate; David, Eric, and Fleur, instead of taking by representation from their respective parents, would take two-ninths each (per capita, not per stirpes).

Had Eric in Example 2.13 predeceased Iris, leaving issue surviving, his two-ninths share would have been divided equally at the next generation with living members, and so forth. Equality is achieved, one might say, horizontally rather than vertically, as under a pure per stirpes distribution, or individually, as through per capita distribution.

Degree of Kinship

The closeness of the relationship to one's (usually blood) relatives, who are referred to as one's **kin** *or* **kindred***.* Many statutes distribute an intestate's property to the next of kin, in the nearest degree.

Usually the first persons to take by inheritance are the surviving spouse and issue of the decedent, if any; next would come immediate ancestors and first- or second-line collaterals, according to a parentelic principle that favors the closest ancestors or their issue. (Such first takers are sometimes called the "inner circle" because they take before and in preference even to persons who are closer in degree of kinship but lack their preferred status.) Some statutes do not look any farther than second-line collaterals, the next step being escheat to the state (see, *e.g.*, UPC 2-103, 2-105); but others consider next of kin if no close parentelic relatives survive.

There are varying versions of **consanguinity charts** that depict, in effect, a "family tree" and the designations that are given to the relationship between one particular person and that person's blood relations. The following chart illustrates such a relationship between a decedent and the

C. Relationship to the Decedent

decedent's ancestors as far back as great-great grandparents and descendants as far forward as great-grandchildren and their contemporaries.

Consanguinity Chart

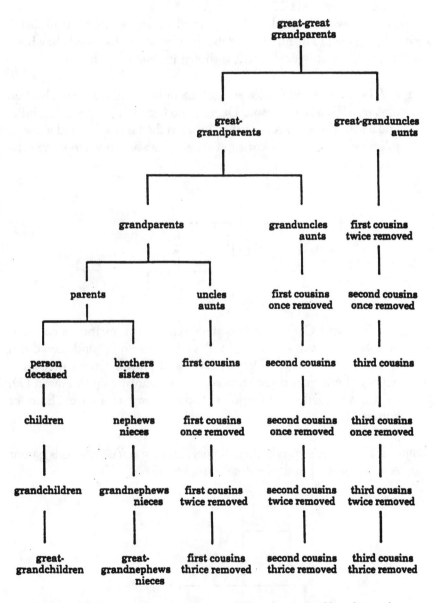

The principal system used for counting degrees of kinship is known as the **civil law system** (a misleading name because of its use by common-law jurisdictions as well). Under this system, one counts the steps, one per generation, between the intestate and each claimant, and the claimant who is the least number of steps from the intestate (the "closest" kin) is entitled to the estate. Counting always proceeds up from the intestate to the nearest common ancestor and then down to the claimant. Thus, for example, on the consanguinity chart the decedent's first cousins once removed and great-granduncles and aunts are all five steps away from the decedent, while third cousins twice removed are 10 steps away.

In the following examples, it is assumed for simplicity that all distribution is by degree of kinship. Parentelic distribution is discussed elsewhere. Also, for simplicity only one parent is shown instead of both.

Example 2.14:   **Bess** and **Carlos** are siblings of Inez. All three are children of **Aaron**. Bess has one son, **Dexter**, and Carlos has a daughter, **Edie**, and a son, **Forrest**. Assume that Inez has died intestate, and we wish to know the degree of kinship between Inez and her surviving relatives.

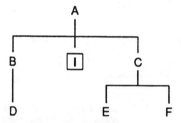

Bess and Carlos are two steps removed from Inez, since it is necessary to count first up to Inez's parent Aaron (1) and then down to Bess or Carlos (2); Dexter, Edie, and Forrest (Inez's niece and nephews) are each three steps removed, counting up to Aaron (1), then down to Bess or Carlos (2), then down to Dexter, Edie, or Forrest (3).

Example 2.15:   Inez's grandfather, **Xavier**, had a son **Yusef**, who is parent Aaron's brother and therefore Inez's uncle:

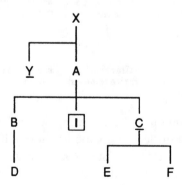

Uncle Yusef is three steps away from Inez, counting up to Aaron (1), then up to common ancestor Xavier (2), then down to Yusef (3).

When, as in the previous two examples, some relatives are the same degree of kindred, some statutes "break the tie" by giving the estate to the one with the nearest common ancestor. (This is called a "parentelic preference.") In Example 2.15, assuming that only uncle Yusef and niece Edie survived Inez, although each is three steps removed from Inez, Edie would prevail because Aaron, the common ancestor of Edie and Inez, is nearer kin to Inez (one step removed) than is Xavier, the common ancestor of Yusef and Inez (two steps removed).

A few states follow the **canon law system** of determining degrees of kinship (so called because it was used by the church to determine who could marry within a family), a system inaccurately but commonly called the "common-law" method. Here one still counts up to the common ancestor and down to the claimant, but rather than combine the two numbers, each is considered separately. The highest of the two numbers for each claimant is the degree of kinship, and the claimant with the lowest degree is, as with the civil law method, the taker.

Example 2.16:   In the family diagrammed in Example 2.15, assume that only uncle Yusef and brother Carlos survived Inez:

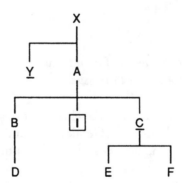

Yusef is one step from common ancestor Xavier, and Xavier is two steps from Inez, making two (the largest of the two numbers between Inez and Yusef) Yusef's degree of kinship. Carlos is one step from common ancestor Aaron, and Aaron is one step from Inez, making one Carlos's degree of kinship. Carlos would thus prevail.

While the above result is the same as under the civil law method, there can be differences:

Example 2.17:   Assume the same family as in the previous examples. Inez is survived only by a grandnephew, Quincy, and a cousin, Zelda:

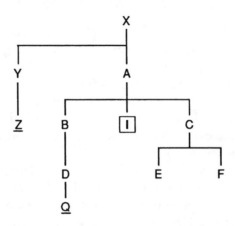

Both Quincy and Zelda would be four steps removed from Inez by the civil law method, and either they would divide the estate equally or, if the parentelic preference was applied, Quincy would prevail because his common ancestor with Inez (Aaron) is closer to Inez than is Zelda's common ancestor (Xavier). Using the canon law method, however, Quincy's degree of kinship is three (the longer of the two branches from Quincy to Aaron and from Aaron to Inez) while Zelda's is only two, making Zelda the prevailing "next of kin."

Parentelic

A method of determining the takers of an intestate estate that gives preference to the intestate's nearest ancestors or their issue.

Example 2.18:   Intestate Ivy has daughter Hepsibah, siblings Ellen and Felipe, niece and nephews Gerald, Jan, and Kermit, father Cory, grandmother Alison, aunt Bonnie, and cousin Dan:

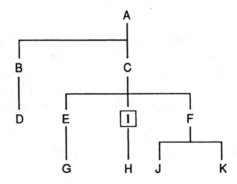

Ivy's issue (here only daughter Hepsibah) are considered to be in the "first parentela." Ivy's parents and *their issue* (other than Ivy and Hepsibah, *i.e.*, Cory, Ellen, Felipe, Gerald, Jan, and Kermit) would be in the second parentela, and Ivy's grandparents and their issue (other than Cory, Ivy, and Hepsibah, *i.e.*, Alison, Bonnie, and Dan) would be in the third parentela.

If a parentelic principle is applied, those surviving relatives in the first parentela (surviving issue) would take ahead of all others; if none survived, those in the second parentela would take, and so forth, all regardless of degree of kinship as reckoned by any other method (that is, no matter how many steps removed from Ivy).

Many statutes use a parentelic principle only for the first or second parentela, and perhaps the third (grandparents and their issue). Thereafter, in the absence of any such relatives surviving, either the property escheats to the state or it goes to the nearest relation as determined by degree of kinship. See UPC 2-103, 2-105.

Note the following overlapping (and possibly confusing) terminology: issue of parents are in the second parentela, but they are considered to be "first-line collaterals"; issue of grandparents are in the third parentela, but are "second-line collaterals," and so forth. (Issue of parents are first, because one's own issue are not collateral relatives.) A look at the "branches" of the diagram above illustrates the reason for this terminology.

D.   LIMITATIONS ON INHERITANCE

Section C set out the usual order of priority and pattern of distribution among family members of an intestate. This section explains the various doctrines that either change that pattern or account for circumstances in which the usual intestate takers are not available.

Escheat

The process whereby property of an intestate passes to the state, for want of any relatives who qualify to take. Statutes differ as to how distant a relative is permitted to take and, therefore, as to when the state takes instead. Many modern statutes, for example, such as UPC 2-103, do not permit relatives to take if they are more remote than second-line collaterals (issue of grandparents), whereas others allow any next of kin, no matter how remote, to take if they can prove their kinship. Very remote relatives are sometimes called **laughing heirs** because it is assumed that they are so little affected by the intestate's death that they "laugh all the way to the bank." Of course, whatever the level of relatives permitted to take before the state, property passes to the state only if none of those designated relatives survives the intestate, can be located, and can prove the necessary relationship. Large estates have drawn hundreds or even thousands of persons claiming to be the intestate's next of kin, and courts have sometimes taken years to sort out the claims. This is one reason a state may prefer escheat to permitting claims by distant relatives.

Advancement

A payment or gift to an heir intended to be part of any eventual intestate share of the donor's estate that might be due the heir. Just as a mother might give her son an "advance" on his allowance before he is due to receive it, reducing to that extent the amount he will receive when the allowance is due, she might also give him an advancement (note the different terminology) on his inheritance, reducing the amount to which he will be entitled if and when she dies intestate.

Advancements usually are limited to payments to a person's children or other descendants, but some statutes include payments to spouses, collateral relatives, or other heirs as well. The doctrine of advancements does not usually apply unless there is total intestacy, on the theory that if there was a later valid will, the testator probably took any advancement into account when executing it; or if there was an earlier will, the testator took its provisions into account when making the payment. Some states, however, do apply the doctrine to partial intestacy.

The two major issues surrounding advancements are determining whether a payment was intended to be an advancement or an outright gift (or perhaps even a loan), and the effect of the payment if it was an advancement. Although early law presumed that any payment to a child (or one in the position of a child) was an advancement, modern statutes often reverse the presumption, and some require that there be a writing specifically indicating the donor's intent that the payment be an advancement. Obviously, these latter statutes result in very few payments being considered advancements. UPC 2-109, which applies to both total and partial intestacy and to any heir, requires a contemporaneous writing by the decedent or a written acknowledgment by the heir.

Assuming that a payment is found to be an advancement, it is taken into consideration when the intestate's estate is distributed. In effect, any person who wishes to take part of the estate that remains on the intestate's death must be willing to credit the estate with the amount of the advancement in order to equalize the distribution among those (usually only children or issue) who received an advancement and those who did not. The process by which this equalization is effected is called **hotchpot**, or "going into hotchpot."

If a child chooses not to claim any of the estate, the doctrine does not attempt to force that child to remit any of the advancement previously received. For this reason a child will claim a share of the estate — will go into hotchpot — only if the amount of the advancement was sufficiently small that the recipient will still receive a share of the estate even after deduction of the advancement. The process is illustrated in Example 2.19.

Example 2.19:   Assume that during his lifetime intestate Isaac made advancements (that is, payments or gifts that were later determined to have been intended as advancements) with a value of $20,000 to son Arlen, of $160,000 to daughter Babette, and nothing to daughter Cindy. He then died intestate with a net estate (at the time of death) of $200,000.

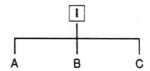

Arlen now claims his share of the estate, and so goes into hotchpot. He credits the estate with his $20,000 advancement (generally valued as of the time he received it, even if it is worth substantially more or less now), making the theoretical total available to distribute $220,000. This is divided by the number of claimants. As we will see, Babette will choose not to make a claim, so there are only two claimants, Arlen and Cindy. Each is allocated $110,000, half of the total. Arlen then subtracts from this augmented share the amount, $20,000, that he received as an advancement, and he takes $90,000; Cindy, who received nothing in advance, takes a full $110,000 share. As a result, Arlen and Cindy are now theoretically treated equally, since each received a total of $110,000, although Arlen received part of his earlier. As for Babette, she will stay out of hotchpot and forgo any claim on the estate. If she were to add her $160,000 back in, and take a one-third share of the resulting $360,000, she would receive less than the amount of the advancement. Clearly she will keep her advancement, stay far away from the hotchpot (an ocean cruise might be suggested), and let Arlen and Cindy divide up the remaining estate.

Note that because of valuation as of the date of receipt, in the above example Arlen and Cindy may not in fact end up with equal amounts; but most states do not attempt to achieve perfect equality. Furthermore, because Arlen put his $20,000 into hotchpot only theoretically, for the sake of calculation, he does not actually have to produce any of the money or property that Isaac advanced to him — a good thing, since it may already have been spent.

If an advancement is made to a child, and that child dies survived by issue, the latter usually are bound by the advancement, but generally only if the advancing parent is survived by other children. UPC 2-109 does not take an advancement to a predeceasing recipient into account unless the decedent's contemporaneous writing indicates otherwise.

Example 2.20: Assume that in Example 2.19 Arlen predeceases parent Isaac, leaving his own child Daisy:

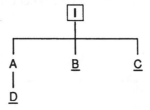

Daisy is bound by the advancement just as Arlen was, because Isaac was also survived by children Babette and Cindy.

Had Isaac died testate (or, in most jurisdictions, even partially testate), both Arlen and Babette would have been entitled to their full share of Isaac's estate (whatever was given them in his will), regardless of the advancements. However, a doctrine of satisfaction applies when a testator gives a legatee what is in effect an advance on a legacy. Thus even if the donor dies testate, it is possible that a pre-death transfer will be credited against the recipient's gift under the will.

If an heir such as Arlen agrees with Isaac that his advancement will take the place of his entire share of the estate, no matter how much that share would otherwise be, the heir has, in effect, given a release of his expectancy to his ancestor.

Expectancy

A mere hope or possibility of receiving a benefit from the death of another. An heir apparent or heir presumptive, or the beneficiary of the will, of a person who is still alive all have no present right to that benefit. However, because they stand to receive property if nothing (such as predeceasing the intestate, execution of a valid will by the intestate, or the testator's change of mind) intervenes to defeat their claim, these holders of expectancies are for some purposes able to deal with their hoped-for future benefits as if they held a true property interest. They may assign it or release it, and they may be protected against fraudulent or other improper tampering with it by others.

Release of Expectancy

The giving up by an heir of a potential claim to an intestate estate (an expectancy). Generally this refers to a release by a child, given to the parent, the latter being referred to as the "source" (of the potential inheritance). Because the expectancy may never come to fruition and is not technically a property right, a release of it can be enforced only in equity and only if fair consideration is given for it. One theory explaining the enforceability of a release is that it is merely a liquidated advancement, a prepayment of an inheritance to an heir with the mutual understanding that it will be the heir's entire share of the estate.

Jurisdictions vary as to the effect of a release on those who would take if the releasor (heir) predeceases the intestate. Commonly a releasing child's children are bound by the release, especially (and under many statutes only) if other children of the source (the releasor's parent) survive.

Assignment of Expectancy

The transfer by an heir of a potential claim to an intestate estate. Because technically the heir has no property interest to transfer, the assignment can be enforced only in equity and if there is a fair consideration for it.

Unlike an advancement or a release of an expectancy, an assignment is a transaction not with the source of the expected benefit but with a third party. For this reason, it does not affect the rights or obligations of anyone except the parties to it (the assignor/heir and the assignee). If the assignor predeceases the source, the assignor's children are not bound by the assignment and they may take their share by representation of their parent; in such a case the gamble by the assignee that the assignor will live to receive an inheritance is lost. The result is similar if the assignor survives the source but still receives no benefit, perhaps being disinherited by the source's will.

Slayer's Statute

A statute that prevents a person who has killed another from inheriting or otherwise benefiting from the latter's estate. (In some states the rule is one of common law, not statute.) States vary as to the types of killings that will disqualify the slayer from taking the victim's estate, but the most common limits the rule to intentional killings without lawful excuse (such as murder or willful manslaughter). Also varying are the types of benefits that the slayer will be denied, from intestate succession to joint tenancy survivorship to appointment as a fiduciary. UPC 2-803 applies broadly to virtually all benefits under a will, statute, or joint tenancy, or any other "wrongful acquisition" of a property interest.

Some statutes do not prevent the benefit passing but instead impose on the killer a constructive trust in favor of the next-entitled taker. This avoids interfering with the usual order of succession while preventing the killer from receiving a benefit.

As the purpose of these rules is to prevent the killer's gaining any advantage from the crime, it usually is said that any further deprivation (such as disallowing a benefit that the killer would have received regardless of the killing) would be a punishment, in the nature of a forfeiture, which should be left for the criminal law to administer.

3

Execution of Testamentary Instruments

A. INTRODUCTION AND OVERVIEW OF CHAPTER

Chapter 3 is in some respects the heart of the course in estates, as it covers the formalities of executing a will. It begins with a discussion of the various instruments that can act as a will, from the basic formal "last will and testament" drawn by an attorney and attested by witnesses, popularly imagined (and often actually) covered in blue vellum and tied with ribbon, to formal or informal instruments that serve the same purpose with different formalities or serve special purposes in limited situations. (Some are not wills at all.) Next the elements of a will are enumerated, including both the parts of the instrument and the persons to whom they relate. Finally, the principal doctrines associated with execution of wills are explained and compared, including those universal to all wills statutes and several that are less uniform or only recently proposed.

Only the law of the formalities of execution is within the scope of this chapter. Such related matters as the effect of fraud or coercion, the formalities of revocation, and legal restrictions on testamentary powers, as well as the use and validity of various "will substitutes," are covered in subsequent chapters.

B.   TESTAMENTARY INSTRUMENTS

There are many different formats for a will, and many different instruments of which property can pass at death. This section discusses first the basic, garden-variety will and codicil, and then some of the more specialized variations or those that lack some or all of the formalities usually associated with a will.

Will

An instrument or declaration by which one directs the disposition of one's property after death. A will is also known as a **testament**, a term that originally referred only to a disposition of personal property. Today the phrase "last will and testament" is a redundancy.

Although usually required to be in writing, certain wills can be oral nuncupative wills and "soldiers' and sailors' " wills); and although usually required to be witnessed (attested), some jurisdictions allow a limited form of unattested holographic wills.

A will is, by definition, ambulatory, or subject to change until the death of the testator. (Therefore even if the testator calls the document a "last will," it is nevertheless subject to change and will be the "last" only if the testator dies before executing another.) A will is valid only if it is executed with the formalities required by the relevant jurisdiction's law. Although most wills statutes contain basically the same formalities, specific requirements can vary greatly depending on both the jurisdiction and the type of will. (See Section D.)

UPC 1-201(56) defines "will" very broadly, to include codicils and testamentary instruments that merely appoint an executor, nominate a guardian, or exclude a person or class from taking an intestate share (a "negative bequest").

Codicil

A supplement to a will that adds or deletes provisions or otherwise changes the will. It is subject to the same formal requirements as a will and, occasionally, to such additional criteria as physical attachment or specific reference to the will. Modern statutes generally do not distinguish the formalities of a will from those of a codicil — a codicil is merely a later will that does not wholly supersede a previous one. There can be as many codicils to a will as a testator desires to execute, each either superseding prior codicils or leaving them intact and further supplementing the will.

A codicil is said to republish the will, meaning that it brings the will's provisions up to the date of the codicil, as if both documents had been executed on that later date. This can have important implications for doctrines under which the date or relative timing of execution is relevant. (See *Republication*.)

Holographic Will

A will (sometimes called an "olographic" will) wholly or in substantial part handwritten by the testator. Jurisdictions that permit holographic wills (about half of the states) do not require that they be attested, although they must contain the testator's signature and sometimes are required to be dated. Depending on the jurisdiction, either the entire will (that is, every word intended by the testator to be incorporated in the will) or only its "material provisions" need be in the testator's handwriting. The latter doctrine is also sometimes known as the "judicial scissors" theory, since the court will, figuratively, "cut out" all non-handwritten provisions to see if the testator's dispositive scheme and testamentary intent can be derived only from those that remain. See UPC 2-502(b).

Nuncupative Will

An oral will. Many states recognize some limited form of oral wills, but usually they are restricted to passing personal property of relatively small value. Other restrictions may be placed on the conditions under which they can be made, such as only during the "last illness" of the testator. Nuncupative "soldiers' and sailors'" wills may be exempted from such restrictions. In Louisiana under the civil law, nuncupative wills are those that are orally declared but then reduced to a formal written document.

Soldiers' and Sailors' Wills

A special category of wills allowing persons in military service and mariners at sea to make wills that lack the usual formalities. Generally these wills may be oral (nuncupative) and need not be formally witnessed, but they usually can pass only personal property. Traditionally, they had to be made in time of war (except in the case of mariners at sea), but today this restriction may be omitted.

Self-proving Will

A will whose due execution is recited in an affidavit contained in or appended to the will itself and signed before a notary public by the testator and the attesting

38

witnesses. In some states, the affidavit can be used as a substitute for the usual signature and attestation clauses of the will. The affidavit permits the will to be probated without further proving (through witnesses) that it was properly signed, raising either a conclusive or a rebuttable presumption to that effect. While the will can still be attacked for other deficiencies, such as fraud or undue influence, by obviating the need for proof of the formalities of execution the affidavit can save a great deal of time and trouble in the probate process. See UPC 2-504, 3-406.

Form Will

A will that is printed with standardized provisions, including spaces for a testator to fill in names of beneficiaries and other specifics. Also referred to as "stationers' wills" because they can be purchased at stationery stores, these wills are usually inexpensive and intended — wisely or not — to be used without the services of an attorney.

Most form wills are intended as formal, attested instruments. A common problem that form wills raise when for some reason they are not attested is whether the handwritten insertions, devoid of the printed matter, constitute sufficient "material provisions" to qualify as a holographic will. The answer will depend on both the nature of the words inserted and the strictness of the court's adherence to the "all in testator's handwriting" requirement.

Statutory Will

A form will prescribed by statute. A few states have promulgated statutes that contain the text of a standardized will (or will with trust), usually with some mandatory and some optional or alternative provisions. Form wills containing these provisions may be purchased by individuals for a nominal cost. To use the statutory will, a testator must select which provisions are desired, indicate those selections (such as by initialing an adjacent space), fill in the names of beneficiaries and fiduciaries and descriptions of property, and execute the will in the usual manner. (The Uniform Statutory Will Act takes a different approach, providing statutory language that can be incorporated by reference in a testator's own will.)

Statutory form wills are intended to be formal attested documents, filled out and executed with the assistance of an attorney. As in the case of stationers' (nonstatutory) form wills, lack of attestation will cause the instrument to fail unless it can qualify as a holographic will. (See *Form Will.*)

Duplicate Wills

Wills that have been prepared in duplicate and each executed with the requisite formalities, so that each is an original instrument (not a copy) and can be probated as such. Generally, revocation of one duplicate will serves as a revocation of both.

Conditional Will

A will that is intended to be operative only on the occurrence of a specified condition or event, failing which it is of no effect. In other words, such a will has been executed with a conditional testamentary intent.

A key question that arises in considering conditional wills is whether the testator intended to state a true condition or only a reason for the will's execution.

Example 3.1:   Prospector Pete's will begins, "In case I don't make it back from Snake Creek, all my property goes to my partner Sam." This might have been intended to pass the property to Sam if and *only* if Pete in fact died at Snake Creek, or as an unconditional bequest regardless of where or when the testator died. In the latter case, the phrase "In case I don't make it back" would represent only a statement of Pete's reason or motivation for executing his will at that time — his fear that he might die while prospecting — and not a limitation on Sam's gift to such an eventuality. Usually extrinsic evidence will be needed to resolve such an ambiguity.

Living Will

Not a will at all, but an instrument directing that the signer's life shall not be prolonged by extraordinary medical procedures when there is no expectation of recovery. Most states permit living wills, although they may have to be executed in a specific form.

Joint Will

The wills of more than one person (usually husband and wife) executed in a single physical document signed by both. **Mutual wills**, on the other hand, are separate wills that contain reciprocal or identical provisions for disposition of each testator's property.

Example 3.2:   (a) Jay leaves all his property to his wife, Amanda, for her life, remainder to their children. Amanda in turn leaves all her property to Jay for his life, remainder to their children. The reciprocal provisions make these mutual wills.

(b) Jay leaves all his property to Amanda for her life, remainder to their children. In the same instrument, Amanda leaves all her property to Tad. Both execute the document. The use of a single instrument makes this a joint will.

While (as illustrated in the above examples) a joint will need not contain reciprocal or identical provisions, and mutual wills can be (and usually are) executed as separate documents, a **joint and mutual will** has the characteristics of both. The latter term usually is used to indicate a will that not only has reciprocal provisions but also was executed pursuant to an agreement by the testators.

Either joint, mutual, or joint and mutual wills may have been executed pursuant to a will contract providing that neither testator will revoke without the agreement of the other. But if the existence of such a contract is not expressed in the will itself and one testator does revoke after the death of the other, it may be difficult later to determine whether such a contract in fact existed. Of course, wills are not usually identical or reciprocal by coincidence; they are the result of at least an informal agreement between the testators to include particular provisions. However, the likely existence of an agreement to execute such wills is not necessarily indicative, much less presumptive, of a further agreement not to revoke them once executed. See UPC 2-514.

C. ELEMENTS OF TESTAMENTARY INSTRUMENTS

This section concerns the operative elements of the documents that govern testamentary dispositions, and the persons and things to which they relate. Some, like a testator, are essential to any form of will. Others, such as a bequest or an attestation clause, are found in nearly every will, although they may not be required in any. A few, like a writing or witnesses, are either mandatory or optional, depending on the type of will in question.

Estate

Either the total property of a decedent that passes by will or intestate succession, or the nature and extent of an interest in real or personal property. The first sense is that used in the title of this book (and of an estates and trusts course). In its broadest connotation it even can encompass the entire probate ("estate") process; but usually it is meant more narrowly as a person's accumulated real and personal property. While a person may be said to "have an estate" before death, the more technical usage is confined to property remaining at death and prior to its being distributed to testate or intestate takers.

In the sense of accumulated property, "estate" does not necessarily encompass all the property that passes at the testator's death. If the context is that of the probate of a will or distribution under the intestacy laws, usually only the probate estate is included, that on which by law the decedent's will or the intestacy laws can operate. It thus excludes so-called nonprobate assets, such as life insurance proceeds and property held in joint tenancy. This distinction is especially important if the term is used in a statute providing, for example, for some benefit (such as the share of an omitted spouse or child) to be taken from the "estate" of the decedent, since this may not be construed to include nonprobate assets.

An example of the second, "property law" (as opposed to "probate law") sense of the word "estate" would be such "freehold estates" in land as a fee simple absolute or a life estate. An estate may be legal or equitable. Here the term does not describe the general array of property that a person owns at death, but it does determine the nature and extent of ownership of each separate item of property that the decedent held or that passes at death. In other words, a person's overall "estate" may consist of, and pass, various interests in property, and each of those interests may be in the form of any one of the established legal or equitable "estates"; for example, "Tom's estate was distributed this month; it consisted of his house and his farm; he had owned a fee simple estate in his house, but gave Becky only a life estate and Joe the remainder in fee simple."

Testator

A person who has died leaving a valid will. The term is used also to refer to one who has executed a will but is still alive (and the will is thus still inoperative). The equivalent designation for a woman is **testatrix**, although today "testator" (usually pronounced to rhyme with "test taker") is commonly used for either gender. A testator is said to have died **testate**, as opposed to one who has died without leaving a valid will, or intestate.

Beneficiary

One who receives a gift or other benefit under a will or trust. Depending on the type of gift received, a will beneficiary may be referred to as a **devisee** (one who receives a devise of real property) or a **legatee** (one who receives a bequest of personal property), although today the real/personal distinction is often disregarded.

UPC 1-201(3) includes in its broad definition the beneficiaries or transferees under nonprobate instruments such as insurance policies and deeds.

Bequest

*A gift of property under a will, also called a **legacy**, technically limited to personal property.* The corresponding verb is "bequeath." The equivalent term for real property is **devise** (both noun and verb). In modern usage all three terms can be used to refer to property of any type, and often the more general term "gift" is used instead.

Historically, a distinction was drawn between testamentary gifts of real and personal property, with different rules attaching to each type, and in some jurisdictions such distinctions are still drawn for certain purposes; thus the difference in terminology. Although one still encounters in wills the trilogy of "give, devise, and bequeath," in most circumstances they are redundant and only one need be used, whatever type of property is passed.

Testamentary gifts are classified according to the manner in which they describe the property transferred, and these classifications have important implications in the construction of the will and the doctrines of abatement and ademption. See, *e.g.*, UPC 3-902 (abatement). A **specific gift** (legacy, bequest, devise) is of a particular thing that can be identified as part of the testator's estate ("I give my house at 1901 Cherry Lane to X"). A **general gift** is of a certain quantity or type of property, but it does not refer to, and is not payable out of, any particular asset of the estate. The most common type of general gift is one of money ("I give the sum of $1,000 to Y"). However, any property can be the subject of a general gift ("I give any good used car to Z," in which case the executor would be obligated to purchase such a car out of the estate's assets and deliver it to Z), and money can sometimes be the subject of a specific gift ("I give the $1,000 in silver dollars that will be found in my safe deposit box to A").

Less common is a **demonstrative gift**, which combines the characteristics of both specific and general gifts. Like a general gift, it is of a quantity or type (but not a specific item) of property; but it is to be satisfied out of a specific fund or asset source if available, otherwise from the general assets of the estate. An example would be, "I give to A $1,000, to be paid from the sale of my house on Cherry Lane if available, otherwise from any funds of the estate." (Unfortunately, demonstrative gifts are seldom so precisely worded, and it may be a difficult question of interpretation to decide whether a gift such as "$1,000, to be paid from the sale of my house" was so intended.)

Finally, a **residuary gift** is of whatever remains in the estate after the payment of specific, general, and demonstrative gifts. The fund it represents is referred to as the **residue**.

Writing

An instrument expressing ideas (such as testamentary provisions) in the form of visible letters or characters. Most wills (except for nuncupative or soldiers' and sailors' wills) must be written. If a will is required to be in writing, it generally can be handwritten, printed, typed, or any combination of these. (An exception is a holographic will, which must be all, or substantially all, handwritten by the testator.) It can be written on virtually any surface, and wills have been admitted to probate written on a petticoat, a tractor fender, and many other unconventional surfaces. The only restrictions on the type of writing relate to such practical considerations as legibility and preservation.

(Writing a will on the side of a cow (see "The Negotiable Cow" in A. P. Herbert's *Uncommon Law*) might be ill advised.)

The person who actually writes (drafts) the will, usually an attorney, is referred to as the **scrivener**.

Signature

The affixing of one's name or mark to an instrument for the purpose of authenticating it. A written will must contain the testator's signature. Although usually this means the handwritten full legal name of the testator, far less (initials, nickname, etc.) generally will suffice, so long as there is **animus signandi**, the intention that it serve as the testator's signature and, as such, authenticate the instrument as the signer's will. A **signature by mark** (such as making an "X") is commonly considered valid. Another person may append the testator's name (a **signature per alium**), although usually this is permissible only in the testator's presence, at the testator's direction and request, and accompanied by the other person's signature as well. See UPC 2-502.

End (or Foot) of Will

Either the physical or the logical conclusion of a will. A statute may require that the testator's name be **subscribed** (literally, written at the end) or that the signature be placed "at the foot or end" of the will. This can lead to difficult questions as to the meaning of "end," particularly whether the statute intends the physical or logical end of the will. The latter refers to the conclusion of the will's provisions in the order they are intended to be read, even if the last provision is written in a place other than at the end of the last page (such as in a margin or on the back of the first page).

Witness

One who observes the testator's signing of the will and who also signs the will to attest to that fact. (See Attestation; Attestation Clause.) The attesting witnesses to the will must be distinguished from those who ultimately may be called on to testify as witnesses when the will is proved in court. While these may be (and often are) the same persons, there is no such requirement, and practically there could not be because the will's attesting witnesses often are themselves deceased or unavailable when the will comes to probate.

Usually a statute requires **competent witnesses**, which means they must meet the requirements for testifying in court (although, as indicated, they may never have to do so). See UPC 2-505(a). Competence is determined as of the time of the will's execution, even if the witnesses thereafter become incompetent. Even a perfect stranger to the testator can be a competent witness to a will, as indeed is often the case when a will is executed under emergent circumstances or in a hospital or other place where the testator has no immediate access to friends or relatives. As indicated elsewhere, under modern statutes a witness may be competent although interested in the estate; but in many states such witnesses will lose any benefits they might have received under the will. (See *Interested Witness*.)

Most statutes require two witnesses to a will; often three are used to add a margin of safety.

Attestation Clause

A clause at the conclusion of a will that recites the due execution of the instrument. It is placed after the testator's signature and is signed by the witnesses to the will. Although not required in any state, an attestation clause serves two important functions: It constitutes evidence of the carrying out of the execution procedures recited in it, sufficient to take the place of the testimony of absent witnesses and even possibly to withstand the contrary testimony of a subscribing witness; and it acts as a checklist of the requirements of due execution, to assure that all such requirements are carried out. Thus while a will is valid without an attestation clause (or, for that matter, without any recitation of due execution), it stands a better chance of being declared valid if such a clause is included.

Interested Witness

A person who would receive some benefit under a will to which that person has acted as an attesting witness. Because a witness who has a personal stake in the will's validity might be tempted to attest falsely to due execution, at Common Law not only was an interested witness denied any benefit under the will, but the witness was considered incompetent to attest and (in the absence of sufficient disinterested witnesses) the entire will was declared invalid. Although under modern statutes interested witnesses are competent to attest and thus to validate the will, in many jurisdictions such witnesses still lose (are "purged" of) any benefits under the will (or of any benefits that exceed those they would have received were the will not valid), thus removing their "interest" and the incentive to attest falsely. Such a statute may be called a **purging statute**.

Some modern statutes (such as UPC 2-505(b)) ignore a witness's interest, on the theory that purging the benefits has no deterrent effect on truly unscrupulous witnesses, and it may cause some innocent beneficiaries who attest in ignorance of the purging statute to lose their benefits unfairly.

A few recent statutes take a middle ground and raise a presumption of fraud or undue influence by an interested witness, putting the onus on such witnesses to prove their innocence or lose their benefits under the will.

As indicated above, a witness's interest is irrelevant if the will was attested by the requisite number of competent and disinterested witnesses. This renders any interested witness a **supernumerary**, an "extra" signatory whose attestation is superfluous and can be ignored because it constitutes more than the number needed. Thus if a statute requires two witnesses, but three sign, including one who is interested, the latter is a supernumerary and will not suffer any disadvantage; but if two of three are interested, neither is a supernumerary and both may lose their benefits.

States differ in their interpretation of who is "interested." Clearly included are those directly receiving gifts under the will. Inclusion is less clear, and states differ, when a witness is the spouse of a beneficiary. Generally an indirect recipient of a will's benefits (such as a member of an organization that receives a benefit) and the appointed executor of the will or trustee under its provisions are not considered interested. Interest usually is determined as of the time of attestation, even if the witness/beneficiary later disclaims any benefits under the will.

D. FORMALITIES OF EXECUTION

A formal will requires adherence to the several formal steps required for a will to be validly executed. Most of these formalities are uniform throughout the common-law world, having originated in sixteenth century England and passed through the centuries almost unscathed (see generally Chapter 1). Nevertheless, there are significant variations in the required execution ceremony; while generally strict adherence to the letter of each formal requirement is an absolute necessity, in a growing number of jurisdictions modern reforms make such strictness less critical.

In this section are set out the traditional and still prevalent formalities, some or all of which may be part of the execution ceremony in a given jurisdiction, together with the emerging doctrines that offer relief from the Draconian consequences of straying from the well-worn path of those formalities.

Execution

The signing of the will by the testator. More generally, execution may refer to the entire execution ceremony, including signing by the testator and attestation by the witnesses, all according to prescribed formalities. Courts or statutes may also refer to **due execution**, meaning execution that has followed all the statutory prerequisites, or formalities, for a valid will.

Attestation

The act of observing, or bearing witness to, the execution of a document such as a will. The term commonly is used to include also the act of subscribing one's name to the document as evidence of having witnessed its execution; statutes generally require both observation and subscription to validate the instrument. Attestation requires not just a physical act but also a state of mind: an intent to act as a witness to, and thereby validate, the instrument (**animus attestandi**). Thus an **attesting witness** to a will is one who has observed its execution and who then signs the will, usually following an attestation clause, as an act of validation.

It is not clear in some jurisdictions whether the witness attests the document itself or only the testator's signature. In either event, it is generally sufficient that the testator have acknowledged the signature to the witnesses even if they did not see the act of signing.

To be valid, the attestation must conform to whatever requirements are set out in the local statute, such as signing in the presence of the testator or other witnesses, or at the direction or request of the testator. The attestation clause should recite that these steps were taken.

Re-execution

Execution, with the requisite formalities, of a will that has already been executed but for some reason has ceased to be in effect. Re-execution is the primary means of reviving a will that has been revoked. It is sometimes confused with the related concept of republication, which it may be a means to accomplish.

Republication

Re-establishment of a will, either after it has been revoked or, although it is still valid, to reassert its terms as of a later date (usually by a codicil). The term generally does not refer merely to a subsequent "publication," or oral declaration that the instrument is the testator's will, which is only one of many formal requirements in the execution of a will; it refers rather to a complete re-execution, with the same formalities originally required by the statute.

Acknowledgment

An indication to witnesses that one's will has been signed. Most states, requiring the testator to sign before (in the "presence" of) witnesses, permit acknowledgment as a substitute for that requirement. Almost any word or gesture is sufficient if it communicates to the witnesses that the testator's signature is on the will; but if the statute is interpreted as requiring that the testator's signature, rather than the will itself, be witnessed, a court may require that the witnesses actually be able to see the signature at the time of acknowledgment. See UPC 2-502(a)(3) (testator may acknowledge either signature or will).

Presence

A requirement that the testator and witnesses of a will be in some type of proximity when one or the other signs the will. Many statutes require that wills be signed by the testator "in the presence" of the witnesses or that the witnesses sign (attest) "in the presence" of the testator or one another. Clearly, even in ordinary speech the term "presence" may mean anything from "adjacent" ("immediate presence") to "in the general vicinity." In probate law presence generally is defined as either within the "line of sight" or within the "conscious presence" of the testator (or witnesses). The former test can be quite mechanical, requiring that the person in question actually see the signing or be able to see it (without changing position or removing some intervening object) if desired. The latter, more liberal test requires only that the person be in the general vicinity of the signer (perhaps in the next room) and be aware of the signing taking place, through the senses of sight or sound or simply a "general consciousness" of its occurrence. Courts vary as to such technical matters as whether the signing or only the signer must be visible. Even strict jurisdictions make allowance for such circumstances as a blind testator's obvious inability to "see" the signing.

Publication

The testator's declaration to the witnesses that the document to be attested is his or her will, a requirement of due execution in some states. Usually publication is accomplished by a simple statement ("This is my will"), but any word, gesture, or other manifestation that communicates this fact to the witnesses, directly or indirectly, will suffice. Only the identity of the document, not its contents, need be communicated. (Note that the term "republication" does not refer to a subsequent act of publication, but it generally implies a full re-execution of the will or the execution of a codicil.)

Testamentary Intent

*The intent (**animus testandi**) that an instrument or declaration serve as one's will, that is, have dispositive effect at one's death.* It is perhaps the most important prerequisite to the validity of any type of will, although it is seldom listed as a statutory requirement.

While testamentary intent may be taken for granted in the case of a

...mally executed will that is regular on its face, it may be very much in ...estion if the will is at all casual in form, such as a holographic (hand-...tten) will contained in an informal letter or a nuncupative (oral) will. ...n if a will appears to be regular in form, it may be proved to be a **sham** ... intended as a joke or for some other nontestamentary purpose, or a **specimen will** intended as a sample or reference for later drafting of the true will. However, lack of testamentary intent behind an apparently regular instrument may be difficult to prove if prevented by rules of construction excluding any extrinsic evidence that contradicts the will's contents.

Substantial Compliance

Sufficient compliance with the formalities of execution to permit a will to be admitted to probate despite lacking total compliance with all the formalities.

Traditionally, a will can be (and often has been) declared invalid if any, even a technical, formality has been omitted or incorrectly carried out, and despite the court's conviction that the will represents the testator's true intent. There have been some recent attempts at liberalization by courts and some statutory reforms to provide at least limited relief for such errors. Most employ a phrase such as "substantial compliance" or "harmless error," intended to limit such relief to instances in which the instrument contains substantially all the formalities considered fundamental to validity (such as a signature or a writing) and when a court is convinced (usually with a very high standard of proof, such as "clear and convincing evidence") that the instrument in question was indeed intended to be the testator's will.

A more liberal approach is to give a court a so-called **dispensing power** to a will proved to represent the testator's intent even in the absence of substantial compliance with the formalities. The latest versions of the Uniform Probate Code and the Restatement of Property adopt this approach. See UPC 2-503. A dispensing power, although it can avoid the hardship of a will's invalidity for inadvertent "technical" omissions, gives a court considerable discretion in excusing noncompliance with will formalities and makes the validity or invalidity of even a substantially noncomplying will much less predictable.

4

Grounds for Contest: Impediments to Testamentary Capacity and Intent

A. INTRODUCTION AND OVERVIEW OF CHAPTER

This chapter could more precisely, if less elegantly, be called "Conditions That Affect a Testator's Mind and, by Impairing Testamentary Capacity or Intent, Undermine the Validity or Effect of the Testator's Execution of a Will." Many circumstances, most of which are technically "grounds for will contests," affect the validity of a will. Prominent examples are the failure to follow the formalities of execution (Chapter 3) or the establishment of a later, superseding instrument or other form of revocation (Chapter 5). The grounds covered in this chapter, however, concern the mind and person of the testator and are variations on the common themes of testamentary capacity and testamentary intent: Did the testator execute the will with a

51

sound mind, free of impediments resulting from disease, senility, coercion, or misunderstanding (innocently or intentionally induced)?

These grounds of contest overlap, of course, and often they are alleged and found to exist together. Some forms of fraud are very close to or may even constitute undue influence; a mistake may be induced by a third party's fraud, the testator's mental derangement, or innocent error; and all forms of coercion are more easily practiced on — as mistakes are more easily made by — a testator whose mind is weak. Thus these particular grounds for upsetting a will are properly, and necessarily, considered together.

After an analysis of the general topic of will contests, the chapter considers the testator's mental state when executing the will, in terms of inherent mental capacity and the internal or external forces that can affect the testator's mind or ability to carry out the mind's true intent. As will be seen, some of these influences are grounds for overturning an otherwise valid will, while others are not.

B. CONTEST IN GENERAL

Will Contest

An attempt to prevent a will from being admitted to probate, or to rescind probate once granted. A will contest generally is an in rem proceeding, "against the world" as opposed to a specific party, and it must be brought in a particular court usually within short time limitations. The party bringing the contest is the **contestant**, the person defending the will the **proponent**; any person who is "interested" (has a pecuniary stake) in rejection of the will can contest.

In addition to lack of proper execution or alleged revocation, the primary grounds for contest have to do with the testator's mind or influences upon it: mental incapacity, mental derangement (insane delusion), fraud, and undue influence. Jurisdictions vary as to whether the burden of proof is on the contestant or the proponent, but commonly the proponent has the burden on questions of proper execution, the contestant on issues of testamentary capacity, mental derangement, fraud, and undue influence. See UPC 3-407. Presumptions often aid the parties in meeting their burdens.

In some states, probate and contest are quite separate matters taken up in different proceedings, while in others they may be combined. Technically, questions of construction (*e.g.*, ambiguous language), the propriety or validity of particular will provisions (*e.g.*, violations of the Rule Against Perpetuities), and the rights or incapacities of particular beneficiaries (*e.g.*, pretermitted heirs) are not matters of contest and may be resolved in a different forum. Whether a challenge is denominated a "contest" may determine not only when and where it is heard but also whether it is precluded by a will's no-contest clause. In many states, there is no right to a jury in a will contest.

The issue in a will contest sometimes is referred to by the Latin phrase *devisavit vel non* (literally "he devises or not," with a long "a" in the first word). Formerly this was the proper designation of the issue sent by a chancery court to a court of law to determine the validity of a will.

C.   SPECIFIC GROUNDS OF CONTEST

This section sets out the various mental states and capacities of the testator that could affect the validity of the execution of a will. They all concern what (or whether) the testator thinks, knows, or believes, or the reason that the testator thinks, knows, or believes it.

Testamentary Capacity

A general term for the mental state and other factors prerequisite to a person's ability to execute a valid will. Although at early common law many classes of persons, such as women and aliens, lacked capacity to make a will simply because of their status, the only factors that remain prerequisites are sufficient age and mental capacity.

The minimum age to execute a will is generally the same as a state's age of majority for other purposes, although a different age sometimes is specified. See UPC 2-501 (18 years). This requirement may be waived if the testator is married or in military service at the time of the will's execution.

A testator may lack mental capacity either because of a mental deficiency or because of some form of mental derangement.

Mental Deficiency

Lack of sufficient memory or understanding to execute a valid will, a form of testamentary incapacity. The standards for mental deficiency of a testator may be more or less strict than those applied to other transactions such as the execution of a valid contract.

Although the test of mental deficiency varies among states, generally execution of a valid will requires at least the ability to know and understand the nature and extent of one's property, the "natural objects of one's bounty" (those persons whom a mentally sound testator would be expected to favor, such as a spouse or children or other close relatives), and the disposition that the will makes of one's property; and to understand the relationship among all these elements. Note the term "ability": The testator need not actually *know* these things but must have the ability to know them.

Example 4.1: At the time Tessa executes her will, she has forgotten the names of some of her 17 grandchildren and the acreage of the private island she owns. She never knew the total value of all her shares of stock in various corporations, nor even which companies' stock she owned, having left most of these details to her financial advisors. None of this renders Tessa mentally deficient so long as she is *capable*, at the time of executing her will, of knowing and understanding these matters and how they relate to her will, were they to be brought to her attention.

Mental Derangement

A mental incapacity in the form of an **insane delusion** *that prevents an otherwise competent testator from making a valid will.* Unlike mental deficiency, mental derangement does not necessarily entail the ability to know the nature of one's property, one's family, or the disposition one is making.

An insane delusion is a false belief to which the testator clings in the absence of rational supporting evidence and, sometimes, in the face of incontrovertible argument or evidence to the contrary. This is not to say that a testator's belief must be those of the ordinary "reasonable person" as that term is applied in tort law, but only that they must not be so unfounded and bizarre as to be explainable only as the product of mental illness.

Example 4.2: (a) Arthur disinherits his daughter Pearl, who lives in a distant city, because he has heard and believes (incorrectly) that she is living with a man not her husband. Arthur may have been "deluded" (mistaken), and perhaps we could say a reasonable person would not have acted so harshly on such thin evidence; but his delusion is unlikely to be found "insane."

(b) Arthur disinherits his daughter Pearl because he mistakenly believes that she has borne several illegitimate children, despite the fact that Pearl has always lived at home and has never shown any signs of pregnancy. Arthur probably is suffering from an insane delusion.

Perhaps because of the impossibility of knowing exactly what motivated a testator's dispositions, not to mention the understandable desire of some courts and juries to rectify an obviously unjust result, the cases in this area tend to be very unpredictable.

Even if an insane delusion is found, it will invalidate the will only to the extent it is shown to have affected the will's dispositions, provided the unaffected parts can be separated.

Example 4.3: Arthur's first will gives $100,000 to his daughter Pearl and the residue to charity X. Arthur then executes a second will that reduces Pearl's gift to $50 and changes the charitable gift to charity Y. If Arthur's insane delusion about Pearl caused him to reduce her gift but had no effect on the other gift in the will, usually only the parts affected by the delusion would be invalidated.

If, in Example 4.3, it can be shown that despite Arthur's belief about Pearl, he gave (or denied) her the same gift as he otherwise would have, the insane delusion will not affect the validity of either the will or Pearl's share in it.

As can be seen from Example 4.2 (a), a delusion that is not insane — that is, a mere mistake — is not a ground for invalidating a will. (See *Mistake*.) Nor are strange beliefs or behavior, eccentricity or misanthropy, short of a specifically directed delusion, considered mental derangement for these purposes.

Undue Influence

An act that has the effect of overcoming the testator's free will in the execution of a testamentary instrument. Undue influence invalidates a will if it caused the challenged disposition.

The exertion of influence is not itself undue just because it has the effect of swaying the mind of the testator. Rather, there must be some element of fraud or coercion, mental or physical, which overrides the testator's volition and substitutes that of the influencer. (Fraud and undue influence, while distinct grounds for contesting a will, often overlap.)

Example 4.4: (a) Florentyna pleads with her strong-willed father, Abel, to leave her his entire estate because of her years of love and devotion to him. If she manages to convince Abel to do so, she clearly has influenced his testamentary decision, but there is nothing "undue" in what she has done, even if the result is "unjust" to other potential beneficiaries who were not so influential.

(b) Florentyna holds a gun to Abel's head, or threatens to throw herself from the window, unless he signs a will in her favor (or, more subtly, she contrives to keep other potential beneficiaries from seeing her weak and susceptible father while telling him lies about how they hate him). Florentyna's influence now would likely be considered undue. That Abel thought he was following his own free will is of no importance if he actually was being manipulated by Florentyna.

The person who exerts the undue influence is not always the one who benefits from it; nonetheless, the will generally is invalid even when the beneficiary is an innocent party.

By its nature, undue influence usually is exercised under conditions that make direct evidence of it unavailable. Typically the actions and words of the influencer are neither witnessed nor recorded; moreover, the person influenced is, of course, no longer available to testify. For this reason, courts have recognized the need to rely on circumstantial evidence of undue influence, and they tend to look for common circumstantial factors. Thus in Example 4.4 above, a court deciding whether Florentyna exercised undue influence over Abel might consider whether: (1) Abel was a person *susceptible* to being influenced (because of ill health, age, and the like); (2) Florentyna had an *opportunity* to exert her influence; (3) she was *disposed* (had a motive) to do so; (4) she took an active part in *procuring* the will (as by drafting it); and (5) the resulting will has the *appearance* of having been influenced by Florentyna (for example, she takes the entire estate, to the exclusion of other natural objects of Abel's bounty; that is, the will seems "unnatural" in its disposition of Abel's property). Not all courts articulate or use all these factors, and not all need be found to permit a finding of undue influence.

If the testator and the alleged influencer shared a **confidential relationship**, and especially if one or more of the above "suspicious" factors (such as procurement of the will) also is present, a presumption of undue influence may be raised, shifting the burden of proof or production to the confidant. Any relationship of trust and confidence may be sufficient to trigger this presumption; a fiduciary relationship is not required, although the strongest case exists if the attorney who drafted the will takes an "unnatural" benefit under it. And while in Example 4.4 the mere relationship of father and daughter usually would not be considered a confidential relationship, if Florentyna were especially close to her father and acted as his financial or spiritual advisor, this clearly would be sufficient.

Fraud

Intentional deception of the testator by another in such a manner as to affect the terms of the testator's will. The deception must be intentional; mere innocent misrepresentation by a third party, even an interested one, usually will not upset the will.

Fraud in the inducement refers to a misrepresentation to the testator as to facts that serve as an inducement for the execution of the will or the inclusion of certain provisions.

Example 4.5: Testator Iva's spiritual advisor Samuel tells her, falsely, that he can communicate with the spirits of the dead. He then tells Iva that the spirit of her deceased husband, Miles, has spoken to him and wishes her to execute a will in favor of Samuel. If Samuel did this knowing the statement to be false and intending that Iva act upon it, and if Iva is deceived and because of this deception she does then execute a will in Samuel's favor, any gift to Samuel may be invalidated for fraud in the inducement. (While all these "if's" need be present, some may be inferred from the presence of the others.)

Fraud in the execution concerns deception as to the nature or contents of the document that the testator signs.

Example 4.6: Samuel makes no false claims about testator Iva's deceased husband, Miles (see Example 4.5); rather, he prepares a document containing a substantial gift to himself and surreptitiously substitutes it for Iva's actual will. Iva executes the will under the mistaken impression that it represents her true intent. The gift in Samuel's favor can be nullified for fraud in the execution.

Note that if Iva is sufficiently gullible to be easily deceived by Samuel about Miles or what she is signing, she may also lack the requisite mental capacity for executing a valid will (see *Testamentary Capacity*), or Samuel may be found to have exercised undue influence over her. Undue influence and fraud are often virtually interchangeable doctrines, fraud being one manner of unduly influencing a testator.

The above material assumes that the testator was intentionally misled by the perpetrator of the fraud. Innocent, and even negligent, misrepresentation is not generally a ground for upsetting a will any more than is a testator's self-deception (see *Mistake*).

Example 4.7: Samuel honestly — if unreasonably — believes his assertion to Iva that he can communicate with the dead. Iva is induced by that assertion to provide for Samuel in her will. If a court accepts Samuel's claim of good faith (and this is a big "if"), the provision is valid. It is likewise valid if Samuel intended to deceive Iva but she made the gift only because she liked Samuel, not because of his claim of spiritual power.

Mistake

An inadvertent, usually self-induced misconception of fact or law that has an effect on the testator's will. Generally mistakes by the testator cannot be corrected by the court.

Mistake in the inducement occurs when the testator is mistaken about some matter of fact or law and is thereby induced to execute a will in a certain way.

Example 4.8:   Hugh incorrectly believes that his friend Stephen has died, and for that reason he leaves Stephen out of his will. The error cannot be corrected after Hugh's death. This is generally true whether the source of Hugh's error was a simple error on his part or an innocent misrepresentation by Maud, Stephen's cousin, who was herself mistaken. (In contrast, if the reason for Hugh's mistake is an *intentional* deception by Maud, the will or a part of it may be invalidated. See *Fraud.*)

Mistake in the execution exists if the testator is mistaken as to the nature or content of the document executed.

Example 4.9:   Hugh signs his life insurance policy thinking it is his will, or (as is more common) he and his wife, Aline, execute reciprocal wills but each mistakenly signs the other's will. The mistakenly signed instrument cannot be probated, nor can the will generally be probated that is unsigned or signed by the wrong person.

If a jurisdiction has adopted a "dispensing power" or permits "substantial compliance" with will formalities, at least some mistakes can be overlooked, possibly including signing the wrong will.

If only a part of an instrument was included by mistake, even a strict court might correct the mistake by denying probate to that part only.

Despite the usual rules denying reformation of mistakes, once a will has been admitted to probate, many mistakes can be corrected in the process of construction. A court is usually more willing to strike mistakenly included language, on the theory that it lacked testamentary intent, than to add an inadvertently omitted gift, because the latter would have lacked the formalities of execution. And if an ambiguity can be found, mistakes often can be corrected through the admission of extrinsic evidence of the testator's actual intent. (See Chapter 7.)

Mistake, or innocent delusion, must be distinguished not only from fraudulently induced error but also from insane delusion, a testator's misapprehension which is irrationally held and is the product of mental illness. (See *Mental Derangement.*)

5
Revocation and Revival

A. INTRODUCTION AND OVERVIEW OF CHAPTER

Revocation of a will, like its execution, is valid only if the testator follows certain formalities set out in a jurisdiction's probate statute. Although the formalities for revocation can be much less onerous than for execution (and may even seem casual), they are no less necessary to accomplish the testator's purpose. This chapter discusses the meaning of revocation and its manner of accomplishment. It then concludes with the doctrines that nullify or render ineffective an otherwise valid revocation.

B. METHODS OF REVOCATION

Set out here are the formalities of the revocation "ceremony," from a formal written document to a very informal physical destruction. Although the rules may be easier to follow than those for execution of the will (see Chapter 3), they must nonetheless be followed to the letter. One of the difficulties in this regard is determining just what that "letter" is, especially with respect to the various means of physical destruction.

Revocation

The act of rendering an otherwise valid will of no further effect. Revocation can be effectuated in two principal ways: by some physical act upon the will, and by a subsequent instrument. Under some circumstances a will also may be revoked by operation of law.

It is the nature of a will to be revocable, or **ambulatory**, always subject to change and able to include property newly acquired. (As the term suggests, a will " 'walks along" with the testator from the time of its execution throughout the testator's life, until death makes it final and irrevocable.)

Revocation of a will's codicil does not revoke the will, although in many states revocation of a will automatically revokes its codicils. Revocation of one duplicate will revokes all.

Revocation by Physical Act

Revocation of a will by something done to or upon the document. A state's probate statute will list the types of act that qualify to revoke it. When one of those acts is accompanied by a contemporaneous intent to revoke (**animus revocandi**), revocation is accomplished. See UPC 2-507.

Compared with a will's execution, revocation by physical act is almost informal, although the testator still must carefully follow the statute's enumerated procedures. Most statutes permit revocation by such acts as "burning," "tearing," "cancelling," and "mutilating," or just plain "destroying." Acts such as burning or tearing generally need not result in the destruction of the entire will, while "destroying" may require more thorough measures.

Cancellation traditionally refers to drawing lines through the terms of the will (think of the cancellation of a stamp); writing "cancelled" in the margin will not suffice, any more than would writing "destroyed." (The 1990 Uniform Probate Code, however, would permit a cancellation that leaves the words of the will untouched. UPC 2-507(a)(2)). Note that if the state allows holographic (handwritten, unattested) wills, words written in the margin might qualify as a revocation by subsequent instrument.

Because a valid revocation by physical act can be carried out without witnesses, and because a physical act is considered to be inherently ambiguous as to its meaning, extrinsic evidence usually is admissible to ascertain not only whether the burning or other act of destruction took place but also whether it was intended, at the time, as an act of revocation. (The testator might, for example, have mistaken the will for some other document.) If a will that was last known to be in the testator's possession either cannot be found after the testator's death or is found bearing indications of physical revocation (such as being torn or burned), it is presumed that the will was destroyed or mutilated by the testator with intent to revoke, and it is up to the will's proponent to demonstrate to the contrary.

The statute may permit an act of revocation to be carried out by a third person, usually adding such requirements as that it be done at the direction, and in the presence, of the testator, or before one or more witnesses.

While many states allow **partial revocation** physical act, as by striking out a single word or clause, some do not. Others may allow such a partial revocation only if it does not have the effect of increasing, without the usual execution formalities, a general or specific gift. Increasing the residue or intestate estate usually is permitted.

Example 5.1: Charles leaves a general gift of $150,000 to be equally divided among "William, Murray, and Daisy." He then crosses out ("cancels") the name "William." This leaves a gift of $150,000 to "Murray, and Daisy," increasing these two gifts from $50,000 to $75,000 each, a change that a court may not allow. But cancellation of the entire $150,000 gift, which increases the residue or (in the absence of a residuary clause) the intestate estate, might be allowed even by a court that would not permit the cancellation of William's gift alone.

Note that if, in Example 5.1, Charles had torn out William's name and burned it, and if no copy could be found, the court might be unable to restore the will to its unrevoked form and thus be forced to choose between considering the entire will revoked (which Charles had no intention of doing) and permitting the partial revocation.

Revocation by Subsequent Instrument

Revocation of a will by another writing, expressly or by implication. A later will always should begin with the statement that it "revokes all prior wills and codicils," if that is the intention of the testator. The revoking instrument generally need not itself be a will (containing dispositive provisions) so long as it is executed with the same formalities. If the subsequent instrument's provisions are inconsistent with those of the prior will, the prior should be considered revoked by implication because the later disposition always prevails. UPC 2-507 presumes an intent to revoke (replace) a prior will entirely, or to revoke only inconsistent provisions, according to whether or not the subsequent will makes a complete disposition of the testator's estate.

A will may be partially revoked by a subsequent instrument, which would then be acting as a codicil. Partial revocation could be express or implied by partially inconsistent provisions.

Example 5.2:   Charles executes a will giving his house and car to his wife, Carrie. He then executes another will that makes no mention of the first but gives his car to his new friend Sarah. This should have the same revocatory effect on the first will as if Charles had executed a codicil expressly revoking the gift of the car to Carrie.

Revocation by Operation of Law

Revocation of a will by virtue of some statutorily defined triggering event or circumstance. Most statutes contain one or more provisions for revocation of a will, or part of it, upon the occurrence of certain events or changes in circumstances. (These are instances of revocation "by operation of law" because they operate automatically and without regard to the actual intent of the testator.)

The most common of these statutory provisions revokes a will upon the testator's subsequent marriage. Such so-called **post-testamentary spouse statutes** usually revoke the earlier will only to the extent necessary to give the subsequent spouse an intestate share of the estate, although this share could well be the entire estate. There usually is no revocation if the will makes some provision for the spouse or indicates that no such provision is intended, or if a transfer in lieu of a testamentary provision is made outside of the will. Extrinsic evidence of an intentional omission may or may not be admissible. Because these statutes generally do not apply to a spouse who was provided for in the will, they often are called **omitted spouse** (or even "pretermitted spouse") **statutes.** See, *e.g.*, UPC(69) 2-301. The 1990 Uniform Probate Code, taking a different approach, does not require that a post-testamentary spouse have been omitted from the will, if the other requirements are satisfied. UPC 2-301. In a few states (following the common-law rule) a will is automatically revoked only by marriage and the birth of children.

A related type of statute revokes any gift or other benefit to a spouse whom the testator has divorced. *E.g.*, UPC 2-804. Some of these statutes, in addition to revoking the spouse's benefits, deem the spouse to have predeceased the testator, in effect to have suffered a "civil death," or to have disclaimed any provision. If the statute provides for revocation but does not expressly deem the spouse to have predeceased or disclaimed, problems may arise if the will also contains gifts to other beneficiaries that are contingent on the "death" of the spouse. As the spouse is neither dead nor able to take, it is left to the court to decide what the testator would have intended in this situation.

Example 5.3:   (a) Charles executes his will in 1980 while married to Carrie. It contains a gift of $10,000 to Charles's church, $1,000 to the Children's Fund, a charity, and the rest to Carrie, "but if Carrie should predecease me I give her share to the Children's Fund." The will expressly disinherits their daughter, Lily. In 1985 Charles and Carrie are divorced. If the state has a revocation-upon-divorce statute, Charles's will is automatically revoked to the extent of the gift to Carrie (as is Carrie's will if it contains a gift to Charles), but it remains valid as to the gifts to the church and the Children's Fund. If the statute deems Carrie to have predeceased Charles, the Fund takes the balance of the estate as well. If the statute is silent on this point, the court must decide whether the revoked gift should go to the Fund or to Lily, as intestate taker. Here the fact that Charles apparently did not want Lily to benefit from his estate may indicate that the Fund should take; but it is seldom so easy a matter to resolve.

(b) In 1986 Charles marries Sarah. If Charles dies without making a new will, his 1980 will (already revoked as to Carrie) would be revoked again, this time by a post-testamentary spouse statute, to the extent necessary to give Sarah an intestate share of the estate. The rest of the will remains valid, and other shares of the estate abate either according to the usual state pattern or proportionally ("ratably").

A testator can avoid revocation in favor of a spouse-to-be, as well as the revocation of provisions for a divorced spouse, by an express statement in the will to that effect.

Example 5.4:   In 1986, knowing he is about to marry Sarah, Charles makes a new will that either provides for Sarah as his future wife or states that "I wish to make no provision for my wife-to-be, Sarah." This expression of contrary intent, negating the possibility that Sarah has been omitted inadvertently, prevents the subsequent marriage from revoking the will.

Under most statutes, divorce revokes only the benefits given to the divorced spouse and not to others, even if they are "in-laws" related to the spouse and not to the testator. In a few states gifts to certain in-laws are revoked; under the Uniform Probate Code's complex new provision, benefits (including those outside of probate) in favor of anyone related to the former spouse but, after divorce, no longer related to the testator, are revoked as well.

Children born subsequent to the will's execution are generally covered by the state's pretermitted heir statute, which technically may not be a revocation statute but acts in much the same way in favor of inadvertently omitted children.

A beneficiary's intentional killing of the testator generally revokes, by operation of law, the killer's benefits under the will or other instrument. See *Slayer's Statute*.

Lost Will Statute

A statute setting out the conditions under which a will that cannot be found after the testator's death can nevertheless be probated.

A will that has been lost or destroyed without the testator's intent to revoke (animus revocandi) technically is not revoked and can be probated. In some states, however, "lost will statutes" may prevent otherwise valid, unrevoked wills from being probated because they are not physically available. Some of these statutes are very technical, requiring that the will be proven to have been "in existence" at the time of the testator's death or "fraudulently destroyed" before then. (Note that if a will that cannot be found was last known to be in the testator's possession, a presumption usually arises that the testator destroyed it with intent to revoke. See *Revocation*.) The likelihood that a lost, unrevoked will might be denied probate depends in these jurisdictions on how broadly the courts are willing to read the terms "in existence" (does it mean "legal existence" or physical existence?) and "fraudulently destroyed" (is accidental destruction by the testator "constructive fraud"?).

Lost will statutes also may contain strict evidentiary requirements, such as two witnesses to the contents of the will. Most modern statutes, however, either eliminate these provisions or modify them greatly.

One of the anomalies that strict lost will statutes can produce is their effect on the doctrine of dependent relative revocation. Under that doctrine, discussed in detail elsewhere, a will destroyed by a conditional act of revocation may be deemed valid and unrevoked if the condition fails; a lost will statute, however, may still prevent the destroyed will from being probated merely because it cannot be physically produced. Some states have modified their lost will statutes to avoid such a result.

C. REVOCATION REVOKED

Revocation of a will, even if seemingly effective, may sometimes be overcome by subsequent actions or nullified by closer examination of its circumstances. This section is perhaps slightly misnamed, in that of the two doctrines set out only the first, revival, is a true "revocation of a revocation." The second, dependent relative revocation, merely declares a purported revocation to have been a nullity at the outset, thus obviating the need for its later rescission. (As you will see, the term "merely" may also be somewhat misplaced as applied to the latter doctrine.)

Revival

Bringing back to life a will that has been revoked. This might be accomplished by revocation of an instrument that itself revoked the will, or by express statement of an intent to revive in a later testamentary instrument, or by re-execution of the revoked will.

Example 5.5: Ralph executes a first will, leaving his estate to Alice. A year later he has a fight with Alice and executes a second will, expressly revoking the first and leaving his estate to Trixi. But then, as often happens in such relationships, Ralph makes up with Alice and revokes his second will, intending the first (which he had kept intact) to be effective again. Assuming the second will is validly revoked, whether his first will has been revived depends on the local law and perhaps whether he revoked his second will by subsequent instrument or by physical act.

In some states, following the English and common-law rule, Ralph's second will in Example 5.5 would be considered to have been merely "covering" the first until it (the second) became effective upon Ralph's death, and until then the first was not really revoked; thus when Ralph tore up the second, the first was still valid. Other states, however, would consider Ralph's first will to have been revoked as soon as the second was executed, and revoking the second could not by itself revive the first. These states are said to have "restrictive revival statutes," or "antirevival statutes," under which the only way to revive a revoked will may be for the testator — Ralph, in this case — either to re-execute his first will (which is the same as executing a new and identical one) or to execute a codicil to the first will, thereby republishing it.

Many states take a middle position, permitting revival if an intent to revive can be proven. Such an intent may be found in the instrument that revokes the second will or, if the second will is revoked by physical act, in the testator's oral statements accompanying the act. See UPC 2-509.

Note that in Example 5.5, if Ralph intended but failed to revive his first will by revoking his second, a court might apply the doctrine of dependent relative revocation to nullify the revocation because of the failure of the "condition" of revival. (See Example 5.6 below.)

Dependent Relative Revocation

A doctrine of conditional revocation that permits a court to disregard a purported revocation of a will.

This doctrine is one of the most difficult for law students and lawyers to understand, in part because of its confusing name. (For example, it has nothing at all to do with dependent relatives.) Briefly, if a will (or part of one) is revoked by a testator under a mistake as to some material fact or as to the effectiveness of some new disposition that the testator had intended to substitute for the revoked one but that turned out to be invalid, a court applying the doctrine will assume (1) that the revocation was conditional ("dependent") on the existence of that fact or the effectiveness of that alternative disposition, and (2) that since the condition failed, the testator did not intend the revocation to take effect at all. Lacking the necessary animus revocandi, the revocation is ineffective and the will can be probated.

Note carefully that, while we assume that the testator was in fact mistaken as indicated, it is highly unlikely that the testator had any actual "condition" in mind at the time of revocation. The condition is a fiction, an inference by the court that had the testator been asked whether the revocation should be valid regardless of the mistake, the testator would have said "no." Therefore, if properly — and not just mechanically — applied, the doctrine should nullify a revocation *only* if it appears that the mistaken fact would indeed have been a condition to the will's revocation had the matter occurred to the testator; that is, that knowing the truth, the testator would not have revoked the will.

Courts generally apply dependent relative revocation only when there is some "alternative scheme" (such as an attempt to make some other gift by subsequent will or perhaps by reviving an earlier will) that has failed, although there is some precedent for applying it to a simple mistake of extrinsic fact (such as revocation of a gift under the mistaken impression that the beneficiary is dead). Some courts refuse to apply the doctrine to an express revocation by subsequent instrument but will apply it to revocation by physical act because such an act is inherently ambiguous; here the court will allow extrinsic evidence to demonstrate not only whether the testator intended to revoke but also whether such intent was "conditional."

Example 5.6:   Bertram has executed his will, giving various gifts to friends and relatives and "five thousand dollars to my dear Aunt Dahlia." Dahlia, although Bertram's favorite aunt, is not one of his heirs (that is, she would not take any of his estate if he died intestate). Subsequently, Bertram and Dahlia have a terrible argument and he executes a second will, revoking the first and giving only $500 to Dahlia. (Otherwise the wills are identical.) Bertram and Dahlia then make up and Bertram tears up the second will, telling Dahlia that the gift is back to $5,000 again. Unfortunately, Bertram does not realize that (under the law of his state) his first will cannot be revived merely by destroying the second (see *Revival*), and Bertram dies under the mistaken impression that his first will still stands. In fact, if the second will was validly revoked, he has died intestate. Dependent relative revocation would permit a court to consider Bertram's intention to revoke his second will conditional upon effective revival of his first will, as if Bertram had stated at the time: "I hereby revoke this second will, on the condition that my action revives my first one; if I am mistaken, however, and the first cannot be revived, I want my second will to stand." Bertram's condition for revocation having failed (the first will was not revived), the revocation of the second will fails and it can be probated.

As indicated above, dependent relative revocation should not be applied to nullify a revocation unless it appears from the evidence that this would have been the intent of the testator. In Example 5.6, the court probably will conclude that because Bertram desired Dahlia to have a large gift (of $5,000), he would prefer her to take $500 under the second will rather than to take nothing by intestacy. (There is also a presumption against intestacy. In addition, intestacy may eliminate gifts to others whom Bertram intended to benefit under both wills, a further reason to prefer the second will.) But the evidence could as easily point to the opposite conclusion, as illustrated in Example 5.7.

Example 5.7: As in Example 5.6, Bertram makes a $5,000 gift to his Aunt Dahlia, has a falling out with her, executes a new will with a $500 gift, then tears up the latter will. Assume, however, that Aunt Dahlia is Bertram's only heir at law; if Bertram dies intestate, Dahlia takes his entire estate, worth $50,000. Now the court must decide whether Bertram, had he considered the possibility that the revocation of the second will could fail to revive the first (which he likely did not), would have preferred Dahlia to take the smaller sum of $500 under the second will or the larger one of $50,000 under intestacy. The answer may depend in part on what other provisions Bertram made in his wills, as they too would fail, together with Dahlia's $500 gift, if the revocation is declared unconditional and effective. If, for example, there was a $45,000 gift to a favorite charity, Bertram probably would have chosen to retain that gift and sacrifice the bulk of Dahlia's.

You may ask why the court doesn't simply declare the revocation of Bertram's *first* will invalid, considering that the first will, with its $5,000 gift to Dahlia, is the one Bertram really preferred at the time of his death. This is not possible, however, because while arguably Bertram's revocation of his second will was "conditional" (even if the condition is a fiction), the written revocation of his *first* will was absolute at the time it was done, based on no mistake of fact or law and subject to the effectiveness of no other disposition.

That Bertram changed his mind at a later time and wished he had not revoked his first will does not render its revocation conditional. As its revocation was absolute, it must be revived to be again effective; this can be accomplished only by the means prescribed for revival in Bertram's state.

That leads to another important point. If Bertram's state had allowed revival by revocation of a revoking instrument (as some states do — see *Revival*), then not only would his first will have been revived, giving Dahlia $5,000, but the revocation of his second will would have been valid, the condition (revival of the first will) having been met and no mistake having been made. In such a case, the first will would have been valid because of the doctrine of revival, not because of dependent relative revocation, which would not have been needed and would never have entered the picture. When dependent relative revocation is invoked, it does not "revive" a will; it merely nullifies as ineffective *ab initio* a will's purported revocation. Never having effectively been revoked, that will need not be — and cannot be — revived, just as a person who has not died cannot be brought back to life.

Another common error is to assume that if Bertram had executed his second will, expressly revoking the first, but the second had been invalid (as for want of proper execution), the first would be reinstated by dependent relative revocation, Bertram having "conditioned" his revocation of the first will on the validity of the second. Here again there is no place for the doctrine. The first will is indeed still valid — but only because when the second will failed its revocation clause failed with it, leaving the first will unaffected. Dependent relative revocation applies only to situations in which, but for its application, the will in question would have been validly revoked. If something else (such as the revoking instrument's invalidity) prevents the revocation from occurring, there is no need to apply dependent relative revocation.

Example 5.8 demonstrates the operation of dependent relative revocation in the case of an attempted partial revocation.

Example 5.8: Bertram executes the first will with a gift of "five hundred dollars to Aunt Dahlia." Then, having become even more fond of Dahlia, he crosses out the word "hundred" and writes above it "thousand," under the impression that he has raised her gift to $5,000. However, assume that while in Bertram's state a will can be partially revoked by cancellation, the word "thousand" was not accompanied by the formalities necessary for a valid will or codicil. That means the word "hundred" was validly revoked, but nothing was validly added to replace it. This leaves a gift to Aunt Dahlia of only "five dollars" unless the court can invoke dependent relative revocation. Because it appears that Bertram wanted Dahlia to have an even larger gift than $500, he likely would (if he had thought about it) have preferred the original will to stand, giving Dahlia $500, than to have

C. Revocation Revoked

it partially revoked, leaving Dahlia only five dollars. (Compare the more equivocal situation, however, if Bertram, after an argument with Dahlia, had crossed out "five hundred" and written in "250.")

Finally, the doctrine's relationship to a lost will statute should be noted. As discussed elsewhere, such a statute prevents a will that cannot be located after the testator's death from being probated unless certain strict conditions are met, sometimes including proof that the will was in existence at the testator's death or was "fraudulently destroyed" before then. As just explained, under dependent relative revocation the purported revocation of a will by destroying it may sometimes be nullified if the testator was under a mistaken impression that some other testamentary scheme would replace it. If, however, a court declines to stretch the meaning of "fraudulently destroyed" to include "destroyed by the testator, under the mistaken impression that a different plan would take effect," it is quite possible that a will deemed unrevoked and thus perfectly valid by the application of dependent relative revocation would nevertheless be denied probate because it was not "in existence" or destroyed "fraudulently." Fortunately, most states have repealed their lost will statutes or have modified them to permit probate of a will destroyed by the testator by mistake.

6

Changes in Circumstances

A. INTRODUCTION AND OVERVIEW OF CHAPTER

Many circumstances may change before or after the testator's death such that the dispositive plan of a will is altered. These changes may be brought about by the testator or occur without the testator's intervention; some may even occur after the testator's death. The changes may be in property or in the intended beneficiaries. In addition, certain adjustments must be made in the distribution process to take into account the circumstances that exist at the testator's death and that may change the amount or nature of the property to which a beneficiary is entitled.

This chapter divides changes such as those described according to whether they are changes in property (or entitlement to property, the two sometimes being difficult to separate) or in the beneficiaries themselves. Many of these changes, especially those in entitlement as a result of payment of debts or mortgages, could as easily be discussed in the chapter on administration, as they are part of the process of administration and distribution of the estate's assets. You therefore may want to review the entries in this chapter in conjunction with those in Chapter 11.

B. CHANGES IN PROPERTY OR ENTITLEMENT

Changes can occur, both before and after the testator's death, in the nature of the testator's property or the amount or character of property to which a beneficiary may be entitled. These range from actions by the testator, such as an inter vivos gift to a beneficiary, to unintended changes in the nature of property, such as stock splits, to the payment of such obligations as mortgages or estate taxes. Some doctrines dealing with these changes, like exoneration of mortgages, are quite narrow in their application; others, such as abatement to satisfy prior obligations, apply quite broadly.

What these doctrines have in common is the need, if one of them is applied, often to make adjustments in what appears to be the intended testamentary plan of the testator.

Ademption

The nullification of a bequest of property because it is no longer in the testator's estate at the time of death. Also called **ademption by extinction** (to distinguish it from "ademption by satisfaction," discussed elsewhere), this doctrine applies to specific gifts of items that were a part of the testator's estate at the time the will was executed but were removed from the estate between that time and the date of death. This removal may have been by the intentional act of the testator, such as by sale or inter vivos gift, or by some unintentional circumstance, such as theft or accidental destruction.

Under most current versions of the ademption doctrine, the testator need not have intended to **adeem** the bequest: If the bequeathed item is not in the estate at the time of death, it cannot pass to the legatee. (This is known as the "identity theory," or **Lord Thurlow's Rule**, for the judge who first rejected the older notion of seeking the testator's intent.) A testator who did not intend to adeem a gift and wishes to reaffirm it usually can do so by codicil after the fact. Partial (or "pro tanto") ademption occurs if only a part of a gift is missing from the estate at death.

Ademption does not affect general, demonstrative, or residual gifts, and often it is a close question whether a gift was intended to be specific or general and thus was or was not adeemed.

Example 6.1: George executes a will leaving to Martha "my house in Mt. Vernon and 100 shares of stock in American Enterprises, Inc." At the time, George owns both such a house and 100 shares of American Enterprises stock. A year later, George's house burns down. It was insured, and with the insurance proceeds he builds a new house. The house would appear to be adeemed, since it clearly is a specific gift and is no longer in existence at the time of his death.

That George had no intention to adeem Martha's gift of the house in Example 6.1, had no control over the manner in which it occurred, and promptly replaced it with a similar item using the insurance proceeds, are of no importance if the state follows the "identity theory." (Some states revert to the "intention theory" for involuntary dispositions such as this and would give Martha the insurance proceeds, at least if they are still unpaid at death.) There is one caveat, however: If George built the new house in Mt. Vernon, a court could construe the will's language as giving Martha whatever "house in Mt. Vernon" George owned at the time of his death, rather than the one owned at the time of execution. If so, Martha takes the new house. If, however, the new house was not in Mt. Vernon, it would not fit the description and such a solution would not be possible. On the other hand, had the gift been worded "my house and 100 shares of American Enterprises, Inc.," the new house would have fit the description wherever it was located. (See *Construction.*)

Example 6.2: Having executed the will set out in Example 6.1, George sells the American Enterprises stock for cash. With the proceeds he buys a savings bond, saying at the time that "now Martha will have a sounder investment when I die." The stock also is adeemed, but only if the gift is construed as specific, that is, if George intended (at the time of execution) to give Martha the specific 100 shares of American Enterprises that he then owned, and not simply any 100 shares of the company.

Here again George's language is crucial: By using the term "my," it seems he had in mind the specific shares he owned at the time of execution, resulting in ademption. However, had the gift simply been worded "100 shares of American Enterprises," a court might construe it as general, giving

Martha the right to have any 100 shares purchased from estate assets and avoiding ademption. (This construction would be certain, of course, if the gift had been of "any 100 shares.") Also, it is important to consider what property George had in his estate when executing his will: If he had no (or fewer than 100) shares of the named stock at that time, a gift of "100 shares" seems more clearly to be general.

Note that in the above example George's intent *at the time of execution* is clearly relevant in determining what type of gift he made to Martha, even under the identity theory; it is only his intent *at the time of sale* that is irrelevant under that theory.

A gift is not adeemed if the property given has merely changed form rather than substance. For example, most courts consider a stock split (in which two or more shares in a company are substituted for each existing share) to be only a change of form because the new shares represent the same ownership interest in the company as did the fewer old ones before the split. Similarly, if in Example 6.1 George had completely remodeled the Mt. Vernon house, so that it became virtually a different house, this would still be a change in form and not in substance, probably even if he then moved it to Schenectady (it still being the same item identified at the time of execution as the "house in Mt. Vernon").

Even states that generally ignore the testator's (lack of) intent when ademption is involuntary may make an exception and reject ademption when the property in question is disposed of by the guardian or conservator of a testator who is incompetent and therefore can neither prevent the disposition at the time nor later execute a codicil or a new will to re-establish the gift.

The pre-1990 Uniform Probate Code had modified the doctrine of ademption to take into account such circumstances as sales by conservators and a testator's death before receipt of the proceeds of a sale, condemnation, or casualty loss. The new Uniform Probate Code, following the lead of a few recent decisions, abandons the identity theory and replaces it with the intent theory. UPC 2-606. In effect, a specific devisee is given property that has replaced property specifically devised, and even if there has been no replacement the devisee receives the equivalent in value unless the evidence or circumstances indicate that ademption was intended. In other words, not only is intent determinative, but there is a presumption against an intent to adeem. A state adopting the new UPC would find no ademption in either Example 6.1 or Example 6.2, in the latter case even absent any express statement of intent.

Satisfaction

The abrogation of a bequest by an inter vivos gift made by the testator to the legatee. Satisfaction (or **ademption by satisfaction**) is analogous to the doctrine of advancement of an intestate share; in both instances the owner of the property has made a pre-death gift intended to take the place of one at death. Unlike the traditional approach to ademption by extinction, a bequest is satisfied only if the testator so intended at the time of the gift. Such an intent usually is presumed if property of a similar nature to that bequeathed is given to a beneficiary who is a child of the testator or if the testator stands "in loco parentis" (in the position of a parent) to the beneficiary. Under UPC 2-609, satisfaction requires that the testator's intention be found in the will or a contemporaneous writing, or that the devisee acknowledge the satisfaction in writing. The post-1990 version also provides for satisfaction of a devisee's gift by a transfer to someone other than the devisee.

Satisfaction usually applies only to general gifts, not to specific or demonstrative gifts, again in contrast to ademption. (In some states it applies to residuary and even demonstrative gifts.) In fact, in most cases of satisfaction the bequest and the gift are both of money, and in some states it is confined to such gifts. There can be a partial satisfaction, like a partial ademption or a partial advancement.

Note that while there usually cannot be satisfaction of a specific gift (unless there is a clear expression of such an intent), if the testator makes a lifetime gift of the very item bequeathed to the beneficiary, since that item will no longer be in the testator's estate at the time of death this works an ademption by extinction.

By the doctrine of **ejusdem generis** (it rhymes with "be just, then generous"), if what is given inter vivos is not of the same nature as the thing bequeathed, a satisfaction will not be presumed. Thus a gift of a house will not be presumed to satisfy a bequest of $1,000 cash. ("Ejusdem generis" is also a rule of construction, stating that if property is both specifically enumerated and generally described, it is presumed that reference is only to the kind of items enumerated. See *Construction*.)

Modern statutes apply satisfaction to gifts of either real or personal property, although traditionally it applied (and still applies in many states) only to personal property.

Accessions and Accretions

Additions to or increases in the value of bequeathed property that accrue before the death of the testator or before distribution to the beneficiary. (The terms are technically different but often are used interchangeably.) Typical would be interest on a bond, dividends on shares of stock, and even improvements to real property. See UPC 2-605 (limited to securities).

Usually pre-death additions such as interest and dividends on securities do not pass to the beneficiary. However, additions to a specific gift that accrue after the testator's death do belong to the beneficiary; it is, at that time, the beneficiary's property, even if not yet distributed.

As in the case of ademption, whether accretions pass to the beneficiary may depend on whether the gift is construed as specific or general. (UPC(69) 2-607 was limited to specific devises; UPC 2-605 is not.) For example, a specific gift of a certain number of shares of stock usually will include any additional shares acquired by the testator through a stock split, there having been no change in the ownership interest of the testator but simply an increase in the number of shares that represent that interest. A cash dividend (and in some instances even a stock dividend), however, does not pass with the stock. In many states even a general gift of stock includes additional shares acquired through a stock split, again because of the equivalence of ownership interest.

Abatement

Reduction of a testamentary gift in order to pay some other obligation of a higher priority. Abatement may be necessary any time the testator's estate is insufficient to pay all the estate's obligations. If an estate has insufficient assets, clearly not all the gifts in the will can be honored in full; abatement is the process of determining which gifts will be reduced, in what order, and by what amount. See UPC 3-902.

The usual order of abatement is as follows: (1) intestate property (that not passing under the will), (2) residuary gifts, (3) general gifts, and (4) specific gifts. Demonstrative gifts usually abate with specific gifts to the extent of the fund from which they are to be taken, and with general gifts for amounts beyond that. Gifts in the same category usually abate ratably, or in proportion to their relative values.

Example 6.3:   Nick's will gives $100,000 to his wife, Nora, and his 1947 Buick to Nick, Jr., residue to Charles. At Nick's death, however, his estate contains only his car and $50,000, and he has run up debts of $10,000. Assuming that Nick's entire estate passes under his will, the first source of payment of the debts would be Charles' residuary gift. If that were not sufficient (and here there is nothing in the residue), Nora's general gift of $100,000 would be taken next, and she loses $10,000. With only $40,000 and the car left, Nick, Jr., loses nothing because his gift is specific, and Nora takes only the remaining $40,000. (Note that even without the debts, the estate was not large enough to pay all the bequests.)

In the above example, if Nick, Jr.'s gift is construed as general rather than specific ("*any* 1947 Buick"), both he and Nora would have general gifts, and the gifts would then abate ratably. If a 1947 Buick is worth $10,000, the ratio of their gifts would be 10:1, and Nora would lose $10 for every $1 involuntarily contributed by Nick, Jr.

Some jurisdictions do not follow the above order of abatement, especially in certain special situations. For example, a typical variation abates last any gifts to a spouse, or sometimes spouse and issue, regardless of the type of gift (specific, general, or residuary) they are given. This is especially important in the common instance of the spouse, who usually is the testator's most favored beneficiary, being given the residue of the estate. Under the traditional abatement scheme, that spouse's gift would abate ahead of all others (except intestate property), whereas under a variation favoring spousal gifts it would abate last. (Thus in Example 6.3 Nick's $10,000 debt would be paid from Nick, Jr.'s share to the extent possible, not from Nora's, whether Nick, Jr.'s gift was specific or general.)

Other preferred classes of gifts may be those for support of a relative or to benefit creditors. Special abatement schemes also may apply to such statutory estate obligations as a spouse's election against the will or a claim by a pretermitted heir; often payment is assessed ratably against all beneficiaries, regardless of type of gift.

At common law all personal property abated before any real property, but most states no longer draw this distinction.

Whatever might be the statutory order of abatement, it can be changed by specific direction in the will. Often a testator will direct that taxes or other classes of obligations, or even all debts, be paid out of a particular fund or not be taken from a particular gift. In some states even an implied intention to avoid the usual order of abatement will be followed, if it can be ascertained.

Retainer

Deduction from the share distributed to a beneficiary of an amount owed by the beneficiary to the estate. See UPC 3-903. In some jurisdictions, even a debt that is barred by the statute of limitations can be retained by the personal representative. The right of retainer is sometimes referred to as a **set-off**.

The effect of retainer is to reduce the share distributed to one beneficiary and leave a greater amount available for others, somewhat as application of the doctrines of advancement and satisfaction require a beneficiary who has received payment in advance to account for it to the estate and to the other beneficiaries.

Charge

A burden imposed on property for the payment of an obligation. A testator may charge a specific item or class of property with certain obligations of the estate such as payment of taxes or of other legacies. A charge may be express or only implied by the will's provisions; the latter especially may be enforceable only in equity (an "equitable charge"). (See also *Trust.*)

Exoneration

Payment of encumbrances on certain property in the estate out of other estate assets. Exoneration treats a mortgage or other such liens merely as debts of the testator, to be paid like other debts; thus it applies only if the lien was a personal obligation of the testator.

At common law it was presumed that the testator intended all devises of real property and specific legacies of personalty to be exonerated from the general personal assets of the estate (usually the residuary personalty) unless the testator directed otherwise. Some modern statutes, however, such as UPC 2-607, have abolished exoneration except to the extent expressly directed by the testator.

Election

A beneficiary's choice between taking a benefit under the will and taking instead some other benefit. The beneficiary who chooses to give up the will's benefits is said to take "against the will." An election may be put to the beneficiary in the will either expressly or by implication, or it may be mandated by statute.

A common express election is the spousal (or so-called **widow's) election**, under which a surviving spouse in a community property state must choose between a limited interest in a greater amount of property and a full interest in a lesser amount.

Example 6.4: Pam and Jerry live in a community property state: Each can devise only half of his or her community property at death (because the other half already belongs to the surviving spouse). For tax reasons (which cannot be explained briefly) Jerry wishes to devise all the community property — his and Pam's — to their children. He recognizes that, with respect to Pam's half, this plan would require Pam's agreement. Jerry's will thus purports to establish a trust of all the community property (and perhaps his separate property as well), with a life estate in Pam and remainder in their children. Pam, of course, can refuse to permit her half of the community property to be included in the trust, and keep that half for herself; but if she does refuse, she must give up the life estate in Jerry's half (and his separate property) as well. She must, in other words, "elect" either to retain a fee interest in her half of the community property, and thus receive none of Jerry's property, or to transfer her half to the trust in exchange for a life estate in all the property (Jerry's and her halves of the community and any of Jerry's separate property he has included).

If in the above example (and as is usual) the will requires that Pam make a choice between her property and Jerry's, it is a "forced" widow's election; if she also has the option both to keep her half of the community property and to take the life estate in Jerry's, it is a "voluntary" election (and, by the way, it loses the tax benefits, although there may be other reasons for using it).

If Pam and Jerry lived in a state without a community property system, there likely would be an "elective share" (or "forced share") statute under which Pam would be entitled to a certain fraction of Jerry's estate, regardless of what, if any, provision Jerry made for her by will. However, assuming that Jerry's will did contain some provision for Pam, she again might have to choose — to "elect" — between the will and the statutory share; she could not have both, unless this was Jerry's intent. (Statutes vary as to whether a need to elect is presumed. It usually is.) See *Elective Share*.

Not all elections are between spouses. An **equitable election** requires any beneficiary whose property the testator has purported to give away to choose between that property and the property of the testator.

Example 6.5:   Pam and Jerry are not married. Jerry wants to devise to his friend Bill a cabin owned by Pam. To induce her to let Bill have the cabin, Jerry includes in his will a gift of his diamond ring to Pam. Upon Jerry's death, and even if Jerry's will says nothing about her having to choose, Pam would be put to an equitable election between taking under the will (receiving the ring but making a gift of her cabin to Jerry's friend) and taking against the will, thus keeping her cabin but giving up the ring.

In equitable terms, in the above problem it would be unfair to let Pam choose among the provisions of the will; she must take all the provisions — favorable and unfavorable — or leave them. (Of course, if Jerry wants Pam to have the ring whether she keeps or gives up the cabin, he need only say so in the will.)

When a spouse elects against the will and in favor of some benefit such as a statutory forced share, it may be necessary to abate other gifts under the will in order to pay the spouse. In addition, if the surviving spouse gave up a life (or any other) interest under the will, the question arises what to do with the renounced interest. In the case of a life estate, a court may decide to **accelerate** the remainder interest, giving it to the remainderman immediately rather than at the end of the surviving spouse's life; or it may decide to **sequester** the life estate during the spouse's lifetime, treating it as still existing and distributing its benefits to any beneficiaries who have lost part of their legacies, through abatement, in order to pay the surviving spouse's elective share. Often the decision whether to accelerate or sequester depends on which, if either, would reach the most equitable result, or which seems most in keeping with the testator's intent.

Example 6.6: Jerry's will gives a life interest in all his real property (most of his estate) to his wife, Pam, remainder to their children, and the residue (about $10,000 in cash) to his friend Bill. State law provides Pam a forced share of one-half of Jerry's estate, which she can elect to take outright. If she does so, however, she surrenders the life interest under the will and there is a life estate (in the remaining portion of the real property) that is without an owner. Bill loses his residuary gift, which is abated to pay part of Pam's forced share. The court will decide whether it would be more equitable, under the circumstances, to accelerate the remainder to the children, leaving Bill with nothing, or to sequester and give all or a part to Bill, the disappointed legatee.

Disclaimer

A refusal to accept the benefits under a will or intestate succession statute. At common law, "disclaimer" referred to a refusal by a will beneficiary to accept a legacy, while a refusal by an heir to accept an intestate share was a **renunciation**.

Most modern statutes use the terms "disclaimer" and "renunciation" interchangeably. (In fact, UPC(69) 2-801 used "renunciation"; the 1990 revision substitutes "disclaimer.") The distinction was important, however, because in theory an heir inherited property by operation of law, instantaneously upon the death of the intestate, so that a renunciation could not prevent the property passing to the heir; it could only transfer it from the heir to the next person entitled to it. A legatee, on the other hand, was seen as receiving a testamentary gift from the testator and could refuse (disclaim) it just as any other donee of a gift could do. In recent times this had the effect that upon renunciation of an intestate share, there was deemed to be a taxable transfer to the heir from the intestate and then from the heir to the next recipient; whereas in the case of disclaimer of a legacy the property bypassed the disclaimant entirely, passing directly to the next recipient. This has now been rectified by the federal tax statute (I.R.C. §2518), which treats a so-called **qualified disclaimer** of either type of interest as bypassing the disclaimant.

The disclaimer provisions of UPC 2-801 now apply to nonprobate transfers as well as testate and intestate succession, and (unlike the original version) they permit disclaimer by a deceased person's personal representative.

Subject to statutory time limits (usually nine months from death), a disclaimer can be made at any time before the recipient accepts the disclaimed benefit, and usually it "relates back" so that it is treated as if it had occurred immediately upon the death of the decedent. The disclaimant is deemed to have predeceased the decedent.

C. CHANGES IN BENEFICIARIES

Changes may occur in a will's beneficiaries as well as in the estate's property. Here we are dealing primarily with the doctrine of lapse, taking into account the death of a beneficiary before that of the testator, and the matter of the simultaneous deaths of the testator and one or more beneficiaries. What is to become of the gift that was intended for a beneficiary who died before or at the same time as the testator, or even before the execution of the will?

Lapse

The termination of a testamentary gift because the beneficiary predeceased the testator or is unable or unwilling to accept the gift. The term "lapse" usually refers only to the beneficiary's death before the testator, but technically it also includes disclaimer and other causes of a gift's failing to reach the beneficiary. A gift to a beneficiary who has already died when the will is executed is a **void gift**, traditionally treated differently from lapsed gifts; but modern statutes treat void and lapsed gifts alike for most purposes. See generally UPC 2-603. (More typical is the much simpler approach of UPC(69) 2-605.)

If a gift lapses, it "falls" into the residue, if there is one, or it passes by intestacy. A lapsed residuary gift remains in the residue for any surviving residuary takers, unless the jurisdiction applies the older rule that there can be "no residue of a residue," in which event a residuary gift that lapses must fall out of the residue and into intestacy.

Most states have **antilapse statutes** (sometimes confusingly called "lapse statutes"), which save lapsed gifts and give them to other persons. It is important to remember, however, that an antilapse statute saves the gifts of only those beneficiaries whom it specifically mentions, and then only if specified alternative takers survive. Statutes vary greatly as to the beneficiaries whose gifts are saved, from the testator's descendants or other relatives to almost all beneficiaries. (UPC(69) 2-605, for example, was limited to the testator's grandparents and their descendants, whereas revised UPC 2-603 adds the testator's stepchildren as well.) Most statutes pass the lapsed gift only to the beneficiary's surviving issue, although some substitute the beneficiary's estate. Typically statutes do not save gifts to the testator's spouse, causing them to lapse and pass through the testator's estate rather than to pass to the deceased spouse's own issue or estate. All these statutory provisions can be defeated by a contrary expression of intent in the will.

Example 6.7:   Theodore's will gives $100,000 to his brother Wallace, residue to June and Ward. Wallace predeceases Theodore, survived by no issue but leaving a will in favor of his friend Edward. Wallace's gift would lapse and pass under the residuary clause of Theodore's will to June and Ward, and a typical antilapse statute would not save it for Wallace's estate because Wallace left no issue surviving.

If in the above example Wallace had died leaving issue, and if the statute was broad enough to apply to gifts to brothers, Wallace's issue would have been substituted for Wallace and they would have taken the $100,000 instead of June and Ward. Even then, however, if Theodore's will had said "to Wallace only if he survives me," under most statutes (including the original Uniform Probate Code) and court decisions it would be presumed that Theodore wanted Wallace's gift to be effective only if Wallace survived, and therefore he did not wish the anti-lapse statute to save the gift for Wallace's issue. Under revised UPC 2-603(b)(3), however, the result is less certain: Such phrases as "if he survives me" are no longer by themselves sufficient evidence of an intent that the statute not apply. In a state adopting this controversial provision, therefore, only much more explicit language, such as "to Wallace, *and not to Wallace's descendants*," would be certain, by itself and in the absence of other evidence of intent, to avoid substitution. Of course, whatever approach a state might take to these phrases, explicit language is always to be preferred over that which might leave any doubt as to the testator's intent.

Example 6.8:   Theodore's will gives $100,000 to his brother Wallace, residue to June and Ward. June predeceases Theodore. Her residuary gift would lapse unless saved by the antilapse statute; if June were Theodore's mother and she left issue surviving Theodore, most statutes would save it for them. If not saved by the statute, the gift would lapse and either pass to Ward, as the surviving residuary taker, or (if the state followed the "no residue of a residue" rule) pass intestate (probably to Wallace or Ward or both, depending on the statute and Ward's relationship to Theodore).

Class gifts present a special problem. Technically, a class gift ("to my children," for example) cannot really lapse because it has a "built-in" survival provision: By definition it goes to those members of the class, and only those members, who survive the testator. However, many antilapse statutes include, or have been interpreted to include, class gifts, placing policy considerations ahead of technical consistency. (In some states, a void class gift may not be saved even if a lapsed gift is; this is the case because presumably the testator did not intend to include in the class someone known to be already deceased at the time of execution.) It thus may be necessary to consult both the statute and local case law to determine whether a class gift is saved.

Example 6.9: Theodore's will includes a class gift of $100,000 "to my brothers and sisters," of whom Theodore had several when his will was executed. Wallace predeceases Theodore, leaving issue. Whether Wallace's gift would be divided by the surviving siblings or would be saved for Wallace's issue would depend on whether the state's anti-lapse statute was construed to apply to class gifts.

Simultaneous Death Statute

A statute that alters distribution of an estate when the decedent and the beneficiary have died at the same time. Under the Uniform Simultaneous Death Act, adopted by most states, the decedent's estate is distributed as if the decedent (testator, intestate) had survived the beneficiary. This is done because if the beneficiary were considered to have survived, the gift would pass needlessly through the estate of a person who is not alive to enjoy it, possibly with adverse tax consequences and other attendant expenses and inconveniences.

Example 6.10: Melrose's will leaves $100,000 to his friend Richard. Richard's will leaves his old Ford to Melrose. Both are killed instantly when Melrose's Rolls Royce misses a turn on a country road. Both gifts lapse, as under Melrose's will Richard is deemed to have died first, and under Richard's will Melrose is considered the first to die. The same rule would apply in intestacy if one were the heir of the other.

Under the pre-1991 Uniform Act, death would be presumed simultaneous if there was "no sufficient evidence" to the contrary. Unfortunately, this led to difficult (and sometimes macabre) trials seeking to prove that one person died a split second before or after another so that the statute would not apply. Under the 1991 Act and many other modern statutes, therefore, a beneficiary is required to survive a decedent by 120 hours (5 days) in order to take under a will, intestacy, or an instrument such as an insurance policy. See UPC 2-104, 2-702. The Uniform Act (and the 1990 revision of UPC 2-104) also requires "clear and convincing evidence" of survival for the requisite period. (Note that, for the same reasons motivating the Uniform Act, often the will itself by express provision requires a beneficiary to survive the decedent by a stated number of days.) Of course, any contrary language in the governing instrument takes precedence over the statutory period.

In the case of joint ownership with right of survivorship, each co-owner generally is deemed by simultaneous death statutes to have survived as to one-half of the property.

7

Construction and Interpretation

A. INTRODUCTION AND OVERVIEW OF CHAPTER

This chapter concerns the very important subject of how the language of a will is construed. One might think that wills generally would be clear and straightforward, leaving little need for difficult questions of interpretation. In reality, however, a will poses far more opportunities for ambiguity or uncertainty than one might suspect; even when the language appears to be clear, its legal effect may be governed not by the apparent, "plain English" meaning of the words but by some statutory or common-law rule of construction or "term of art" definition. Moreover, in some instances the testator's intent, even if abundantly clear, will not change that legal effect.

The chapter begins with rules of construction that apply generally to wills, including whether and when extrinsic evidence may be admitted to aid in the construction process. Class gifts, which present particular difficulties, are treated separately.

The next part of the chapter is devoted to future interests, a subject that strikes terror in the hearts of many law students (and lawyers), though needlessly so in most instances. In order to discuss future interests, however, it is first necessary to consider present possessory interests, from which they differ but from which they necessarily derive.

Finally, separate entries describe many of the common-law rules that govern the construction of gifts couched in particular language or having particular characteristics, sometimes regardless of the apparent meaning or the testator's intention. Some of these rules are arcane, most are outdated, but all can be critical if and when they apply.

B. RULES OF CONSTRUCTION IN GENERAL

When the proper interpretation of the language of a will is in question, a court may turn to many formal "rules of construction" to determine the testator's intended meaning. This section discusses these rules and their application in a general way, including the admissibility of extrinsic evidence to ascertain the testator's intent. It does not attempt to list and discuss all the specific rules that a jurisdiction might follow, but it does provide several examples of those that are most often applied and the occasional difficulty in reconciling them. Separate entries explain the special rules for class gifts.

Construction

The process of determining the meaning of a will. In the construction phase of the probate process, a court interprets the will's language and, if necessary, applies certain "rules of construction" to ascribe a meaning to the testator's words. The term "construction" commonly is used (and will be used here) interchangeably with **interpretation**, although technically the two differ: Interpretation is an attempt to ascertain the actual intent of the testator, whereas construction is the attribution of a meaning according to some external principle when interpretation has failed to reveal the testator's actual intent.

Every will, even if clear and unambiguous, requires some degree of construction, if only to ascertain what persons and objects fit the testator's descriptions. Thus a gift of "my car to John" is clear enough, but we still have to fit the terms "car" and "John" to an actual automobile and a real person in order to carry out the gift. Furthermore, many of the doctrines that apply to a will's provisions involve or depend on the construction process: A bequest, for example, may be adeemed only if it is construed as a specific rather than a general gift, or it may avoid lapse only if it is construed as a class gift rather than a gift to an individual; an entire will may fail if it is construed as being conditioned on, rather than merely motivated by, a given event.

A court may construe a will, just as it may construe a statute, "liberally" or "strictly," reading the will's language broadly and flexibly in an attempt to reach a result in keeping with the testator's presumed intent, or narrowly and technically as the language appears to dictate.

Rules of construction may be general (such as "seek to give effect to all parts of the will") or quite specific (such as the presumed meaning of terms like "heirs"). See, *e.g.*, UPC 2-701-711. The Code also broadly classifies such doctrines as ademption, lapse, and satisfaction as "rules of construction." UPC 2-601-609.

Will construction is more an art than a science, and often conflicting and overlapping rules can be found to apply to any factual situation. Because of this, a court may reach a desired result by selecting the appropriate rule or rules and ignoring others. For the same reason it often is futile to seek "the" rule that applies to a case; rather one should identify all those rules — conflicting and consistent — that seem to apply and should seek to resolve the construction in their (sometimes flickering) light.

It often is said that the primary rule of construction is to seek and give effect to the testator's (actual or presumed) intention, and in theory most other rules are merely specific applications of that principle, although some rules are outright applications of public policy. The testator's intent initially is sought from the "four corners" of the will, and if it cannot be found there, under some circumstances extrinsic evidence is admissible to aid the process. If, however, neither the bare language of the will nor admissible extrinsic evidence reveals the testator's true intention (or if the testator simply had no intention regarding the particular circumstance that has arisen), one or more rules of construction may be applied to attribute a meaning to the language.

As indicated, rules of construction can be complementary or conflicting. For example, a typical rule of construction ascribes a technical meaning to technical language; but according to another rule technical knowledge will not necessarily be ascribed to a lay drafter, and a drafter's "personal usage" will be applied if it is discovered. Similarly, a court will presume that the testator intended to make a valid disposition and did not intend to die intestate as to any part of the estate; but partial intestacy will be dictated if most in keeping with the overall dispositive scheme of the will. We are enjoined to give effect to the later of two or more inconsistent provisions; but inconsistent provisions will be reconciled before one will be disregarded, in order to give effect to every part of the will.

One particularly confusing pair of rules provides that a will speaks as of the time of death (which merely means that a will is ambulatory, not final until the testator dies); but the testator's intent is determined, and the testator's circumstances are viewed, as of the time of execution (thus disregarding subsequent changes of mind or circumstances). To illustrate:

Example 7.1: Ann's will gives $1,000 to "my maid." At the time of executing the will, Marcella was Ann's maid; at the time of Ann's death, her maid is Babette. If the will "speaks as of Ann's death," Babette takes the gift; if her "intent is determined according to circumstances existing at the date of execution," it seems Marcella should take. Usually it would be assumed Ann intended at the time of execution that whoever was her maid at her death should take the gift; but were evidence properly admitted that she meant Marcella only, this intent should prevail. And if it were proved that Ann always referred to her older sister Rebecca, who as a child complained of always having to clean up after Ann, as "my maid," Rebecca might have an even better claim to the gift than either of the two housemaids.

Many more such rules exist, and the above examples should demonstrate the variety from which a court can choose.

Extrinsic Evidence

Evidence of facts and circumstances beyond the words of the will. The provisions of a will must be written and executed with the formalities required by statute, and in most instances evidence of the testator's intentions beyond what is indicated in the formal will is excluded.

For some purposes, however, it is always necessary to look beyond the "four corners of the will" to the circumstances surrounding its execution. No matter how clear the language of a will, one must look to the outside world to identify the persons and property to which it refers. If the testator has left "my car to my employee Millie Perkins," nothing can be distributed until we discover what car the testator owned and who is this Millie Perkins to whom the will refers.

Beyond the need for identification, the will may contain an **ambiguity** whose resolution requires resort to extrinsic evidence. Ordinarily, if the words of the will make an unambiguous statement or seem clearly to identify a particular person or thing later found to exist, courts will not admit extrinsic evidence at variance with this language. This is sometimes known as the **plain meaning** (or **single plain meaning) rule**. But if an ambiguity can be found (and courts have become much more willing to consider seemingly "plain" language to be capable of multiple meanings), extrinsic evidence may be admitted to resolve it.

An ambiguity may be **patent** or **latent**. A patent ambiguity appears on the face of the will (for example, "my car to _____"). Merely reading the will reveals the ambiguity or uncertainty. A latent ambiguity, however, does not appear until extrinsic evidence is introduced, usually in the identification phase. Thus "my car to my employee Millie Perkins" is perfectly clear and unambiguous until one looks outside the will to identify Millie and the car, and the extrinsic evidence reveals that the testator had no car but only a truck, and he had two employees named Millie Perkins (or perhaps no employees of that name but one named Millie Parkins and another named Minnie Perkins). The latter type of latent ambiguity, in which the description fits more than one person or object equally well (or equally poorly), is known as an **equivocation**.

At common law a latent ambiguity could be resolved by the introduction of extrinsic evidence, courts saying that because extrinsic evidence revealed it in the first place, additional such evidence could be introduced to resolve it. A patent ambiguity, however, could not be resolved in this way, and a gift lacking sufficient clarity would fail. This was probably a product of courts' reluctance to add anything to a will, as discussed below. Many courts still draw the patent-latent distinction, but others now admit extrinsic evidence to clear up either type of ambiguity.

When extrinsic evidence is admitted, usually only facts and circumstances surrounding the execution of the will — those that put the court in the place of the testator — will be considered. Direct statements of intent by the testator are excluded. When equivocation is present, however, statements of intent usually are admitted to clarify which of the persons or objects was meant.

Sometimes it appears, from the face of the will or by extrinsic evidence, that the testator has made a mistake in the will's provisions. Usually mistakes cannot be corrected, and courts are especially reluctant to add words to a will — to "make a will for the testator." Under some circumstances, however, wills can be reformed and mistakes rectified in the process of construction, especially if the court need only ignore words mistakenly inserted and not add those mistakenly omitted. One example already mentioned is the resolution of an equivocation where two or more persons answer a description. Another common instance is application of the principle **falsa demonstratio non nocet** (literally "a false description is harmless"; "ratio" is pronounced like the English word so spelled, and "no-cet" to rhyme with "no set"): If a person or object can be identified clearly, the fact that the will's description is imperfect does not invalidate the gift. Thus if Millie Perkins is referred to as "Minnie," or the testator's 1957 Chevrolet is incorrectly described as a 1958 model, and it is clear that no other person or car could have been intended, Millie will still get the Chevrolet.

Sometimes a court (or an attorney particularly enamored of legalese), in referring to the admissibility of extrinsic evidence, will use the term evidence (or matters) **dehors** the will. It is simply a fancy way to say "outside" the will. (The "s" is silent — this is Law French, not Latin.)

The admission or exclusion of extrinsic evidence may be crucial to the application of many specific doctrines that depend on the testator's intent. For example, post-testamentary spouse and pretermitted child statutes apply, at least in theory, only if the testator did not contemplate the marriage or have the child in mind when executing the will. Some statutes permit extrinsic evidence of the testator's intent and some do not; some might admit it with regard to spouses but not children; or only certain types of extrinsic evidence may be allowed. Compare, *e.g.,* UPC 2-301(a)(1), 2-301(a)(3),

2-302(b)(1), 2-302(b)(2). See generally *Post-testamentary Spouse Statute; Pretermitted Heir Statute.*

Class Gift

A gift to be divided proportionately among a distinct group (or "class") of persons. More precisely, a class gift is a gift of an aggregate sum to a group of persons, the number of persons to be determined at some later time and the amount of the proportionate share of each to be dependent on the ultimate number in the class.

The simplest example of a class gift is one of "$1,000 in equal shares to my nieces and nephews":"$1,000" is an aggregate sum, to be divided in a specific proportion, equally; and by the usual rules of construction "to my nieces and nephews" is shorthand for "to those of my nieces and nephews who are alive at my death," a group uncertain in number until that time. If at the testator's death 10 nieces and nephews survive, each takes $100; if only one survives, he or she takes $1,000. (Note that in some jurisdictions a gift to a predeceased member of a group may be saved by an antilapse statute.) In contrast, a gift of "$1,000 to each of my nieces and nephews" is not technically a class gift (it is called a **per capita gift**); although the gift is still to a "class" of persons to be determined at the testator's death, a fixed sum goes to each member of the group regardless of the total number who survive. Nor is "$1,000 equally to Ike and Mamie" a class gift. Although it is of an aggregate sum in a definite proportion, it is to two named individuals whose number will not fluctuate: No one else can be added to the "group," and if one of them dies before the testator, the proportion of the gift passing to the other will not thereby increase. If the size of the group cannot fluctuate — either up or down or both, it is not a class gift.

While such examples are fairly easy to construe, it often is a difficult question of construction whether a class or an individual gift was intended. In the gift to nieces and nephews, if through construction it became clear that the testator meant to include only those alive at the date of execution of the will, the gift would be to those persons as individuals, and not as a class. This in turn could have important implications for such issues as whether the niece or nephew must survive the testator in order to take part of the gift, and whether the gift violates the Rule Against Perpetuities.

Closing of a Class

The determination that after a certain time or event no one further may be added to the group that shares in a class gift. One of the difficult issues in construing class gifts is to decide when the class closes, thus excluding those who did not meet the class description (usually because they were not yet born) until after that date.

Example 7.2:   (a) Jimmy's will includes a gift of "$1,000 to my nieces and nephews." Jimmy had only one nephew, Gerald, and one niece, Betty, at the time he executed his will. If both of them survive as his only nieces or nephews at his death, they divide the $1,000 equally. If Betty predeceases Jimmy and only Gerald survives, he takes the entire amount. (See *Class Gift*.)

(b) Same facts as (a), except Richard is born to Jimmy's brother Billy after execution of the will but before Jimmy's death. If the class remains "open" until Jimmy's death (as it ordinarily would), Richard is added to the group and if he survives Jimmy, he takes an equal share. If, on the other hand, the class had already closed when Richard was born, he takes nothing.

A class may close simply because, for example, it is physically impossible for any more members to appear. In Example 7.3, in which Jimmy's will included a gift of "$1,000 to my nieces and nephews," all of testator Jimmy's siblings (and his parents) might die before Jimmy, thus closing the class of nephews and nieces "naturally" through the impossibility of any more being born.

Suppose, however, that brother Billy survives Jimmy and nephew Richard is not born to Billy until after Jimmy's death. Will the class be held open for him, and for any other nieces or nephews who might come along, until all of Jimmy's brothers and sisters have died and there cannot be any more nieces or nephews? Usually the answer is no: Under the **rule of convenience**, the class will close and no one else will be admitted once there is at least one person to whom the property can presently be distributed. In other words, at Jimmy's death whatever nieces and nephews are then alive, and no others, are entitled to distribution of their share of the estate. It would be very "inconvenient" if afterborn nieces and nephews could take a share, because there would be no way of knowing how many nieces and nephews would eventually be born, and so into how many shares to divide the aggregate sum of $1,000 and how much to give the existing members of the class at the testator's death. (They might, for example, have to take their shares subject to a promise to give some back if more class members appeared later.) Usually, only if Jimmy's will clearly states that the class should include afterborn nieces and nephews will a court so interpret it.

Note that while no one can be added after a class closes, members may be deleted after that time. If one thinks of a class gift in terms of students sitting in a classroom run by a professor very strict about punctuality, when the period begins the classroom door is closed and locked and no one else can get in. However, fire regulations require that the locks permit opening from the inside for students to exit in an emergency. Therefore when the class closes no one else can get in, but it is still possible to get out.

Example 7.3: Jimmy's will makes a gift of "$1,000 to the children of my brother Billy." If Billy was alive at the time of execution but died before Jimmy, the class would close "naturally" at Billy's death (because no one else could thereafter be added to it, with the exception of a posthumous child); yet a child of Billy could still die before Jimmy and thus "fall out" of the class (survival being a presumed condition precedent to taking a class gift).

In fact, any condition precedent to a member of a class taking a gift introduces the possibility that a person will fail to meet the condition and thus be absent from the class when it finally receives its gift.

Example 7.4: Jimmy's will gives $1,000 "to my nieces and nephews who reach the age of 21." The class would not close until Jimmy's parents and siblings died or, under the rule of convenience, at least one niece or nephew reached 21 and could claim his or her gift. If little Richard was born to Billy after Jimmy's death but before any other niece or nephew reached 21, he would be admitted into the class; but if he thereafter died before reaching 21, he would fall out of it again (and those who survived to 21 would receive an additional amount).

When the gift is of a *future interest*, the rule of convenience still operates.

Example 7.5: Jimmy's will makes a gift of $1,000 to his brother Billy in trust for 20 years, remainder to Billy's children. The class of children would not close until either Billy died (so no more could be born) or his estate for 20 years ended and under the rule of convenience the existing children were ready to take their shares. Jimmy's death before Billy would not close the class because no member would then be ready to take. (Whether the children must survive Billy or only Jimmy in order to qualify is a separate, though important, question of construction.)

There are exceptions to the rule of convenience. If Jimmy's will gave $1,000 "to the children of my brother Billy," and at the time of Jimmy's death (when the class ordinarily would close) Billy was alive but had no children, the class would not close until Billy's death, no matter how many children he had before then. (Yes, it could close when Billy's first child was born, but once we accept the "inconvenience" of waiting beyond Jimmy's death, we might as well wait for all possible members to join the class, perhaps a victory of common sense over consistency.) Also, although a per capita gift ("$1,000 to each child of Billy") is not technically a "class gift," it is still a gift to a class of persons and is subject to closing (as when Billy dies). However, because we know how much each member is to receive at the time of distribution, no inconvenience generally arises in paying one member before the eventual size of the class is known; thus the rule of convenience does not apply to per capita gifts.

C.   CONSTRUCTION OF PRESENT AND FUTURE INTERESTS

One very important aspect of construction of a will (or any instrument of transfer, especially of real property) is establishing the nature of the interests in property that beneficiaries have been given. In most instances, of course, a gift is of the total ownership interest in property: a ring, a house, cash, and so on. When, however, the gift is of a more limited possessory interest or of a future interest, it is necessary to determine the nature of the interest the donor intended to give, as well as to understand the implications of that determination.

Detailed discussion of the various estates in land is a subject of the course in property. Here enough is said about present possessory estates to provide a foundation for understanding future interests. In addition, key constructional concepts (such as "vest") that apply beyond but are especially crucial to future interests are separately explained. Powers of appointment and the Rule Against Perpetuities, both of which fall under the general topic of future interests, are the subjects of Chapters 14 and 15, respectively.

Words of Purchase or of Limitation

Language in a conveyance that describes either persons who take an interest in the property conveyed or the extent or quality of that interest. In the conveyance "to John for life, remainder to Marsha," the phrases "to John" and "to Marsha" are words of purchase, while the phrase "for life," which qualifies John's estate, is an example of words of limitation.

The distinction between words of purchase and limitation is important because it determines whether a person named in a conveyance has actually been given an interest in the property. Thus for reasons more historical than logical, in a conveyance "to John and his heirs" the phrase "and his heirs" is always construed as words of limitation, not of purchase: They define the quality of John's estate — a fee simple absolute — rather than the persons who have been given an interest in the property. If John's heirs (when they are determined) are to take such an interest, it will have to be by John's will or by intestate succession: They take nothing (except an expectancy) by virtue of the wording of the original gift.

A related use of the term "limitation" should be noted: In the conveyance "to Marsha for life, remainder to John," the remainder is sometimes called a **limitation** or **limitation over** (or **gift over**) to John, and in a fee simple determinable ("to Marsha so long as she lives in America") the condition is a **special limitation**. Thus usage merely refers to an interest that follows (and limits) a prior interest.

Possessory Estate

The interest of one who has a present right to possession or enjoyment of property. It stands in contrast to the future interest of one who has only a postponed right to possession or enjoyment. Together, the holders of the possessory estate and the future interest(s) have total ownership in the property.

Example 7.6: Siegfried devises Skeldale House to Tristan for life, remainder to James. Upon Siegfried's death Tristan owns the possessory estate and James a future interest in Skeldale.

The principal possessory estates are a **fee simple absolute**, which is the total interest in the property, the most one can own ("to Tristan and his heirs" — see *Words of Purchase or of Limitation*); a **life estate**, which is just what it says, an estate lasting for the lifetime of the transferee ("to Tristan for life"); and the limited fee simple estates, the **fee simple determinable** ("to Tristan so long as he uses Skeldale as his residence," the latter phrase being a "special limitation") and the **fee simple subject to condition subsequent** ("to Tristan in fee, but if he ever moves out of Skeldale House, his interest shall terminate and Siegfried may retake possession"). The term **fee** often is used as shorthand for "fee simple," although technically it refers to any inheritable estate. Note how a small difference in wording can change a special limitation into a condition subsequent, thus changing the nature of both the possessory estate and the future interest that follows it. (See *Future Interests in Transferors.*)

Of lesser import are the **term of years** ("to Tristan for 40 years, then to James") and the life estate **pur autre vie** ("to Tristan for the life of James"; it means "for another's life" and is pronounced to rhyme roughly with "poor Joe, a 'B'". Finally, a **fee tail** ("to Tristan and the heirs of his body") is a mostly obsolete estate that purports to pass the property only to the grantee and the grantee's lineal descendants, but which today through various devices is usually transformed into some one or combination of other estates (such as a fee simple in Tristan or a life interest in Tristan and remainder in fee simple in his issue).

Vested and Contingent Interests

An interest that is either fixed and certain in its ownership ("vested") or subject to some uncertainty yet to be resolved ("contingent"). (The Uniform Probate

Code refers to all interests that are not vested as **nonvested interests**. *E.g.*, UPC 2-901.) More specifically, a **vested remainder** is created in an ascertained person and is subject to no **condition precedent** (requirement that must first be met, other than the necessary termination of the preceding estate): "to Peter for life, remainder to Harriet." A **contingent remainder**, then, must be in an unascertained (such as an unborn) person or subject to a condition precedent: "to Peter for life, remainder to Harriet's children" (Harriet having none at the time of the transfer), or "to Peter for life, remainder to Harriet if she survives Peter."

An interest can be **indefeasibly vested** ("remainder to Harriet" leaves no chance she or her successors will not take); **vested subject to divestment** ("remainder to Harriet, but if she moves to America, to Gerald," there being here a **condition subsequent** that follows an otherwise absolute gift and cuts it off if it is satisfied); and **vested subject to open** (or **subject to partial divestment**), which merely means that the remainder is part of a class gift and the class is still "open" to admit further members: "remainder to my children," each present child having a vested remainder in (a share of) the property but subject to their share being diminished ("partially divested") by the birth of more children.

If a contingency may result in either of two persons taking the remainder, each has an **alternate contingent remainder**: "to Peter for life, remainder to Harriet if she marries Peter, and to Gerald if she does not."

Of course, interests other than remainders may be vested or contingent: Executory interests are virtually always contingent, reversions are always vested, and both possibilities of reverter and rights of entry are, of necessity, contingent.

Whether an interest is vested or contingent is often a difficult question of construction, and it may depend on some very technical, perhaps only historically based rules and distinctions. The primary rule of construction here is a preference for a vested interest, but like other such rules it is subject to many exceptions and countervailing forces. Although often dependent on seemingly arbitrary differences in the wording of a gift or on policies that no longer have any justification, the classification of an interest as vested or contingent can have substantial implications, even to the point of validating or voiding the interest, in conjunction with a number of doctrines, from transfer taxation to the Rule Against Perpetuities.

Future Interest

An interest in property that will not come into possession or enjoyment until some later time. The name "future interest" can be misleading, because a future interest is really a present interest — or put the other way, one can presently hold a future interest: Only possession or enjoyment is postponed, not ownership. (The one who holds the present right to possession or enjoyment has a possessory estate, discussed elsewhere.)

Example 7.7:   Siegfried's will leaves $1,000 in trust, income to Tristan for life, then principal to James. When Siegfried dies, Tristan receives a life estate in the fund, which is a present possessory interest, and James a remainder, which is a future interest with possession postponed. James owns the remainder as soon as Siegfried dies, just as Tristan owns the life estate; the only difference is that Tristan can enjoy (go out and spend) his interest immediately, while James must wait to spend his (unless he converts his future interest into immediate cash by selling it to someone willing to wait, which James can do because it is a presently owned and transferable property interest).

Future interests are generally divided into two major categories: those retained by the transferor of the property, and those held by a transferee. Brief definitions of the interests comprising each type are the subject of separate entries below. They are intended only to set out the basic characteristics of the interests; the many and varied qualifications or extensions of these definitions are the substance of the course in property law and are beyond the scope of this work.

Future Interests in Transferees

Future interests held by one or more of the persons to whom property has been transferred.

Example 7.8:   Siegfried devises Skeldale House to Tristan for life, remainder to James for life, remainder to Helen. Upon Siegfried's death Tristan owns the present possessory estate in Skeldale House; James owns a remainder for life, and Helen owns a remainder in fee, both future interests in transferees. James's future interest will not become possessory until Tristan's death; Helen's possession must await the death of both Tristan and James.

A **remainder** is a future interest in a transferee (such as James or Helen) that can become possessory (but may not if it is subject to some condition precedent that fails) at the expiration of all other prior interests (like Tristan's and James's life estates) that were created at the same time (as by Siegfried's will). A remainder must not cut off any prior interest of another transferee before the latter expires of its own accord, and by definition (for reasons more historical than logical) it cannot follow any kind of fee simple. A remainder may be vested or contingent. The holder of a remainder is called a **remainderman** (whether male or female).

An **executory interest** is any future interest in a transferee that is not a remainder. In effect, this means it is a "divesting" interest that either cuts off the interest of another transferee (a "shifting" executory interest: "to Tristan, but if Tristan declares bankruptcy, to James") or cuts off the interest of a transferor at a time when no other transferee is entitled to possession (a "springing" executory interest, so named because it "springs" out from the transferor across the "gap" in ownership between transferor and transferee: "to Tristan for life, and one day after his death to James"). An interest in a transferee following a fee simple determinable is also an executory interest because by definition a remainder cannot follow any kind of fee simple ("to Tristan in fee so long as he remains sober, then to James"). A fee simple followed by an executory interest in a third person (like James, above), which would be a fee simple determinable if the transferor had retained a possibility of reverter, is sometimes called a **fee simple on executory limitation**. With an exception not here relevant, an executory interest is never vested.

Future Interests in Transferors

Future interests retained by persons who have transferred less than their entire interest in the subject property to another.

A **reversion** is a future interest in a transferor that automatically results from having transferred (as by will) a lesser estate than the transferor had.

Example 7.9: Siegfried owns a fee simple absolute in Skeldale House. If he transfers a fee simple absolute to Tristan, he retains nothing; if he transfers a life estate to Tristan and a vested remainder in fee simple to James, he still retains nothing; but if he transfers a life estate to Tristan and no remainder, he (or his successor) necessarily retains what is left after Tristan's life estate ends, a reversion.

Because what Siegfried has is a retained interest in the transferor, it is called a reversion, not a remainder. All reversions are vested interests, although they may or may not eventually come into possession. If Siegfried transferred Skeldale to Tristan for life, remainder to James "if by then James has any children," Siegfried has a vested reversion, but it comes into possession only if James's contingent remainder fails (if James has no children at Tristan's death).

The remaining two future interests in transferors are the **possibility of reverter** and the **right of entry for condition broken** (often called a **power of termination**). A possibility of reverter follows (remains after the transfer of) a fee simple determinable ("to Tristan so long as he remains sober"), while a right of entry follows a fee simple subject to condition subsequent ("to Tristan, but if he ever takes another alcoholic drink, Siegfried may reenter the premises"). Had Siegfried followed either transfer with a gift over to James upon Tristan's insobriety, James (as a transferee) would have an executory interest, as elsewhere defined (see *Future Interests in Transferees*).

The principal differences between the possibility of reverter and the right of entry are that the former operates automatically while the latter requires exercise of the transferor's right (or power), and in some states a right of entry is not alienable (transferable) inter vivos. Also, the distinction may have some significance in applying the Rule Against Perpetuities. Some legislation has abolished the distinction entirely, creating one "power of termination" and placing various restrictions on its exercise and duration.

D.   SPECIAL RULES OF CONSTRUCTION

The only thing "special" about the rules of construction set out in this section is that they apply a predetermined meaning to the use of very specific language. A transfer of property that contains a given phrase or use of words is taken (absolutely or presumably) to intend to pass a particular interest in a particular way.

Most of these rules are based more on history than on logic, and therefore they are a plague to the unwary transferor or practitioner, not to mention the unprepared law student. Modern statutes tend to retain some and reject others or to apply them only to certain forms of property or transfers. Unfortunately, these disparate reforms only make it more necessary to check carefully the local law when encountering the potentially triggering language.

Rule in Shelley's Case

A rule that transforms a conveyance's remainder to the grantee's heirs into a remainder to the grantee.

Example 7.10:   Marsha conveys her house "to John for life, remainder to John's heirs." This becomes a conveyance "to John for life, remainder to John." Because (as is usually the case) there is no intervening estate (such as another life estate) between John's life estate and the remainder, John ends up with all possible interests in the land and they "merge" into a fee simple absolute in John.

The rule's historical justification was primarily related to the feudal system, and it has been abolished in most states, although it survives in some form in a few and may be abolished only prospectively in others. (It should be carefully distinguished from the Doctrine of Worthier Title, which transforms a conveyance from Marsha "to John for life, remainder to *Marsha's* heirs" into a life estate in John and reversion in Marsha.)

The Rule in Shelley's Case (which actually arose before Shelley's Case was decided in 1579) applies only if certain conditions are met: the grantee

(John in Example 7.10) receives a "freehold estate" (actually a life estate or a fee tail) in land; the grantee's heirs are purportedly given a remainder; the same instrument (such as a will) creates both interests; and the interests are both legal or both equitable.

The rule is one of law, not of construction, which means that the transferor's actual intent is irrelevant (similarly to the Rule Against Perpetuities). Even if Marsha intends that John's not-yet-ascertained heirs, and not John, should take the remainder, if she uses the above form to attempt it and the rule applies, she will fail.

Doctrine of Worthier Title

A rule that transforms a gift's remainder or other limitation over to the grantor's heirs (or next of kin) into a reversionary interest in the grantor.

Example 7.11:   Marsha conveys her house "to John for life, remainder to Marsha's heirs." Under the Doctrine of Worthier Title this is transformed into a gift "to John for life, reversion in Marsha."

The historical explanation was that "descent was worthier than purchase": It was more beneficial to the feudal overlord if an heir took by descent (in effect by intestate succession), which carried with it certain incidents of feudal tenure, than by purchase (by direct gift from the grantor).

The doctrine must be distinguished from the Rule in Shelley's Case, which transforms a gift from Marsha "to John for life, remainder to *John's* heirs" into a fee simple absolute in John. Unlike the Rule in Shelley's Case, any kind of estate (life estate, term of years, and so on) may precede the remainder; the remainder to heirs or next of kin may be either legal or equitable; both realty and personality are covered by the doctrine; it is applicable today only to inter vivos transfers; and it is not a rule of law but a rule of construction that can be rebutted by sufficient evidence of a contrary intent. While the doctrine has been abolished in many states and by UPC 2-710, it still is applied in one form or another in several jurisdictions.

Rule in Wild's Case

A rule of construction applicable to gifts such as "to John and his children" (or "his issue"). There are two "resolutions" in Wild's Case: Under the first resolution, if John has no children (issue) at the time of the transfer, John is deemed to have a fee tail; under the second resolution, if John has any children at the time of the transfer, John and his children hold the property as tenants in common in fee (formerly as joint tenants for life). Although originally the Rule applied only to devises of real property, today it may apply as well to inter vivos transfers and any type of property.

Most states still apply the second resolution in Wild's Case, although many now construe the gift as a life estate in John and remainder in his children. Few if any states still apply the first resolution, especially since most have abolished the fee tail and, in any event, it is highly unlikely a grantor or testator intended to create one; most would construe the gift as a fee simple absolute in John or, under the more modern approach, a life estate in John and remainder in his children.

Rules in Clobberie's Case

Rules of construction, named after a 1677 English case, that determine whether, given certain language, a beneficiary must survive to a designated time in order to take a gift. Specifically: (1) If there is a bequest of money "to Marsha at age 21, *to be paid with interest*," even if Marsha dies before reaching 21, the gift is considered vested and her estate would receive the gift in her stead. Because she was to receive accrued interest until that time, it is assumed that the money was meant to be hers from the date of the gift, not just the date of payment. (2) If the bequest is one "*to be paid* at age 21," again it is construed as vesting the gift in Marsha immediately, and if she dies before reaching 21 her estate takes it. But if the gift is worded merely "to Marsha *at age 21*," it is construed as being contingent on Marsha's survival until age 21. (The gift is *given* to her "at 21," not given immediately and just "paid" to her at 21.)

Most states follow the first two of these rules of construction (they actually are the first and third rules as set out in *Clobberie's Case* itself). Courts are more divided as to the last-stated rule because it seems to put great weight on a small difference in language that may have had no such significance to the testator.

"Die Without Issue"

A phrase establishing a particular type of contingency, as in "to John, but if he should die without issue, to Marsha." The usual meaning is simply that Marsha takes the property if, at the time of John's death, he (John) has no surviving issue (descendants). This is called "definite failure of issue." Historically, however, two other meanings could attach to the phrase: "if at any time after his death John's line of issue should die out" ("indefinite failure of issue"); and "if John should die without ever having had issue," a possible but unlikely construction.

Perhaps the most notable application of the "indefinite failure" construction was in the famous (or infamous) case of *Jee v. Audley*, in which the inability to tell at the time of a beneficiary's death whether she had "died without issue" (that is, whether or when her line of descendants would eventually die out) led to a violation of the Rule Against Perpetuities and many subsequent generations of confused law students.

"Heirs" (When Determined)

The date on which it is assumed a person died for purposes of determining who should be considered that person's "heirs." The term "heirs" technically refers to those persons who take by intestate succession at the death of another (see *Heir*). It may, however, refer to those who *would* have taken as heirs at some other time than at the decedent's actual death.

Example 7.12: Marsha conveys her house "to Marsha for life, remainder to John for life, remainder to Marsha's heirs." (Ignore any possible application of the Doctrine of Worthier Title.) Marsha's heirs, whoever they are, will not take possession of the house until after the death of both Marsha and John; and if John survives Marsha, they will not take possession until sometime after (and not immediately at) Marsha's death. At Marsha's death, her sole heir might be her daughter Mary; but by the time of John's death, Mary might have died, and Mary's daughter Melinda might be Marsha's only heir *as of that date*, that is, had Marsha died then. Thus "heirs" could mean either Mary or Melinda, depending upon when they are ascertained. Under the traditional, technical definition, Mary is the true "heir" and she will take the remainder interest, although she will never come into possession, and most likely her interest will pass through her estate to Melinda.

Because Mary would have no real benefit from inheriting in these circumstances, and because a transmissible remainder interest (as Mary would have) is taxable, a court may construe Marsha's intent (if it is not otherwise clear) as meaning "my heirs ascertained as of the time they take possession," in this case Melinda, not Mary. In some states, statutes make this "heirs as of the date of possession" the preferred construction in the absence of a contrary indication. The 1990 Uniform Probate Code adopts this construction as well. UPC 2-711.

There is also a **rule of incongruity** that could lead to the same result under particular circumstances: If a life estate is followed by a gift to the testator's "heirs" and one of those heirs is the life tenant, usually a court will determine the "heirs" as of the date of the life tenant's death rather than the testator's, to avoid the "incongruity" of giving the remainder to the then-deceased life tenant. In other words, if John were one of Marsha's heirs, this rule would determine Marsha's heirs as of John's death rather than Marsha's, assuming John outlived Marsha. (See also *Rule in Shelley's Case* and *Doctrine of Worthier Title*.)

8

Integration, Incorporation, and Related Matters of Inclusion

A. INTRODUCTION AND OVERVIEW OF CHAPTER

This short chapter covers a series of related circumstances that raise the issue of what constitutes the testator's "will." The doctrine of integration concerns what pieces of paper can or should be considered a part of the testamentary instrument. The remaining doctrines begin with the integrated will and address the possibility that other writings (or even events) that clearly are not a physical part of the will might nevertheless be given testamentary effect.

B. DOCTRINES OF INCLUSION

The three concepts explained below really fall into two categories. Integration simply pertains to what pieces of paper are to be probated as the testator's "will." Incorporation by reference and facts of independent significance, on the other hand, both concern giving testamentary effect to documents or circumstances clearly outside of the (integrated) will.

Integration

The inclusion in one whole document, or series of documents, of all the writings that constitute a will. These parts are validated by a single act of execution.

In other words, a will may consist of more than one page, and when the testator executes the will by signing it, all those pages — and only those pages — that are then present and that the testator intends to include as part of the will are thereby integrated into it.

The best evidence of integration — that is, of the testator's intent to integrate particular documents into the will — is some physical bond, such as a staple, holding them together. Similarly, the fact that the language ending one page continues on the next indicates that the two were meant to be read together. (For this reason, it is good practice to fasten the pages of a will together and also to end each pages in mid-sentence so as to provide a contextual link from each to the next. Pages should be numbered, the form "Page ____ of [total number]" should be used, and the total number of pages should be recited in the attestation clause.)

A document that is not present at the time of execution cannot be considered a part of the will in the sense of being integrated, but it can be incorporated by reference or included under the doctrine of facts of independent significance if the requirements of those doctrines are met.

Incorporation by Reference

A process for giving testamentary effect to documents that are not physically a part of the executed will. Through integration, a will consists of all the writings that were present at the time of execution and were intended by the testator to be part of the will. But a writing that is not then present, or that does not become part of the integrated will, still can be given effect if it is properly incorporated by a reference to it within the will. The testator intends that the incorporated document be read with the will but for one reason or another has not included it physically or verbatim in the will's text.

The usual requirements for a valid incorporation by reference are the following: (1) that the document to be incorporated have been *in existence* at the time of the will's execution; (2) that the document be sufficiently *identified* in the will to make it reasonably certain that the document in question is the one referred to; and (3) that the will manifest the testator's *intent* that the document be incorporated. See, *e.g.*, UPC 2-510. Older formulations, still in effect in some jurisdictions, also require that the will refer to the document as being in existence.

Example 8.1: Testator Horace wishes to give to his wife, Hilda, all the rare poetry books from his collection that he purchased himself and to give to his daughter Portia books that he inherited from his father. He could simply describe the two gifts this way, leaving it for the executor to figure out which books are which, or he could list in the will the hundreds of titles given to each. Better yet, if he has kept a record of his purchases over the years, he can simply state in his will that he gives to Hilda "all those books I have listed in my record of acquisitions, dated 1950 to the present, to be found in the top left drawer of my desk." This language clearly identifies the list, states that it is then in existence, and manifests Horace's intent that it be incorporated in his will and used to distribute the books.

Note that if in the above example the will contained more equivocal language, such as "a list that will be found in my desk drawer," this might not satisfy the requirement of sufficient identification, or of reference to the list as being in existence, even should extrinsic evidence show that the list was in fact in existence at the time of execution.

The reason for the principal requirement that the document have been in existence at the time of execution of the will is to assure that the testator cannot make changes in an already executed will simply by writing out a separate piece of paper that lacks the formalities of a will. If Horace wishes to amend his will after the fact, he must execute a formal codicil.

On the other hand, so long as the document is already in existence, it matters not why the testator executed it. Unlike the doctrine of facts of independent significance, therefore, Horace's incorporation by reference would be valid even if the list in question was prepared strictly for purposes of dividing his books at his death, so long as it satisfied the three criteria of time, identification, and intent.

A conceptual dilemma is posed by an attempt to incorporate by reference a printed document in a holographic will. Most courts would permit this, despite the theoretical inconsistency that technically the will cannot then be "all in the testator's handwriting" (as is required for holographic wills). For this reason, however, the result may depend on whether the court considers an incorporated document to be a "part of" the will for purposes of initial probate or only for purposes of construction.

The distinction between the concepts of integration and incorporation by reference can be graphically illustrated as follows:

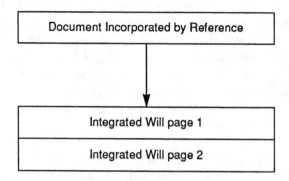

Here the will consists of two "integrated" (probably physically attached) pages; the incorporated document either is physically elsewhere or (even if present) is not part of the text of the will.

Two additional devices for incorporating other documents into a will's provisions do not follow the usual rules of incorporation by reference (or its related doctrine, facts of independent significance). The first, the "pour-over" will and trust, is permitted in every jurisdiction and is discussed fully in Chapter 12. The second, less widely adopted but included in the Uniform Probate Code and gaining popularity, is a separate written list of tangible personal property, handwritten or signed by the testator, that can be incorporated despite being prepared or altered after execution and having no nontestamentary significance. See UPC 2-513. While specific statutory requirements vary, generally such a list is not effective to pass real property, money, or "intangibles" such as securities. This device is a convenience for both attorney and testator, permitting changes of mind over the disposition of items such as paintings or automobiles without the necessity of a formal codicil.

Facts of Independent Significance

A doctrine that gives testamentary effect to facts or circumstances that are not a part of the executed will. It is also called the doctrine of **acts** or **events of independent significance,** or of nontestamentary acts, but it may actually validate nontestamentary writings ("My car to the residuary beneficiary in Uncle Tom's will") and circumstances ("The contents of my safe deposit box to Uncle Tom") as well as acts ("Everything to my wife, should I marry"). See UPC 2-512.

To the extent that the doctrine permits the testator to make use of writings that were not present at the execution of, and thus not integrated into, the will, it is like incorporation by reference. It differs, however, in that it permits reference to writings that were not in existence at the time of execution. The key to the distinction between the two doctrines is in the phrase "independent significance."

Example 8.2:   Horace leaves his estate to Hilda, and in so doing he refers to a list of poetry books that he wants Hilda to have. It is a list of books he has acquired, regularly kept for his tax or insurance records and too lengthy and detailed to insert verbatim into the will. While the list already exists, Horace intends to add to or change it as he acquires or disposes of poetry books. Because the list has an independent, nontestamentary purpose (tax or insurance record), it may validly be included in Horace's overall testamentary plan despite being changed (or even created anew) after execution of the will.

If the list in Example 8.2 had been prepared only for testamentary purposes (that is, to indicate which books Hilda should have), it would not qualify as a fact of independent significance; but even then, if it was in existence at the time of execution and not changed thereafter, it still might satisfy the doctrine of incorporation by reference. No such pre-execution time limitation exists under the doctrine of facts of independent significance: If, by definition, the list (or other fact) referred to has significance to Horace independent of his will, he will not be considered to be "changing his will without formalities" when he later creates or amends the list, but merely to be performing an independent act that also and incidentally happens to affect his will. Of course, if Horace confines his reference to an independently significant list complete and existing at the time of execution, he may (if he uses the proper language) rely on both doctrines together.

Many common testamentary gifts could theoretically be challenged as permitting some later informal alteration of the will, but they generally are accepted without question. Thus if Horace decides to give the books he purchased to Hilda but to give those he inherited to whoever is his law clerk at the time of his death, the latter gift theoretically permits Horace to "change his will" by changing his clerk. Similarly, if Hilda leaves her estate "to any child or children I might have at my death," in theory she could manipulate her testamentary dispositions simply by having children. However, because these are so obviously nontestamentary acts, with significance wholly apart from their effect on the testator's will, they are seldom if ever questioned, and if questioned they would be validated by the doctrine of facts of independent significance. That is not to say, of course, that no eccentric testators are capable of hiring or firing employees or even having children in order to manipulate their testamentary scheme; just that the law generally is willing to overlook such a possibility (at least in the absence of contrary evidence) in the application of this doctrine.

The same graphic illustration may be used to represent the independent significance doctrine as was used to illustrate incorporation by reference:

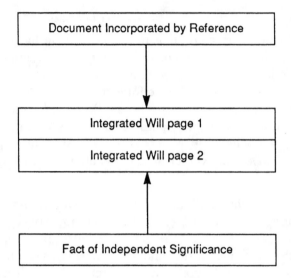

Here both the incorporated document and the independent document or circumstance are either physically or contextually outside of the two pages of the will. Note that, read from the top, this diagram also illustrates the time frame of the three doctrines of integration, incorporation by reference, and facts of independent significance: The integrated will includes documents that are present at the time of execution; document incorporated by reference must have been created earlier than the time of execution; and a fact of independent significance may (although it need not) be created after execution of the will.

9

Restrictions and Conditions

Disabling Restraints
Rule Against Suspension of the Power of Alienation

A.   INTRODUCTION AND OVERVIEW OF CHAPTER

Although the principle of freedom of testation is a strong element in American probate law, there are definite limits on the property a testator may pass and the persons to whom it may be passed. These limitations concern mostly protection of the family, especially a surviving spouse. They may take the form of statutory restrictions on the disposition of the testator's own property, or they may give a spouse full or partial ownership in a part of that property before the testator's death.

Of course, the will itself may contain restrictions imposed by the testator, either on the nature of the property interest given or the persons receiving it. Again, while testators are generally free to impose whatever restrictions they wish, the law imposes certain limitations on restrictions whose implementation is deemed contrary to public policy.

This chapter considers both types of restrictions, those imposed by the law and those by choice. It only mentions, but does not discuss in detail, perhaps the most well-known (and least understood) restriction of all, the Rule Against Perpetuities, to which a separate chapter is devoted in Part 2.

B.   RESTRICTIONS ON PROPERTY AND ITS DISPOSITION

States vary in the degree to which they seek to protect a surviving spouse or other family members against disinheritance by a decedent. They also take different approaches to affording that protection. At one extreme is the community property system, which is not truly meant to protect against disinheritance (although it usually has that effect) but changes the very nature of the marital relationship and the ownership of property within it. At the other is the forced share, which makes no attempt to alter the ownership of property within an existing marriage but assures that when one spouse dies, the survivor receives some minimum share of the decedent's estate. Between these extremes are variations, ancient and new, protecting spouses only or other family members as well.

Community Property

A system of property ownership, derived from the civil law, under which a husband and wife are deemed co-owners of property each of them earned during marriage. It places certain restrictions on the use and transfer of such property, both protecting the nonacquiring spouse's property interest and recognizing the contributions of both spouses to the partnership of marriage. Eight states follow the community property system (and to date one state follows a similar regime under the Uniform Marital Property Act). Noncommunity property states often are referred to as following the "common law system."

The chief characteristic of community property is that it is co-owned by a husband and wife during the lifetime of both; unlike dower and courtesy or the elective share system of common law states, married persons need not wait until their spouses' death to own a share of the marital property. Because ownership is undivided, either community property must be "managed" by one spouse who has control over the interests of both, or both spouses must agree on transfers, especially of community real property. States vary in how these rights are allocated. Property that is not classified as community is called **separate property.** (Under the Uniform Act community property is **marital property** and separate property is **individual property.**)

Perhaps the most difficult issue arising in a community property system is the determination of what property is community and what is a spouse's separate property. The basic rule is fairly simple: Earnings of either spouse during marriage, and items purchased with those earnings, are community property; property acquired during marriage by gift, devise, or inheritance, as well as property that a spouse brings into the marriage, is separate. Problems arise when separate and community property are "commingled," making it difficult to trace their source; when property of one type is maintained or improved with funds of the other type; when there are profits produced by property that is partly community and partly separate; and so forth. For example, real property may be purchased before marriage and later improved with community funds, or a life insurance policy may be acquired before marriage but premiums later paid from community (or mixed separate and community) funds.

Courts have developed rules and presumptions to aid in resolving some of these problems. For example, under the **inception of title** rule, property acquired before marriage is and remains wholly separate, and any later addition to it from community funds entitles the community to reimbursement but to no ownership interest; whereas under the **tracing** (or "pro rata") theory, the property is considered both separate and community in proportion to the contributions that were made (and can be traced) from each type. It should be apparent why modern versions of the community property system, such as the Uniform Marital Property Act, dissociate themselves from the community property system's reputation for complexity by adopting entirely different terminology and never using the term "community property" at all.

Because of the joint ownership of community property, only half can be devised by the first spouse to die, and if the spouse dies intestate usually that half passes to the surviving spouse, who already owns the other half.

The inability of the deceased spouse to deal with both halves of the community property in a single, unified estate plan has led to use of the so-called widow's election, which gives a surviving spouse a choice between keeping only the half of the community property already owned, thus forgoing any part of the deceased spouse's half, and permitting the deceased spouse's will to dispose of both halves, usually in exchange for some benefit from the deceased spouse's half.

Finally, property of spouses living in a community property state may have been acquired earlier, while they were domiciled in a common law state (and so it is classified as separate property because its character is governed by the law of their domicile at the time of acquisition). If the acquiring spouse then dies domiciled in the community property state, which (typically) has no elective share statute, the nonowner surviving spouse could be left with no protection (or property) at all. To address this common situation, the concept of **quasi-community property** was developed. In those few states that follow this rule, property acquired elsewhere that would have been community property if acquired in the community property state is treated for most purposes as separate property of the acquiring spouse during the spouses' lifetimes, but at the death of either it takes on the characteristics of community property. In this way it is like having an elective share with respect to that property. (Under the Uniform Marital Property Act, the equivalent of quasi-community property is **deferred marital property.**)

Elective Share

A *share of an estate (also called a **forced share**)* set aside by law for a surviving spouse, regardless of the provisions of the decedent spouse's will. Typically the share is a fraction such as one-third of the decedent spouse's net probate estate (thus including property acquired outside of the marriage, but excluding nonprobate assets such as life insurance proceeds), although some statutes now include certain nonprobate transfers in order to prevent the decedent spouse from making inter vivos transfers that defeat the surviving spouse's share.

Example 9.1: Frederic predeceases his wife, Mabel, in a state having an elective share statute. He expressly leaves nothing to Mabel in his will. If the state has an elective share statute, Mabel may nevertheless be entitled to some fraction of Frederic's net estate.

Mabel's statutory share in Example 9.1 is a "forced" share because it is available to Mabel regardless of Frederic's will provision or actual intent; it is an "elective" share because Mabel is generally required to choose between her statutory share and any favorable provision in Frederic's will. (See generally *Election.*) The share generally would not be reduced by amounts given to Mabel by Frederic prior to Frederic's death, or by nonprobate assets payable to Mabel, thus permitting Mabel to benefit from Frederic's estate even if well provided for by other, nonprobate means.

Elective shares are meant to protect a person against disinheritance by a predeceasing spouse who acquired and therefore owns all or most of the marital property. They exist only in common law, as opposed to community property, states. Unlike community property, an elective share does not give to one spouse any actual interest in property acquired by the other until the latter's death, although some states impose certain limitations on the manner in which spouses can deal with their property where the result might be to defeat the other spouse's statutory share.

In effect, the elective share is primarily a protective device that secures a surviving spouse against disinheritance regardless of contributions to, or the length of, the marriage; the community property system seeks primarily to recognize the surviving spouse's contributions, and in so doing it makes no provision for the spouse of a marriage that, because of its brevity or the manner of property acquisition, ends with little or no community property having been acquired.

A relatively new concept is the **augmented estate,** found in the Uniform Probate Code (but not yet adopted in many states). The pre-1990 UPC version, UPC (69) 2-201-207, contained a somewhat complex system that in effect — and put very simply — added back into the decedent spouse's estate from which the surviving spouse's elective share was taken various inter vivos transfers (without full consideration) from the decedent to third parties that depleted the estate available to the survivor. It also, however, credited against the forced share certain inter vivos transfers by the decedent to the surviving spouse. Calculation of the augmented estate can involve difficult questions of tracing and valuation.

The 1990 UPC (with several revisions in 1993), UPC 2-201-214, proposed a new augmented estate formula that attempts to implement a rough approximation of the community property notion of a marital partnership. It adjusts the surviving spouse's share according to the marriage's length, up to a maximum of 50 percent after 15 years of marriage. It also, however, redefines the augmented estate to include (again stated simply) not only the decedent spouse's probate estate and gratuitous nonprobate transfers (in the 1990 version called "reclaimable transfers") to third parties but also all of the surviving spouse's assets, however acquired, and whatever would have been included as nonprobate (or "reclaimable") transfers by the surviving spouse had he or she died first. The decedent's nonprobate transfers for consideration, or to which the surviving spouse consented, are excluded. In funding the elective share, credit is given first for property owned by or attributable to the surviving spouse. Thus the surviving spouse who already owns (or has transferred "reclaimably") half the augmented estate gets no elective share in a marriage of any length; the same is true for a smaller fraction in a shorter marriage. This result may or may not resemble that under a community property system, depending on such factors as the nature of the surviving spouse's property and how it was acquired.

Prenuptial Agreement

An agreement made prior to marriage that affects the rights and property interests of the parties after they are married. Such an agreement, also called an **antenuptial agreement** or **antenuptial settlement,** may determine matters of property ownership and control during the marriage and its division upon the marriage's termination by death or divorce. This is especially important when one or both of the parties comes into the marriage with a substantial estate and, perhaps, with obligations to children of prior marriages, and it is desired to avoid the usual division of property that might occur under divorce laws or an elective share statute.

A **postnuptial agreement,** as its name implies, is an agreement that is made by the parties after they already are married. Where, as is often true, the postnuptial agreement is for purposes of property settlement in contemplation of dissolution, it may be referred to as a **separation contract.**

Although these various types of marital agreements are generally valid, they may be closely scrutinized by courts to assure that they are fair and that there has been complete disclosure to a spouse of any provisions favorable to the other. (This may be less necessary for agreements in contemplation of dissolution, since the parties are then presumably dealing at arm's length.) See generally UPC 2-213.

Homestead

A family protection device under which a decedent's property of a certain value, usually consisting of the family residence, is set aside by operation of law for the benefit of a surviving spouse and minor children.

Homestead property is exempt from creditors' claims and protected against testamentary disposition by the decedent spouse. The amount and type of the set-aside varies greatly among the states. It may require a declaration by the owner of the property, or it may automatically attach to every person's residence. The set-aside may be outright or may exempt the property only during the surviving spouse's lifetime. If the state provides for an inter vivos declaration of homestead, it may be protected against creditors and transfer both before and after the owner's death. In some states only a **probate homestead** can be declared after the decedent spouse's death, or an award of cash can be made "in lieu of homestead." See UPC 2-402, 2-402A.

A related concept still in place in some states is the ancient one of **quarantine,** which permits the decedent's spouse (and sometimes minor children) to live in the family house for a certain period of time (originally

40 days) after the decedent's death. This concept may now be incorporated into or superseded by the homestead award. Also related is the **personal property set-aside,** which exempts certain classes of tangible personal property (and in some circumstances intangible property) from creditors' claims during the owner's lifetime or after death. See UPC 2-403.

Like other family protection measures, a homestead generally is taken "off the top" of the decedent's estate, calculated and set aside before the claims of creditors or other claims of the spouse and family; thus a surviving spouse may be entitled to a homestead award in addition to, and regardless of, a substantial gift of property under the decedent spouse's will. For this reason it is necessary that the availability of homestead be taken into account when planning the estate of a married person.

Family Allowance

*A family protection device, sometimes called **family maintenance,** that allocates from a decedent's estate a certain amount of money to help to support the decedent's spouse (and perhaps dependent children) in the period following the decedent's death.* This period may extend for a fixed length of time or until the estate is distributed, but typically not beyond the closing of the estate. Its amount may also be fixed or it may, as under UPC 2-404, depend on the probate court's assessment of the spouse's needs or accustomed standard of living.

Like homestead and other family protection measures, a family allowance generally comes off the top of the decedent's estate and is paid in addition to any other benefits accruing to the protected family members. Surviving spouses who were appointed executors have been known to draw out the estate closing until substantial maintenance awards were made. It thus represents a potentially significant disruption of any estate plan that has not taken it into account.

Dower

A common-law family protection device that gave a surviving widow a life estate in one-third of all the real property of which her deceased husband was seised (essentially that he owned with a right of possession) and which could pass by inheritance to the couple's children. **Curtesy** was a similar right in the husband, with the exception that he received a life interest in all the wife's real property, but only if there were children of the marriage.

Dower attached to real property during the lifetime of the husband as soon as it was acquired (or the couple was married), although the wife's rights remained **inchoate** (merely incipient or unperfected, not yet possessory) until the husband's death. During the husband's lifetime he could not transfer the property, even to a bona fide purchaser, free of his wife's dower interest without her written consent, and at his death he could not devise it in derogation of that interest. But if the wife predeceased her husband, her incipient dower interest was extinguished.

Today most states have abolished dower or retain the name as applied to a wife's statutory elective share. Those that retain dower as a separate right may have changed the wife's life estate to a fee interest and subjected it to the wife's election, so that she might be able to choose among dower, a forced share, and any gift under her husband's will. To the extent curtesy survives, it is now identical to dower. UPC 2-112 abolishes both devices.

Pretermitted Heir Statute

A statute that saves a share of the testator's estate for any child of the testator who was unintentionally omitted ("pretermitted") from the will. The most common statutes are limited to omitted children of the testator (and may be called **"pretermitted child"** or **"omitted child" statutes**), although some extend as well to other potential heirs, especially grandchildren. They generally give to the omitted child (or other heir) an intestate share, which in some instances could be the entire estate. (The Uniform Probate Code takes into account the existence and amount of gifts to other children of the testator. UPC 2-302.)

The theory of a pretermitted heir statute is that, while it is permissible for testators to disinherit their children, they must do so deliberately and not inadvertently. Because it is much more likely that one might forget to make reference to a child who has not yet been born (that is, might fail to anticipate future children and forget to amend one's will when the children are born) than to omit unintentionally a child already in existence, many modern statutes are limited to children born after execution of the will.

An important issue is the type of evidence admissible to prove or disprove the testator's intention in omitting a child. Some statutes, like the UPC, explicitly state whether extrinsic evidence is admissible, but others are silent in this regard. So-called Missouri-type statutes, which mandate an intestate share if the child (or other heir) is not "named or provided for" in the will, generally are construed to preclude admission of extrinsic evidence to determine the testator's intent; "Massachusetts-type" statutes, which provide an intestate share "unless the omission is shown to be intentional," usually are construed to permit such evidence. The distinction is crucial, especially when the will says nothing at all about the reason for the child's omission. Thus while a parent may wish to leave only a small gift to one son and nothing at all to another, if the latter is not mentioned in the will he may end up with a much larger share (his intestate share) of the estate than his more favored brother.

Another problem of construction is what a statute means when it requires that a child be "named or provided for." For example, a court may permit a reference to the intentional omission of the testator's "children" without their actually being named, especially of course when the children excluded are not yet born; and a court may or may not consider a token gift, such as one dollar, a sufficient "provision" for an otherwise omitted child.

Some statutes now consider provision made for a child outside of the will, or even indirectly by providing for the child's surviving parent. See, e.g., UPC 2-302(a)(1), (b)(2).

C. TESTATOR-IMPOSED CONDITIONS AND RESTRICTIONS

A testator may attempt to impose various kinds of restrictions on testamentary gifts, and most are unremarkable. Some relatively common types of restrictions, however, are subject to certain legal limitations. These relate both to the probate process itself and to the interests in property passed under the will. The section begins with a restriction that many testators no doubt would like to include in their wills but that most jurisdictions do not yet permit. (Public policy limitations on restrictions on the beneficial interests in trusts are also discussed under *Trusts* in Chapter 12.)

Negative Bequest

A provision in a will directing that a person who otherwise might be an heir of the testator shall not take any property by intestate succession. This is sometimes referred to as a **negative will**.

In the great majority of states, a testator cannot control by will the devolution of property that passes by intestate succession. Thus although it is generally permitted to "disinherit" a child by express language (see *Pretermitted Heir Statute*), this is a misleading term: If any of the testator's property does not ultimately pass by the will, a "disinherited" child is still eligible to take such property by intestate succession. In a jurisdiction permitting a negative bequest, however, a testator may by appropriate language prevent a person not only from taking under the will but also from taking by intestacy. Such a person is treated as having either predeceased the testator or disclaimed the inheritance.

Example 9.2: (a) Simeon leaves his estate to charity, expressly stating in the will that his son Henry shall take nothing under the will. There is no residuary clause. Because of a mortmain statute, the charitable gift fails, and the entire estate passes by intestacy. Henry survives Simeon and is his only heir. Despite Simeon's attempt to disinherit him, Henry takes Simeon's entire estate. (If only a part of the estate had passed by intestacy because of the failure of one of several gifts,

Henry would have taken just that part.)

(b) Same facts as in (a), except Simeon's will contains a statement that Henry should take nothing either under the will or by intestacy. If the jurisdiction recognizes negative bequests, Henry will be treated as if he had predeceased Simeon and the intestate part of the estate will pass accordingly.

To date few jurisdictions permit negative bequests; but the 1990 Uniform Probate Code does so (UPC 1-201(56)), making likely the adoption of such a provision in other jurisdictions in the future.

No-Contest Clause

A clause in a will that denies some benefit to a person who contests the will. Such clauses are generally enforced by the courts, although in many states they will not operate against a contestant who acts with probable cause. See UPC 3-905.

A clause that penalizes only a "will contest" often will not be enforced against a person who brings a proceeding, such as the assertion of a claim by a pretermitted heir or an attempt to probate a later will, that technically is not a "contest." This becomes a question of interpretation of the testator's language and intent; many courts do not favor such clauses and may be inclined to construe them narrowly.

Testators sometimes forget that a no-contest clause can be effective only against a person who has been given some substantial benefit under the will (or a nonprobate benefit that can be cancelled by the will). Of course, even the threat of the loss of a substantial benefit may not deter a contestant with a good case; if the contest is successful in overturning the will, the no-contest clause will fall with it.

Example 9.3: Edwin's will leaves nothing (or a token such as one dollar) to Angelina, and then it adds a no-contest clause to discourage her from contesting the will. Angelina will hardly be deterred by the prospect of being denied such a "benefit." And whatever she was given under the will, if Angelina succeeds in defeating it, she will receive whatever benefits she is entitled to in its absence.

In other words, a no-contest clause deters only those for whom the risk (the amount and likelihood) of loss if the contest is unsuccessful exceeds the benefits to be gained if it succeeds.

In Terrorem Clause

A clause that seeks to frighten or coerce a person into taking or refraining from some action.

118

In some contexts a provision may be declared invalid if it is deemed "merely in terrorem." It is sometimes said, for example, that a condition attached to a testamentary gift — especially a condition in restraint of marriage — that includes no limitation over (no alternative gift in case the condition is not fulfilled) is "in terrorem" and void because it can have no purpose except to coerce the beneficiary into meeting the condition. (This assumes, of course, that the prospect of the property's passing to someone unknown rather than a named alternative taker will "terrify" the beneficiary into complying with the condition, an expectation that has justly been called "irrational.")

A more cynical explanation of the above doctrine offered by one court is that "in terrorem" is merely "a convenient phrase adopted by judges to stand in place of a reason for refusing to give effect to a valid condition."

Sometimes the term "in terrorem clause" is used as a synonym for a no-contest clause, although the latter is really just one example of a clause with a coercive purpose.

Restraint on Alienation

A provision in a will or trust (or other instrument of transfer) that has the effect of preventing the owner of an interest in property from further transferring (alienating) that interest. In some contexts, this may be called a **disabling restraint**.

Many forms of restraint on alienation are either invalid or narrowly circumscribed. Perhaps the best known example of an invalid restraint is one in violation of the Rule Against Perpetuities; other devices that attempt to prevent transfer, such as spendthrift trusts, also may run afoul of rules that seek to promote the free marketability of property.

The **rule against suspension of the power of alienation,** which originated in New York and exists in only a few states, is another example of a prohibition against restraint on alienation. It declares a provision invalid if, for longer than the statutory period, there are not persons in being who can convey an absolute fee interest in property. The statutory period is the same as that for the Rule Against Perpetuities: lives in being at the creation of the interest plus 21 years. In effect, the rule is violated if the holders of an interest are either unborn or unascertainable, or if there is an express prohibition on alienation, beyond the permissible period.

10

Will Substitutes and Will Contracts

A. INTRODUCTION AND OVERVIEW OF CHAPTER

The probate system — that is, a conventional will and its intestacy counterpart — is by no means the only way to transfer property at the death of its owner. In fact, in many estates today far more property is transferred outside the probate system than within it. This chapter examines the various nonprobate devices that have evolved over time and that continue to evolve as estate planners find new reasons and new ways to avoid probate.

Not only do nonprobate transfers affect those by will indirectly, by passing property that would otherwise have passed by will (or intestacy), but in certain instances they may have a more direct effect on testamentary gifts; or the will may in turn directly affect a nonprobate device. These latter "intersections" of the two regimes are discussed in the chapter's final section.

B.   NONPROBATE TRANSFERS ON DEATH

Nonprobate transfers — those other than by will or intestacy — come in many forms, and those forms are changing and expanding rapidly. This section discusses the nature and implications of many of those currently in use. One important example, the inter vivos trust, is examined here but is also more fully discussed in Chapter 12.

Will Substitute

A term for any instrument or means of transfer that has the practical effect of taking the place of a will. A will substitute passes property without the necessity for (or, in most jurisdictions, the possibility of) probate or administration; it passes neither under the testator's will nor under the intestacy statute. Thus the items transferred are referred to as the decedent's **nonprobate assets,** or nonprobate estate. It is this feature that has popularized some will substitutes, primarily inter vivos trusts, with persons seeking to "avoid probate."

Will substitutes generally require far fewer formalities of execution than do wills, although they may have their own peculiar requirements that are just as strictly applied. They also may avoid many of the statutory restrictions that attach to wills, such as those protecting pretermitted heirs or post-testamentary spouses, and some (such as life insurance) even may be free of the claims of the decedent's creditors.

Although in the past will substitutes were in constant danger of being declared invalid as improperly executed testamentary instruments, today in most states at least the more commonplace will substitutes are permitted to stand despite their admitted quasi-testamentary effect. Some are rationalized as nontestamentary third-party beneficiary contracts or as instruments that transfer a "present interest" to the beneficiary during the transferor's lifetime; others are accepted without rationalization. Recent statutory changes under the Uniform Probate Code and in several states have declared a broad array of common "at death" provisions found in various instruments to be, by definition, "nontestamentary." See, *e.g.,* UPC 6-101. Nevertheless, some states continue to invalidate certain types of transfer that have the characteristics of a will without its formalities.

So many different will substitutes are now used, and are so widely employed, that for many testators their will passes only a small portion of their total estate. Moreover, this proliferation of will substitutes has caused many jurisdictions either to liberalize their will formalities or, in some cases, to apply restrictions and protective devices to will substitutes that formerly had applied only to wills. A will and the various will substitutes remain separate in operation: Will substitutes affect only the nonprobate assets to which they specifically relate, and the testator's will generally cannot affect the transfer on death of nonprobate assets. (For two exceptions to this statement, see Section C below.)

Will substitutes generally fall into two broad categories: those whose transfer-on-death provisions derive from contract, and those that by their nature include a right of survivorship, that is, some form of joint ownership under which the interest of the person who dies first is extinguished in favor of the surviving owner.

Among the most common will substitutes are the following:

Life insurance is perhaps the most widely used and understood will substitute. Although it is a contract executed and effective during the lifetime of the insured, its benefits do not pass until the insured's death.

Example 10.1:   Ralph purchases a life insurance policy from Maritime Insurance Co. and pays the company premiums during his lifetime. Maritime will pay Ralph's wife and beneficiary Josephine an agreed sum upon (but not until) Ralph's death. (Note that, unlike a gift under a will, it is the insurance company's property, not Ralph's, that Josephine ultimately receives.)

Revocable inter vivos trusts, discussed fully in Chapter 12, are the closest equivalent to an actual will because they permit the transfer at death of almost any property owned by the trustor, with retention of virtually unlimited control.

Example 10.2:   Ralph establishes a trust during his lifetime to which he transfers all his real and personal property. He names himself as trustee and retains a life estate in the income and the right to revoke, and he names Josephine the remainderman. Upon Ralph's death, Josephine receives the corpus of the trust. The result is just as if Ralph had executed a will leaving the property outright to Josephine: He retains control of the property and the right to revoke, and Josephine has no practical use of the property unless and until Ralph dies without having revoked. (There are certain differences in Ralph's position under the two alternatives, but they are of little practical effect.)

Various types of bank or brokerage accounts can act as will substitutes. Under a **joint and survivorship account**, two or more depositors may exercise some degree of control over the funds during their joint lifetimes (the degree of control depending on state law), and upon the death of the first of them to die the survivor becomes sole owner of the funds. (A joint account may not have all the characteristics of a true joint tenancy, but it will always have, by definition, a right of survivorship.)

A **P.O.D.** ("payable on death") **account**, in contrast, belongs solely to the depositor until it is paid to the named beneficiary upon the depositor's death. (It is thus a pure will substitute with no pretense of a pre-death transfer or co-ownership; for this reason it was generally considered invalid and has begun to gain acceptance only recently.)

A **Totten Trust** (named for the New York case that first validated it and also called a *savings account trust*, a **tentative trust**, or a "poor man's will") is similar to a P.O.D. account except that the deposit is in the form "Ralph in trust for Josephine." Under traditional rules, a Totten Trust can be revoked or the beneficiary changed by the depositor's (Ralph, the trustor's) will, and the funds are available to the depositor's creditors after his death. Neither is generally true of joint accounts, although some states and the Uniform Probate Code now treat all these accounts alike. See UPC 6-201 *et seq*.

Example 10.3:   Ralph deposits money in the Buttercup State Bank, and although he does not wish to give up control over the funds while he is alive, he wants Josephine to have whatever is in the account upon his death. Depending on state law, he can accomplish this purpose in slightly different ways using a joint and survivorship account, a P.O.D. account, or a Totten Trust.

An infinite variety of contracts contain provisions operative to pass benefits at a party's death. Pension plans, for example, often contain benefits for survivors similar to those in insurance policies. Partnership agreements may include buy-out clauses or other provisions passing either a deceased partner's interest or some similar benefit to a surviving spouse or other beneficiary. Notes, mortgages, and real estate contracts may have clauses forgiving payments of interest or principal upon the death of the mortgagor or the mortgagee.

United States Savings Bonds contain survivorship provisions that are controlled by both federal and state law, and therefore they are valid in every state.

Deeds are a frequent source of dispute when they appear to be testamentary.

Example 10.4:   Ralph grants a parcel of realty to Josephine under a deed that states, "I hereby grant all of my interest in Wetacre to Josephine, effective upon my death, until which time I retain full ownership of Wetacre." Since the deed does not pass any interest at all to Josephine until Ralph's death, technically it is testamentary and generally it must satisfy the formalities of a will. But the deed may be valid as a will substitute if it merely retains for Ralph a life interest, a power to revoke, or the like.

A number of less-common will substitutes have been developed, and more are being created every day by imaginative estate planners. Some, like the **community property agreement**, by which a married couple is permitted to contract with respect to the disposition of community property upon death, are unique to certain jurisdictions; others begin in one state and, if successful, quickly find their way to others. Until such devices have become well established by statute or court decree, however, it is wise to remember the words of one court: "[T]he legal mind is invincibly hostile to the new, the strange, and the unfamiliar."

Joint Tenancy

A form of property ownership under which two or more persons share undivided ownership of the whole property during their joint lifetimes, and the interest of an owner who dies is extinguished, leaving the surviving joint tenant(s) with sole ownership. Although a true joint tenancy has many other requirements, the principal characteristic that sets it apart from other forms of ownership is this **right of survivorship**.

Technically, when a joint tenancy is created there is a present transfer of an interest (which can have significant tax consequences), and at the death of one tenant there is not a transfer to the surviving tenants but merely an extinguishing of the existing competing interest of the decedent. Technicalities aside, the practical effect of joint tenancy is to pass to the survivor a sole interest in the property, immediately upon the death of the first to die, without the need for probate and (in most states) regardless of the terms of the decedent's will; this is the characteristic that makes joint tenancy a popular will substitute.

Generally a joint tenancy can be "severed" by the unilateral action (such as conveyance to a third party) of one co-owner, with the resulting ownership being as tenants in common.

Gift Causa Mortis

A gift made "in contemplation of death" that is revocable until the death of the donor and is automatically revoked (or remains revocable) upon recovery. In most respects the rules for a valid gift causa mortis are the same as those for any other gift — effective delivery, donative intent, and so on. The revocability of a gift causa mortis, however, sets it apart from the usual gift and makes it a will substitute.

Example 10.5: Aline believes she is in peril of imminent death from some source (such as a terminal disease, an onrushing train, or even a planned suicide). She may, if she has time, make a gift of some item of personal property (not realty) to her friend Alexis, and if she then dies of that peril the gift is complete. If Aline changes her mind, however, she can revoke the gift to Alexis.

Under the traditional approach to gifts causa mortis, if the donor survives the peril that prompted the gift, the gift is automatically revoked. In some jurisdictions, it is merely revocable at the donor's option.

While, as indicated, gifts causa mortis require the same formalities as other gifts, including delivery, the circumstances of such gifts often lead courts to accept less than the usual form of delivery. **Constructive delivery** may be found even if actual physical delivery was absent. In this and other ways courts, which tend to favor gifts causa mortis, may relax the rules enough to validate them.

Example 10.6:   Aline is on her deathbed and wants to give her automobile to Alexis. She is not expected to get up, go home, get in the car, and deliver it to Alexis at his home; handing him the keys with appropriate donative words will suffice as constructive delivery, and the gift will be valid.

C.   PROBATE AND NONPROBATE INTERSECTIONS

Although the probate and nonprobate regimes are in most respects distinct, parallel means of transferring property at death, under certain circumstances they overlap. One, the pour-over will, under which probate assets are "poured" into an existing inter vivos trust, is discussed in Chapter 8. In certain limited situations, however, a will may have a direct effect on the very terms of a nonprobate device, or a nonprobate contract may in effect prevail over the apparent terms of a will. These two possibilities are discussed in this section.

Will Contract

An agreement by a testator to execute (or not to revoke) a will containing particular provisions. Usually the consideration for the testator's compliance is the promisee's performance of some service for the testator, such as lifetime care. A will contract also may be found in conjunction with joint and mutual wills if the parties (usually husband and wife), upon executing wills with reciprocal provisions, also agree not to revoke those provisions.

Will contracts may be oral or written, although if oral they may violate a state's Statute of Frauds. As they are not themselves wills, they need not comply with the formalities for wills, and they cannot be probated. Under UPC 2-514, will contracts must be either set out in a will, expressly referred to in a will and proved by extrinsic evidence, or supported by a separate writing signed by the decedent.

If the testator fails to execute (or to leave unrevoked) the promised will, the promise may sue for breach of contract. The actual probate process is not affected by this lawsuit, but its result may nullify that reached by probate law, thus having the same effect as working directly upon the will.

Example 10.7:   Phoebe agrees to leave all her property to Wilfred if he takes care of her for the rest of her life. Phoebe does execute a will in favor of Wilfred, as promised, but she subsequently meets Jack and Elsie, itinerant musicians, who persuade her to revoke that will and execute one in their favor. Wilfred complies with his part of the bargain by caring for Phoebe for several years until she dies, and Wilfred then learns of the revocation and the new will. Wilfred cannot probate the will that Phoebe revoked if she complied with the necessary formalities to do so; nor can he oppose probate of the new will if Phoebe complied with the formalities for execution. The law of wills governs both of those instruments. Wilfred can, however, invoke the law of contracts; if the requirements for a valid contract are satisfied, he can obtain relief in a suit either for damages against Phoebe's estate or for imposition of a constructive trust forcing Jack and Elsie, on receipt of Phoebe's property from the estate, to convey it to Wilfred.

Many courts take a dim view of will contracts because they can pose very difficult problems of proof, especially if they are oral. In the words of Dean Pound, "As one reads these cases he cannot but have an uneasy feeling that general expectations of becoming the object of a testator's bounty often ripen into a contract after testator's death."

Super-will

A will (also known as a **blockbuster will***) that controls the disposition not only of probate assets but also of nonprobate assets, in particular those passing under a will substitute such as a life insurance policy or inter vivos trust.* Absent a statute permitting it, a will normally cannot change the beneficiaries or otherwise alter the disposition under a will substitute. Most states do not yet have a statute permitting super-wills. However, given the proliferation of will substitutes and the continued use of wills, it is likely that many states eventually will adopt some such provision.

11

Probate and Administration

A. INTRODUCTION AND OVERVIEW OF CHAPTER

Once a will (or no will) has been executed and the testator/intestate has died, the estate plan dictated by the will or by statute must be put into effect. This involves not only probate of the will, if any, but also subsequent administration of the estate to carry out the appropriate mandate. Probate and administration are the practical side of estate practice that often is given little attention in theoretical courses. (They are to the theory of these courses what civil procedure is to a substantive course such as torts or contracts.) This chapter covers the terms and concepts encountered in the probate and administration process, from its judicial setting, to the persons who are entrusted with carrying it out, to the types of activities it involves.

It should be noted that one very important aspect of the administration process, that of the powers and duties of the administrator, is discussed in Chapter 17.

B. THE JUDICIAL SETTING

This section concerns the manner in which estate administration is begun: the opening of probate, the appointment of a personal representative, and the various types of proceedings that may be available. In other words, once the decedent has died, the process starts here.

Probate

The process of "proving" a will, or having it declared valid and effective following the death of the testator. (This process may also be called **testacy proceeding**. UPC 3-401 uses the term **formal testacy proceeding** broadly to include proceedings to probate a will, to set aside informal probate, or to establish intestacy.) "Probate" is a multifaceted word, used as a verb, adjective, or noun: One "probates a will" in a "probate proceeding," and as a result a will is "admitted to probate." Admission to probate is generally (but not necessarily) followed by appointment of a personal representative and the commencement of administration of the estate. The term "probate" also is used loosely to refer to this entire process of probate, administration, and whatever ancillary proceedings are necessary to carry out in full the distribution of the testator's estate under the terms of the will. This is the "probate" process that one is said to be avoiding by using will substitutes such as inter vivos trusts.

Gifts under a will are not effective unless and until the will is admitted to probate. (Technically real property may be said to pass to the devisee at the instant of death, without the intervention of the personal representative; but for practical purposes this generally does not diminish the need to establish title through probate.)

Probate (the court proceeding) may be in **common form** or **solemn form**. (Some modern statutes, including the Uniform Probate Code, use the terms "informal" and "formal" to distinguish these types of probate proceedings.) Common form is an ex parte proceeding, with no notice given to those who might wish to challenge the will. There is then a period of time during which interested persons may contest the will and seek revocation of probate. When probate is in solemn form, it is an adversary proceeding, with notice to interested persons; a decree is a final and binding adjudication, subject only to the usual appellate process. In some jurisdictions, however, a will may be contested for a limited period of time even after probate with notice.

With variations depending on the type of proceeding and local practice, admission to probate generally requires some ascertainment or showing of the testator's death, due execution of the will, proper jurisdiction and venue, and perhaps testamentary capacity. Usually the named executor will petition for probate, but any interested person can do so.

Probate Court

The court that hears and adjudicates matters concerning wills and intestate succession, including administration of estates and other aspects of the testamentary process. In some states these courts are called **orphans'** or **surrogate's courts**.

These courts usually have quite limited subject-matter jurisdiction and sometimes are presided over by nonlawyers, although in many states they have more general jurisdiction. Thus, for example, a will may be probated in the state's probate court, but an equitable remedy (such as declaration of a constructive trust because of a beneficiary's wrongdoing) may have to be adjudicated in a separate court of equity. Or a probate court may have jurisdiction over "probate" in the narrow sense of proving the will but not over will contests or proceedings to construe the will's language.

Usually the probate court in the state (and county) in which the decedent is domiciled at death is the proper forum for probate; if the decedent owned real property in another state or county, parallel proceedings, including ancillary administration, may have to be held there.

Administration

The process of collecting, managing, and distributing the property of a decedent in accordance with the terms of the decedent's will or the intestacy statutes. It includes all aspects of management of the estate, such as (and most importantly) payment of taxes and creditors' claims and distribution of the remaining assets to those entitled to them.

Administration is carried out by the personal representative, who acts in a fiduciary capacity. It may be supervised on a continuing basis by the probate court, requiring the personal representative to seek court approval for acts on behalf of the estate. This can be an expensive and time-consuming process, involving in each instance notice, a hearing, and a court order. In some states, however, a testator can specify or the probate court can approve an **independent administration** (also given such designations as **nonintervention administration**). Under this system there is only limited court supervision, occurring primarily at the beginning and the end of the administration process, with no need for the personal representative to come into court for approval of every sale, payment, or other such action. Under the Uniform Probate Code, administration is informal and unsupervised unless the court grants a petition for supervised administration. See UPC 3-501 *et seq*.

The administration process generally begins with appointment of the personal representative and ends with a final decree of distribution. Along the way the personal representative files an inventory and appraisement of estate assets, gives notice to creditors to begin the running of the nonclaim statute, pays estate and inheritance taxes, pays or rejects the claims of creditors, sells property of the estate where necessary, renders an accounting to estate beneficiaries or the court or both, and perhaps makes a partial distribution of assets. The personal representative may have to petition the court for approval before taking steps such as sale of estate assets or for instructions where uncertain about a contemplated act.

In large or complex estates, administration can be quite elaborate and may involve everything from continuing the decedent's business to prosecuting, continuing, or defending lawsuits on behalf of the estate. In very small estates, administration often can be either dispensed with, both creditors and beneficiaries being paid informally, or done through an abbreviated and less expensive **summary administration**. The Uniform Probate Code contains both options in UPC 3-1201-1204.

Usually administration is carried out in the state in which the will is probated, which is the state of the decedent's domicile at death. If the decedent owned real property situated in another state, however, it may be necessary to open a parallel **ancillary administration** in that state, including the appointment of an ancillary administrator. The domiciliary administration then is denominated the **principal administration**.

One function of the probate and administration process, especially important in the case of real property, is the establishment on the record of the fact of the decedent's death and the transfer of ownership following that death. Without such an adjudication, it may be difficult for successors to the property to obtain a clear and marketable title. However, for circumstances in which it is necessary to establish formally the fact of death but probate or administration are not desired, many states provide for a more limited proceeding, called an **adjudication of testacy** (or of intestacy) or given some similar designation, that serves this limited purpose.

Letters of Administration

The formal documentation issued by a probate court to signify that a person has been appointed the administrator of an estate and giving the administrator the powers that accompany that office. **Letters testamentary** are the equivalent documentation issued to the executor under a will. (There are also, among others, letters of guardianship and conservatorship.)

The nature of the letters issued will depend on the type of administrator appointed. Thus there are letters of administration d.b.n., c.t.a., and d.b.n.c.t.a. issued to administrators similarly designated.

C.   PERSONS IN CHARGE

Every estate administration, whether under a will or through intestacy, requires someone to carry it through. That person may be appointed pursuant to the stated wishes of the decedent or, if that is not possible, by the court from a statutory list. Both the designation and, to some extent, the function of the personal representative varies according to the presence or absence of a will and the manner of appointment. This section describes the nature and functions of these persons in charge of probating the will and administering the estate. In addition to personal representatives, it includes guardians and related functionaries, who serve a different purpose but may be vital to the carrying out of the administration process.

Personal Representative

The person appointed by the probate court to administer the estate of a decedent: the executor of a will or administrator of an intestate estate. It is the personal representative (or "P.R." in attorneys' shorthand) who collects and inventories the estate's assets, invests or manages them to the extent necessary, gives all required notices to interested parties, sees that taxes are paid and creditors' claims are satisfied or rejected, and distributes the remaining assets to legatees or heirs. See generally UPC 3-601-3-721.

If the decedent's will nominates an executor, and if the person nominated qualifies for and accepts the office, that person usually will be appointed. If no will exists or no person appointed by the will can or will serve, an administrator will be appointed as personal representative. In either case, there is usually a statutory hierarchy of those entitled to be appointed, with first priority given to close relatives, such as spouse or children, or to devisees under the will. A lower priority is given to creditors, who in the absence of another suitable nominee may have to step in and act as personal representative in order to assure orderly payment of their claims.

A personal representative generally is subject to the continuing supervision of the probate court and must seek court approval for most actions taken and account to the court for their results. In many states, however, the personal representative also may be "independent," that is, subject to only limited supervision of the probate court if the testator so chooses or the court so decides. (See *Administration*.)

Executor

The person nominated in a testator's will to act as personal representative and "execute" its provisions, carrying out the will's directions regarding disposition of the testator's estate. (The feminine equivalent is **executrix**, but "executor" can be used for both genders.) Generally the person nominated in the will is appointed by the probate court and issued letters testamentary, but on occasion that person does not qualify for or declines to accept the office. In this event, the court will appoint an administrator c.t.a. ("with will annexed").

An executor acts in a fiduciary capacity, with duties and responsibilities similar to those of a trustee but of more limited scope and duration. Generally the probate court supervises and must approve the executor's actions, although in some states the testator can specify (or is presumed to specify in the absence of contrary directions) that the executor be independent or the administration be of a "nonintervention" type that requires only limited court supervision.

Executor De Son Tort

At common law, one who intermeddles with the decedent's personal property without legal authority, unlawfully assuming the role of executor or administrator. The executor de son tort ("executor of his own wrong," pronounced to rhyme with "be home more") was subject to liability for any losses resulting from the unauthorized acts. In many states this doctrine as such has been abolished or modified, giving way to other methods of dealing with intermeddlers.

Administrator

A person appointed by the probate court as personal representative to administer (collect, manage, and distribute) the estate of a person who dies intestate. The administrator acts in a fiduciary capacity, as does the executor appointed under a will, and like an executor has powers and duties similar to but more limited than those of a trustee.

There are many different types of administrators. If a will exists but no executor is nominated or available, the court will appoint an **administrator c.t.a.** ("cum testamento annexo," "with will attached"). If an administrator dies, resigns, or is removed before completing the administration, an **administrator d.b.n.** ("de bonis non [administratis]," "of goods not administered") must be appointed to administer the remainder of the estate. And if a will exists and the executor does not complete administration, the court will appoint an **administrator d.b.n.c.t.a.** (for which no further translation should be necessary). (Pronunciations are omitted because the letters of abbreviation are used much more commonly — and with less violence to the language — than the Latin terms themselves.)

Special administrators may be appointed for specific, usually temporary purposes. For example, an administrator might be appointed to serve during the time until the regular personal representative can be appointed and take office. An **administrator pendente lite** ("pending the litigation," with the final "e" on the second and third words pronounced like the "y" in "twenty") might be appointed while a will contest is in progress, especially one involving the nominated executor. Or if a person is needed to act in behalf of the estate in a lawsuit, an **administrator ad litem** (the latter word pronounced to rhyme with "item") can be appointed for that limited purpose.

A state may have a **public administrator**, a public officer whose duty it is to administer any estate that lacks a qualified and available personal representative.

An administrator, like an executor, traditionally is subject to the continuing supervision of the probate court and must seek the court's approval for actions taken on behalf of the estate. In some states, however, the court can appoint an "independent" administrator, who is subject to only limited court supervision.

Guardian

One who is appointed to protect the person or property of an infant (that is, a minor) or of a person who is mentally incompetent or physically incapacitated. The protected person is known as the guardian's **ward.** The Uniform Probate Code contains a comprehensive scheme for both minors and incapacitated persons (UPC 5-101 *et seq.*).

The guardian's role is much like that of a parent, and in fact parents are the "natural guardians" of their children. (Recall those permission slips in school that required the signature of your "parent or guardian.")

Example 11.1: Rose and Robin are married and have a 2-year-old son, Richard. They are concerned that, should they both die before Richard reaches majority, no one will care for him, at least in the manner that they consider appropriate. (Richard could, for example, find himself living with Uncle Despard and Aunt Margaret, whose lifestyle is, to be charitable, eccentric.) Therefore, on their attorney's advice, they execute wills providing that, in the event both of them die before Richard is 21, they appoint their trusted friend Adam as Richard's guardian. This makes Adam a **testamentary guardian**, one appointed by the will of the ward's parents.

While in Example 11.1 a **general guardian** such as Adam would usually appointed, in some circumstances it is necessary or appropriate to limit the powers of a guardian in some way (a **limited guardian**); and sometimes the court will appoint separate **guardians of the person and of the estate** (property) of the ward. Such a limited guardian would also be called a **special guardian**.

Example 11.2: Robin and Rose believe that, while Adam is the best person to look after Richard and see to his proper education and development, Adam is also a very poor manager of money, and they hesitate to put Richard's inheritance in Adam's hands. They then might appoint Adam guardian of Richard's person and Roderic, his financially astute uncle, guardian of his estate. This can, however, have unfortunate consequences if the two do not agree on crucial matters of Richard's upbringing, with Adam deciding to send Richard to an expensive private school and Roderic willing to authorize payment only for the state university.

If a general guardian resembles a parent, a guardian of the estate resembles a trustee, in that the guardian is a fiduciary who may have responsibility for the management or control of the ward's property. Unlike a trustee, however, the powers and duties of a guardian are usually quite narrow, and the guardian does not take title to the ward's property.

A guardian (even if there is only one) may be called a **committee**.

A **conservator** is similar to (and in some states almost identical with) a guardian. Usually, however, a conservator is appointed only for a conservatee's estate (although some states provide for conservators of the person as well) and may take title to the conservatee's property. For a child, a will generally appoints a guardian, not a conservator, who is appointed after a special court proceeding.

A **guardian ad litem** (pronounced like "item"), another form of special guardian, is appointed to protect the interests of a minor, incompetent, or even unborn person in litigation and is given no powers or duties beyond that role. In the context of probate, such a guardian might be appointed when a will is contested and the result of the contest may affect the rights of a minor or as yet unborn beneficiary.

Generally a person who is under the protection of a guardian may nevertheless make a valid will, although of course in a given situation the reason for the guardianship also may be a basis for declaring the testator incompetent to make a will. (See *Mental Competence*.)

D. THE ADMINISTRATION PROCESS

Once the will has been probated or intestacy established, it is necessary to carry out the wishes of the testator (or the dictates of the intestacy statute). For example, creditors must be identified, notified, and paid; legatees must be allocated their share of the estate, against which may be assessed a share of the expenses; a proper accounting must be made to the court and beneficiaries; and the estate must be closed. This section addresses all these functions, together with an alternative method for accomplishing much the same thing in a somewhat different manner.

Nonclaim Statute

A statute that limits the time in which a creditor of a decedent can submit a claim for payment. The period, typically four months, contemplates the giving of notice to creditors, and it usually runs from the date of that notice or the date of the opening of probate or appointment of the personal representative. Upon expiration of the nonclaim period, any claim not properly presented to the personal representative is forever barred, regardless of its underlying statute of limitations.

There also may be a longer period of time — from one to six years, running from the date of death — after which all claims are barred, regardless of the presence or absence of notice. The latter sometimes is called a "long-term" nonclaim statute, as distinguished from the "short-term" statutes first described; more accurately, these are not nonclaim statutes but are probate statutes of repose, analogous to those that apply to products liability actions in tort.

Until very recently, notice to creditors in most states was given by publication only. This practice was declared unconstitutional in 1988 in *Tulsa Professional Collection Services v. Pope*, leading to the amendment of almost every state's nonclaim statute. Many of the new statutes retain the four-month nonclaim period but now require actual notice to known or reasonably ascertainable creditors, as seemingly dictated by the Supreme Court. Some states have eliminated the "short-term" statute entirely, relying on the statute of repose to cut off claims. A few simultaneously have eliminated any form of mandatory notice to creditors; the constitutionality of the latter variation, which leaves it entirely to creditors themselves to learn of their debtor's death, has yet to be determined. See UPC 3-801-803 (recommending only voluntary notice and substituting a one-year "long-term" statute of repose for the three years of the original Code).

A creditor's submission of a claim to the personal representative is called a **presentment**. The personal representative then will either accept the claim and pay it or reject it, leaving the creditor to sue the estate for payment.

Inventory and Appraisement

The collection and evaluation of the property in a decedent's estate by the personal representative appointed for that purpose. Filing of an inventory and appraisement (also called an **appraisal**) is usually one of the first responsibilities of a personal representative, and it is a necessary precursor to subsequent tasks such as payment of creditors and distribution to beneficiaries or heirs. See UPC 3-706.

Estate Taxes

Taxes assessed upon the transfer of a decedent's property at death. Taxes assessed upon the receipt of that property by the estate's beneficiaries are called **inheritance taxes** (also known as **succession duties** or succession taxes). In other words, estate taxes are levied on and payable out of the estate, based on the making of a testamentary gift; inheritance taxes are levied on and payable out of the amount that a particular beneficiary receives, based on that receipt. The taxes generally apply equally to testate and intestate succession.

Federal death taxes are estate taxes, while many states levy an inheritance tax. There also may be what is sometimes called a **pickup tax**: The federal estate tax includes a deduction for taxes paid to the state, up to a certain amount; the pickup tax "picks up" as an additional state estate tax any difference in amount between the state inheritance tax and the federal deduction. This gives the state the full amount of the federal deduction without costing the estate or beneficiary anything extra.

Accounting

A submission by the personal representative of a statement of receipts and expenditures on behalf of the estate. Several periodic interim accounts may be submitted, each covering the period since the previous one. Beneficiaries and certain others who are interested may file objections to the account. On approval, or **settlement**, of the account, the personal representative is protected against future claims with respect to the matters it recites. Upon a final accounting and settlement, the court will issue a **decree of distribution** and the estate will be closed. See UPC 3-1001-1003.

Universal Succession

A system of distribution of a decedent's property under which beneficiaries of a will or intestate successors take title to the property directly, without the need for administration or appointment of a personal representative but subject to the claims of creditors and others with prior rights. In effect, the successors step into the shoes of the decedent with respect to debts and other obligations.

Universal succession, common in Europe and long available in Louisiana under its civil law code, is beginning to gain favor and to be adopted, at least in limited form, elsewhere in the United States. The Uniform Probate Code contains a comprehensive universal succession scheme as an alternative to the more traditional methods of formal and informal administration. UPC 3-311-322. It is not yet, however, the general rule in any common-law state.

PART II

TRUSTS

12

Creation and General Characteristics of Trusts

Honorary Trust
Illusory Trust
Supplemental Needs Trust
Special Needs Trust
C. Elements of a Trust
Settlor
Trustor
Grantor Trust
Trustee
Co-trustees
Qualification
Fiduciary
Fiduciary
Fiduciary Relationship
Fiduciary Capacity
Fiduciary Duties
Beneficiary
Cestui Que Trust
Cestui Que Use
Cestuis Que Trustent
Trust Property
Trust Res
Trust Corpus
Debt
Trust Instrument
Deed of Trust
Trust Indenture
D. Implied Trusts: Trusts That Arise by Operation of Law
Implied Trust
Resulting Trust
Purchase Money Resulting Trust
Constructive Trust
Trust Ex Maleficio
Trust Ex Delicto
Trust De Son Tort
Trust in Invitum
Involuntary Trust
E. Limited Transfer of Trust Interests
Spendthrift Trust
Discretionary Trust
Mandatory Trust
Support Trust
Hybrid Trust
Blended Trust
Protective Trust

A. INTRODUCTION AND OVERVIEW OF CHAPTER

Chapter 12 discusses the creation and operation of a trust. It begins with the general concept of a trust and the different forms in which it can be found (active, passive, testamentary, inter vivos, and so on). It then defines the many components of a trust, including both persons (trustor, trustee) and things (trust instrument, trust res). Next the chapter describes implied trusts, which arise by operation of law, and finally trusts whose interests are not freely transferable. Along the way, entities that are similar to yet different from a trust are compared and distinguished.

B. DEFINITION, CREATION, AND CHARACTERISTICS OF A TRUST

This section defines the concept of a "trust" and discusses its creation and characteristics. It also describes and presents examples of the principal types of trusts based on how they are created, what they contain, or how they are to be administered. Trusts are distinguished both from one another and from other, nontrust alternatives for holding and administering property.

Trust

A fiduciary relationship with respect to property, in which one person (the trustee) holds property (the trust res) for the benefit of another person (the beneficiary), with specific duties attaching to the manner in which the trustee deals with the property.

Example 12.1: Suppose when you were a child you had a younger brother whom you were taking to the circus, and your mother give you the tickets and two one-dollar bills, saying, "The first dollar is for you. Buy whatever you want with it. The other dollar is for your brother. See that he gets a snack, and bring me back any change." You were the complete owner of the first dollar, the donee of your mother's gift. With respect to the second dollar, however, you were in effect only the trustee: Your mother had entrusted the money to you to spend not for yourself but for the benefit of your brother, the beneficiary. You had possession of the money and the right to spend it, but only as you were told; your brother lacked possession, but he had the right to have it spent for his snack. (In trust terms, you had legal ownership, and he had equitable or beneficial ownership.) If you had failed to buy your brother's snack and instead used the second dollar for candy for yourself, your brother likely would have complained to your mother and sought enforcement of the trust — not to mention unspecified penalties for its breach — from your parents.

The modern trust has many different functions, and new uses for its unique qualities are continually being found. Primarily it is used to separate the management of property from its enjoyment — as when parents set up a trust for their minor children, or a charitable trust is established to benefit the needy or for other charitable purposes — or to facilitate the division of property ownership among different concurrent or successive owners, such as life tenants and remaindermen. Trusts also are used to achieve various collateral advantages such as "avoiding probate" (by using a trust instead of a will to pass property at death) or gaining an income tax benefit. Trusts come in many sizes, shapes, colors, and configurations, limited only by the imagination of their creators and the relevant rules of law.

The distinction between property held in trust and that to which the beneficial owner also has legal title may seem only a technical one, especially when the trustee and the life beneficiary are the same person. However, that technical distinction can have extremely important consequences, not the least of which is the fiduciary obligation owed by the trustee to all the beneficiaries when dealing with trust property.

The most common type of trust is an **express trust**, sometimes called a **direct trust**, which arises by virtue of the intentional act of its creator, the settlor. (There are, however, also implied trusts, such as constructive and resulting trusts, which arise by operation of law and without anyone's expressed intention to create them. These are discussed in Section D.) No particular language is necessary to create a trust, although of course it helps to be very explicit and leave no doubt as to intent. The only absolute requirements for the creation of any express trust are the trust property, an intent by the settlor that the property be held by the trustee in trust for the benefit of another, and at least one beneficiary for whom it is to be held. A trustee is ultimately necessary but can be supplied by the court.

Example 12.2: Emma, a wealthy woman, wanting her friend Charles to have the lifetime benefits of her villa but considering him incapable of managing it properly, transfers it instead to her more responsible friend Rodolphe "in trust, for the benefit of Charles." Emma, the settlor, has created an express trust, with Rodolphe as the trustee and Charles as a beneficiary. Rodolphe has legal title to the villa — is the "legal owner" for purposes of sale, encumbrance, and so on — but he can deal with it only for the benefit of Charles.

In the above example, Emma created her trust for Charles alone. More typically, Charles would be given only a life interest in the income, with the remainder to someone else, perhaps Emma's children, free of trust. Any such remaindermen become additional beneficiaries, for whose benefit as well as Charles's the trustee must administer the villa.

Emma created Charles's express trust by transfer of the villa to Rodolphe. Because of the Statute of Frauds, a writing was necessary for the transfer of this real property to be effective. If, however, Emma had wished instead to create a trust of her jewels (or other personal property) for Charles, she could have done so either by transfer or by **declaration of trust**. If by declaration, Emma merely expresses an intent that she thereafter holds the jewels in trust for Charles. No transfer is necessary, and no writing. Under a declaration of trust, Emma becomes the trustee. If Emma wishes to have a third person — such as her friend Rodolphe — act as trustee, she must transfer the trust property to him. Here the requirements of delivery, as for any gift, take effect. Either the jewels themselves or a deed of trust must be delivered to the trustee. If Emma had created the trust by will, it would have had to be in writing whether it involved real or personal property. (See *Secret* and *Semi-secret Trusts*.)

Trusts are distinguished in several other ways. For example, a trust may be **active** or **passive**, depending on whether the trustee has any duties to perform. (Passive trusts were "executed," or converted into legal interests in the beneficiary, by the Statute of Uses; and still today, with some exceptions, a passive trust (also called a **dry** or **naked** trust, although occasionally these latter terms are given slightly different meanings) is ineffective and results in legal title passing to the beneficiaries.) If Emma in Example 12.2 had conveyed her villa to Rodolphe "in trust for Charles" but had given Charles all rights of possession and duties of management, Rodolphe would have been left with no duties to perform and the trust would be considered passive.

One form of seemingly passive trust that is nevertheless valid is the **life insurance trust**, a trust of which the res consists of the proceeds of a life insurance policy, or the policy itself. Its most common use is as the vehicle established inter vivos (during the settlor's lifetime) to receive life insurance proceeds upon the settlor's death. Although if this is its only function and it has no other trust property, it is close to being a passive trust, courts and legislatures have recognized the importance of the life insurance trust as an estate planning device and generally have declared such a trust valid, sometimes reasoning that a trustee who watches and waits for the insured's death is performing "active" duties.

A trust is **testamentary** if created by will, **inter vivos** (literally "between living persons," the third syllable pronounced either as in "virus" or as in "Venus") if created by deed while the settlor is still alive. The latter is also called a **living trust**. Sometimes a testator's will directs that property in the estate be transferred to an existing inter vivos trust. The trust is then termed a **pour-over trust**, and the will a **pour-over will**. Because the receptacle trust might be unfunded until the trustor's death or might have been amended after the will's execution, the validity of pour-over trusts was once in question. Today, however, legislation in all states (most under the **Uniform Testamentary Additions to Trusts Act**) permits pour-over wills and trusts even if the trust is amendable or unfunded, and it declares the post-death trust to be, in effect, a continuation of the existing inter vivos trust. If the trust is revoked before the death of the settlor/testator, the bequest lapses. See UPC 2-511.

Trusts may be private or charitable, depending on their purpose and the nature of their beneficiaries. (In essence, any trust that is not charitable is denominated "private.") They may be **revocable** (if the settlor can choose to terminate them) or **irrevocable**, mandatory (if the trustee must act in a certain way, particularly must distribute all the income) or discretionary. A **sprinkle trust** is a form of discretionary trust under which the trustee is directed to distribute the income but has discretion as to the amount (if any) to be given to each beneficiary — that is, as to how it is to be "sprinkled" among them. It is also known as a **spray trust**. (Discretionary trusts are further discussed in Section E, and charitable trusts are the subject of Chapter 16.)

To the extent that a trust is created as part of the donative process (as an inter vivos or testamentary gift to the beneficiary), its legal rules generally parallel those for other gifts, including such requirements as donative intent and delivery. The trustor is transferring property to the trustee for the purpose of making a gift of the beneficial interest to the beneficiary. Intent to create a trust obligation is crucial; an intent merely to give property to another in the hope, or with the request, that it will be dealt with in a way that benefits a third party will not generally be construed as creating a binding trust. (See *Precatory Trust*.)

Because a trust has the potential to continue well beyond the lifetime of the trustor, public policy places certain limitations on the control that can be exercised by the trustor's so-called **dead hand**. Restrictions relating to the remote vesting of property interests generally invoke the Rule Against Perpetuities, discussed in Chapter 15. But certain conditions placed on the enjoyment of trust benefits may offend public policy for very different reasons. For example, a condition that, after the trustor's death, discourages marriage or induces divorce (particularly if that was its intent) may be declared invalid. Restricting marriage to one of a particular religion, on the other hand, would generally be permitted, at least if sufficient eligible partners were available. Although some such conditions would be unlawful in an inter vivos trust as well, they are particularly disfavored when they continue past the trustor's death, when there is no longer the opportunity for a change of heart through reassessment by or persuasion of the trustor.

An early antecedent of the trust was the **use**, which was really a passive trust employed for feudal purposes beyond the scope of this discussion. After the Statute of Uses "executed" and eliminated these uses, only active uses, uses of personality, and the "use upon a use" survived. It is from these unexecuted uses that our present trust has developed. Although the term "use" is still sometimes employed as synonymous with "trust," it is best confined to its proper historical connotation. (See *Statute of Uses*.)

Some similar relationships should be distinguished here from a trust. An **equitable charge** arises when property is transferred subject to an obligation to make some payment to another person.

Example 12.3:   Emma transfers property to Rodolphe, "subject to the payment of $1,000 per month to Charles." Charles is in a position similar to that of a trust beneficiary, in that he has an equitable interest in the property; however, he actually holds only a security interest, not equitable ownership, and no fiduciary relationship exists between Rodolphe and Charles. So long as Rodolphe does not deal with the property in a manner inconsistent with Charles's security interest, he can sell it or otherwise deal with it as his own. In fact, to the extent of the property's value beyond the encumbrance (or after it is satisfied), Rodolphe is the sole beneficial owner of the property.

Whether a transfer created a trust or an equitable charge is, of course, a matter of intent and depends on the language used and the surrounding circumstances.

Another relationship with similar features to a trust is the power of appointment, which is discussed in detail in Chapter 14. Suffice it to say that while there is a similarity between the donee (holder) of a power and the trustee of a trust, and between the power's objects (permissible appointees) and trust beneficiaries, there is no fiduciary relationship between the donee and the objects (except perhaps in the case of a so-called power in trust) and generally no requirement that the donee act for the benefit of the objects. (See generally *Fiduciary*.)

A **durable power of attorney** resembles a trust in that one person (the attorney-in-fact) has the power to act in the place of another, often with respect to the latter's property interests. A power of attorney, however, is an agency relationship. The attorney-in-fact (agent) does not hold title to the principal's property and usually has only limited powers respecting it; and unlike a trust, a power of attorney does not survive the principal's death. The important estate-planning feature of the *durable* power is that, unlike an ordinary agency relationship, it does not terminate on the incapacity of the principal. Thus the attorney-in-fact can make decisions on behalf of the principal after the latter becomes incompetent, including (if authorized) the creation or funding of a revocable trust that will thereafter provide for the incompetent beneficiary's care. See UPC 5-501-505. A **durable power of attorney for health care**, as the name implies, is limited to the making of health care decisions after the principal has become incompetent.

A **custodianship** for a minor bears a strong resemblance to a trust. It is a relationship governed by statute that allows a gift to be made to a minor with broad management powers retained by the donor or given to another adult. The custodian's powers and duties are set out in the statute. Every state has adopted one of the two custodianship statutes: either the **Uniform Gifts to Minors Act** or the more recent **Uniform Transfers to Minors Act**.

The advantages of these custodianship statutes are ease of creation, since reference need be made only to the statute and its terms automatically attach, and the more extensive powers (and fewer responsibilities) of the custodian as compared with a trustee. The custodianship ends when the minor reaches majority, at which time the property belongs to the donee free of the statute's provisions.

Recently the idea of a custodianship for minors has been extended to adults by the **Uniform Custodial Trust Act**, which provides for creation of a **custodial trust**. By simple designation, a transferor may establish a trust whose terms are set out in the statute. Intended primarily (but not exclusively) for elderly adults, the custodial trust can be controlled by the beneficiary if and while competent, but upon incapacity it becomes a discretionary trust for the benefit of the beneficiary and the beneficiary's dependents. It terminates on the beneficiary's death, with distribution by the custodial trustee according to the (pre-incapacity) directions, if any, of the beneficiary.

Secret Trust

A trust that is created when a will purports to make an absolute gift, but there is an undisclosed ("secret") agreement between the testator and the legatee that the latter will hold the property in trust for another.

Example 12.4: Emma leaves her jewels "absolutely" to Rodolphe, with no mention in her will that Rodolphe has promised her that he will hold them in trust for Charles. The secret trust agreement cannot be recognized directly because it lacks the formalities required of a will; but if it is ignored, Rodolphe will take property that Emma intended — and he promised — would be held in trust for Charles. Usually a court will prevent unjust enrichment of the transferee by decreeing a constructive trust in favor of the intended beneficiary, here Charles.

Note that, in the above example, if Emma forgot to tell Rodolphe of her intention or Rodolphe did not promise to honor it, Rodolphe can keep the jewels for himself, as he is not unjustly enriched.

A related concept is the **semi-secret trust**. As its name implies, this arrangement is only "half-secret": the will states that the gift is in trust and the legatee holds only as trustee, but it does not reveal the terms (or at least the beneficiaries) of the trust, which presumably are known only to the trustee. In Example 12.4, had Emma left her jewels "to Rodolphe, to hold in trust on the terms and for the persons we have previously discussed," she would have created a semi-secret trust. No chance of unjust enrichment arises if the undisclosed trust terms are ignored because a beneficial gift to the "trustee" Rodolphe clearly was not intended. Usually a court treats the gift in a semi-secret trust as an incomplete attempt to create a trust and decrees a resulting trust in favor of the testator's successors (residual beneficiaries or heirs). In England and a minority of states the court decrees a constructive trust in favor of the intended beneficiaries.

It sometimes is difficult to keep clear the distinctions between secret and semi-secret trusts, and for this the following chart may assist:

	Secret Trust	*Semi-secret Trust*
Will Provision:	absolute gift to intended trustee	gift in trust, key terms omited
Oral Agreement:	to be held in trust	beneficiaries' names (or other key terms)
Result if left as is:	"trustee" takes: unjust enrichment	trust fails, heirs/residuary legatees take
Usual remedy:	constructive trust	resulting trust
Who takes:	intended beneficiaries	heirs/residuary legatees

Equitable Title

The interest in trust property held by a beneficiary of a trust. It is in contrast to the **legal title** held by the trustee. Technically and historically the equitable title (or interest) is that which would be protected by a court of equity (and legal title by a court of law). Although this can have certain procedural effects, for most purposes today the importance of the distinction between equitable and legal title is that the former represents the beneficial interest in the trust property — the right under principles of fairness and equity to the enjoyment of its fruits — whereas the latter represents the "official" title. Legal title gives its holder the right to sell, encumber, or otherwise deal with the property, although for the benefit of another. (Note, however, that the holder of an equitable interest, such as an equitable life estate, generally can sell or encumber that interest.)

It is this bifurcated nature of the ownership of trust property, and the separation it entails between the person who holds property and the person who benefits from it, that makes possible such important functions of the trust as property management by one person for another.

Precatory Trust

A trust, or purported trust, employing words of request ("precatory language") rather than of direction. Typical precatory language would be statements that

151

the transferor "desires," "wishes," "hopes," or "recommends" that the trans-feree hold or deal with the property for the benefit of another: "I give to Mary the farm, the profits from which I would hope she shares with her brother."

"Precatory trust" is really something of an oxymoron, as the general rule is that a trust cannot be created by precatory language; a trust is, by its nature, a relationship in which the trustee is required to hold the property in trust, not just requested to do so. The phrase thus often describes a gift (as in a will) that would be in trust if the language were mandatory but fails as a trust because the language is merely precatory. The result is not a trust at all but an absolute gift to the transferee (would-be "trustee").

Another, opposing usage of this phrase is a trust held to be validly created despite the use of precatory language. Here there is a trust, but only because it was decided that, notwithstanding its language, it was not meant to be precatory.

It therefore is recommended that the term "precatory trust" not be used: Either there is a trust created despite the use of precatory language or there is no trust because of that language.

In deciding whether a trust was created despite the use of precatory language, a court will consider such factors as the relationship between the transferor and the purported beneficiary (is the latter someone for whom the former would naturally provide?) or between the transferor and the trans-feree/trustee (is it likely the latter would be intended to take a beneficial interest in the property?). If the gift is testamentary, the court will take into account the overall dispositive scheme found in the will. As always, the fundamental question is one of the transferor's intent.

Example 12.5: Emma's will leaves her villa "to the Provincial Bank, it being my wish that they distribute the income to my beloved Charles and, on his death, the principal to my good friend Rodolphe." Given the relationship between Emma and the "beneficiaries" and the un-likelihood that she would be making a beneficial gift to a bank, her gift would probably be construed as a trust, despite the precatory language of "wishing."

The precatory trust should not be confused with certain other concepts that share some of its characteristics. A trust may be discretionary in some of its terms, giving the trustee permission to decide such matters as whether to make certain payments to a beneficiary; yet the relationship of trustee and beneficiary still must be mandatory: The trustee must hold the property and exercise that discretion on behalf of the beneficiary, not the trustee. Also to be distinguished is the so-called honorary trust (also not technically a true trust), which lacks a beneficiary who can enforce it but which can be car-ried out (upon the "honor" of the "trustee") in certain narrow circumstances.

Honorary Trust

A term applied to a class of trust-like gifts that neither are intended to benefit the transferee nor have specific beneficiaries who can enforce the gift as a trust.

Example 12.6:   Tom's will leaves $1,000 to his brother Archie for the care of Tom's pet cat Mehitabel. Because the benefiting cat is specifically named, this cannot be a charitable trust; and because Mehitabel is not a "person" capable of enforcing Archie's obligations of care, it would fail as a private trust as well.

Ordinarily an attempted trust such as that in Example 12.6 would leave only a resulting trust for the testator's successors. However, the English and some American courts have permitted this and a few other such "trusts" for specific noncharitable purposes to stand, calling them "honorary trusts," to be performed on the honor of the "trustee." In the example, only if and when Archie either attempts to use the property for his own purposes or otherwise fails to carry out the direction of the testator will the court order a resulting trust and take the property away from him. Other purposes that have been upheld as honorary trusts include the erection of a monument or the care of a grave.

It has been pointed out that, to the extent a "trust" connotes a relationship carrying enforceable fiduciary obligations, "honorary trust" is a contradiction in terms: it is really a form of power of appointment. However, the concept is sufficiently close to an actual trust that it seems pointless to quibble over a semantic inconsistency in the name.

Note that because an animal is not considered a "person" for purposes of the Rule Against Perpetuities, an honorary trust for animals can easily violate the Rule unless it contains some limitation on duration other than the animal's lifetime.

The Uniform Probate Code (UPC 2-907) expressly provides for honorary trusts (trusts with specific noncharitable purposes but no ascertainable beneficiary) and separately designated trusts for the care of pets; the former are limited to 21 years, and the latter to the pet's lifetime. The fund cannot be used for the trustee's personal benefit, and the intended use can be enforced by a person designated in the instrument or by another person appointed by the court.

Illusory Trust

A purported trust under which the settlor retains such extensive powers that no interest is really passed to the beneficiary and thus no trust exists at all. The term is used most frequently to describe an attempt to deprive one's spouse of a statutory forced share of one's estate by transferring property to a third person but retaining substantial incidents of ownership. A related term is "illusory transfer."

Example 12.7:   Emma wishes to leave her entire estate to her friend Rodolphe. To do this, she must avoid the local forced share statute that automatically gives to her husband Charles half of her estate upon her death. She knows she can avoid the statute by giving her property away before her death; however, she does not yet want to lose ownership or control of it. She thus "transfers" most of her property to one of her friends, "in trust for" Rodolphe; but she retains the right to spend the income, invade the principal, direct investments, and approve all the trustee's managerial acts. In effect, Emma has retained virtually all indicia of ownership, and in some states the purported trust would be considered illusory and invalid, and Emma would die intestate.

Supplemental Needs Trust

A type of discretionary trust designed to benefit a disabled person without affecting the beneficiary's eligibility for public assistance. It is also commonly called a **special needs trust**.

A disabled person may be receiving some form of public (that is, government) assistance, or may be institutionalized in a state hospital. Eligibility for assistance may depend on the availability of private resources, and these resources may be reachable by the government to reimburse it for institutional care. An ordinary discretionary trust, if created by a third person and truly beyond the reach of the beneficiary, may be protected from the state's reach. If, however, it can practically or theoretically be accessed by the beneficiary for support, it may also be reachable by the state. Supplemental needs trusts are clearly limited to needs of the disabled person that the state cannot or does not provide, and where permitted they prevent the state from realizing the benefit of a third person's gift.

Some states by statute expressly permit or prohibit supplemental needs trusts, or certain of their forms.

UPC 2-212(c)(2), governing election on behalf of an incapacitated surviving spouse, requires (for states adopting the appropriate language) that expenditures under a custodial trust for the incompetent spouse take into account the availability of need-based governmental assistance.

C.   ELEMENTS OF A TRUST

A trust consists of many separate components, both human and material. Each trust is a little like a story: There are several roles to fill, although one person often may play more than one part, and there are also the objects of which a trust is composed, from the property it concerns to the document in which it is set out. This section describes these elements — first the dramatis personæ and then the "props" — and the relationship of each to the others.

Settlor

The person who creates a trust. The settlor is also called the **trustor**. These terms are applicable to persons who create either testamentary or inter vivos trusts, although some authorities use "settlor" for an inter vivos trust and "trustor" for a testamentary trust.

The settlor of a trust may also be its trustee; this is always true when the trust is created by declaration rather than transfer. (See *Trust.*) The settlor also may be a trust beneficiary, although if the sole trustee were also the sole beneficiary (living or potential), the terms of the trust could not be enforced, and it would fail.

A trust under which the settlor, or "grantor" (since by definition it cannot be a testamentary trust), is a beneficiary may be called a **grantor trust**. In tax law, a grantor trust is one under which the settlor retains such powers of management or control as to cause the settlor to be deemed the owner of the trust property and the income to be attributed to the settlor rather than to the beneficiary.

Trustee

The person who, in a trust relationship, holds and deals with trust property for the benefit of another (the beneficiary). The role or office of trustee is a fiduciary one, and the duties owed by the trustee to the beneficiaries — and the attendant liabilities — can be quite onerous; therefore the position must be voluntarily accepted and will not be forcibly imposed on one (except in the case of resulting or constructive trusts, which arise by operation of law).

The trustee of an express trust holds legal title to the property, while the beneficiary holds equitable (beneficial) title. The trustee may be a natural person or an entity such as a bank or trust company, and there may be one trustee or several **co-trustees**. The trustee also may be a beneficiary (and in fact may be both a beneficiary and the settlor), although if the sole trustee is also the sole beneficiary (living or potential), no one can enforce the trust against the trustee and it will fail.

While it is necessary that a trust have a trustee, it is said that "a trust will not fail for want of a trustee" because if no trustee has been appointed, or the appointed trustee disclaims, dies, resigns, or is removed, a court will simply appoint another (unless the trustee's duties are of a personal nature that only the named trustee could properly carry out).

After accepting the trust, the trustee must take title to and possession of the trust property. In some states, the trustee also must qualify. **Qualification** entails the performance of various acts that are specified by statute or prescribed by the settlor or the court, such as the taking of an oath of office or the giving of a bond.

Fiduciary

As an adjective, founded on the utmost trust and confidence; as a noun, a person (such as a trustee) who stands in a position of great trust and confidence toward another, with a duty to act in good faith for the benefit of that person. In the legal terminology of trusts and estates, trustees, executors, and other administrators or personal representatives all are "fiduciaries": They stand in a **fiduciary relationship** with their beneficiaries; they act in a **fiduciary capacity**; and they have strict **fiduciary duties** toward the beneficiaries.

The law assumes that beneficiaries can and will trust and confide in a fiduciary and will expect the fiduciary to act faithfully to protect and further the beneficiaries' interests. The law therefore requires fiduciaries to act in accordance with this expectation of good faith, to perform selflessly and not to abuse or take advantage of their position and the trust that has been placed in them. This means that they are precluded (under most circumstances) from "self-dealing," or entering into transactions — even "fair" ones — between themselves in their individual and their fiduciary capacities, since this necessarily would involve a division of their loyalty between their personal interests and those of the beneficiaries. In other words, they generally cannot "wear both hats" (individual and fiduciary) in the same transaction.

Example 12.8: Emma transfers her villa to her trusted business advisor Rodolphe, as trustee, to hold it in trust for her good friend Charles, the trust beneficiary. Rodolphe's duties will include maintaining the villa and its rental so as to produce an income for Charles. Rodolphe has always coveted Emma's villa and would like to rent (or purchase) it for himself. As a trustee, however, Rodolphe stands in a fiduciary relationship to Charles, and one of his principal fiduciary duties is that of undivided loyalty to the trust's beneficiaries. In practical effect, the duty of loyalty prohibits Rodolphe's purchase from, sale to, or other transaction with the trust for his own account.

Many relationships other than between an executor or trustee (a "fiduciary" as such) and a beneficiary are considered to be of a fiduciary nature. Common examples are guardian and ward, principal and agent, corporate director and shareholders, and attorney and client.

A fiduciary relationship is sometimes contrasted with a confidential relationship, a more general concept that shares with it many characteristics, and sometimes the terms are used interchangeably. If, however, the law declares a relationship to be "fiduciary," using the latter as a term of art, the responsibilities of the trusted person and the consequences of a breach of that trust may be more serious than if the relationship is merely "confidential." Thus in some jurisdictions if it is alleged that the donee of a gift exercised undue influence over the donor, the existence of a fiduciary relationship (such as that of trustee and beneficiary) between the parties will create a presumption of undue influence, whereas existence of a confidential relationship, such as business advisor and advisee, will not.

Beneficiary

The person who is entitled to the benefit of property held in trust and to whom the duties of the trustee are owed. A trust may have one or more beneficiaries; they may include anyone capable of holding an equitable interest in the trust property, including the settlor. Beneficiaries may hold either concurrent or successive interests; if the latter, typically one beneficiary will hold a life estate or term of years and others will hold future interests.

Another common term for a trust beneficiary is **cestui que** (pronounced either "sest we key" or "set tea cu(t)") **trust**. The equivalent term for the use is *cestui que use* (pronounced like the verb "use," not the noun). The proper plural is "cestuis que trust," although one occasionally sees the more daunting and somewhat pretentious **cestuis que trustent**.

A trust must have definite, ascertainable beneficiaries such that it is clear (or will be when enjoyment of their interest would begin) who is included and who is not, and therefore who has a right to enforce the trust. If the description of beneficiaries is omitted or too vague and indefinite (such as "my friends"), and it cannot be interpreted to mean some more definite class of persons (such as "the three friends to whom I previously referred"), the trust will fail. (Compare a charitable trust (Chapter 16) or a power of appointment (Chapter 14), for which the beneficiaries need not be as definite.)

Trust Property

The property that is held by the trustee in trust for the benefit of the trust's beneficiaries. It is also commonly referred to as the trust **res** (pronounced to rhyme with either "peas" or "ace"), the trust **corpus** (literally "body"), the trust estate, the subject matter of the trust, the trust fund, the trust assets, or the trust principal (watch the spelling!). The last term reflects the fact that the res often is cash or other income-producing property; the distinction between principal and income thus becomes an important one. (See also *Uniform Principal and Income Act*.)

Every trust must have some specific, ascertained (or ascertainable) property, tangible or intangible, as its subject matter. Any recognized and transferable property interest will suffice, although it must be in existence before the trust can come into being. Thus a trust of "all the money I earn from garage sales next year, should I hold any" would be ineffective. In an express trust, the trustee holds legal title to the trust property, and the beneficiaries hold equitable title.

It is the existence of specific trust property, identifiable and segregated and intended to be held by the trustee for the benefit of the beneficiary, that most clearly distinguishes both a trust from a **debt** and a trustee/beneficiary relationship from that of debtor/creditor: A debtor owes money to a creditor but is not holding any specific money or other property belonging to the creditor. The debtor therefore owes no fiduciary duties to the creditor, merely a duty to repay the debt from whatever source the debtor chooses. Moreover, profits or losses attributable to property held in trust belong to the beneficiary, not the trustee; those attributable to borrowed property belong to the debtor, not the creditor.

Example 12.9: Emma transfers $10,000 to Rodolphe, as trustee for her friend Charles. Rodolphe must put the money into a separate trust account, for it is Charles's property, not his. (See *Duty to Segregate and Earmark.*) If he (properly) invests it in Ajax Pharmaceuticals, Inc., and Ajax triples in value, the extra $20,000 belongs not to Rodolphe but to Charles, the beneficial owner of the original amount. If, however, Ajax goes bankrupt, it is Charles who has lost $10,000, not Rodolphe. Had Rodolphe *borrowed* the original $10,000 from Charles at 5 percent interest, the borrowed money would have belonged to Rodolphe and he would have been free to put it into his personal account; whether his investments soared or sank, he would still owe Charles the original $10,000 plus interest, no more and no less.

Note that a debt (of a third party — Rodolphe's "I.O.U.") can be the subject matter of a trust, although one cannot hold one's own debt in trust because a debtor has no claim against himself and so no property interest to hold as trustee.

While bailment, like a trust, involves the transfer of specific property, it is only for a temporary, limited purpose or use by the bailee, and the bailor retains general legal title. Bailment, like debt, is not a fiduciary relationship.

Trust Instrument

The document that embodies the terms of a trust. A trust need not be in writing unless it is testamentary or it concerns real property. One form of trust instrument is a **deed of trust** ("trust deed"), which generally refers to an instrument giving to a lender a security interest in real property (comparable to a mortgage) but also is used to refer to any written document of transfer in trust. (If the transfer is gratuitous, the instrument is technically a deed of gift.)

Typically, the trust instrument would begin with a transfer or conveyance by the trustor to the trustee of the described trust property, "to hold in trust [usually together with other property the trustee may acquire under the terms of the trust instrument] for the following purposes and subject to the following terms: . . ." This would be followed by a recital of the terms of the trust (the beneficiaries, their respective interests, and so on) and the powers, duties, and compensation of the trustee. The instrument might conclude with miscellaneous provisions such as those for successor trustees, irrevocability, or governing law.

The term **trust indenture** (from the ancient practice of executing a deed in two parts on one page and tearing it in two, leaving a ragged or "indented" edge for later proof of authenticity by matching the parts) also may be used to refer to a document of transfer in trust, especially in reference to corporate finance documents.

D.   IMPLIED TRUSTS: TRUSTS THAT ARISE BY OPERATION OF LAW

Most trusts are express trusts: The trustor intends to create a trust and performs some act toward that end. In a few circumstances, however, the law will imply a trust relationship that was not necessarily intended. This section discusses the types of implied trust, the circumstances under which they are implied, the purposes they can serve, and the differences in function between them and express trusts.

Implied Trust

A trust that arises by operation of law, implied from the circumstances, and not through the express intent of a settlor. Implied trusts are thus distinguished from express trusts. The two types of implied trust are the resulting trust and the constructive trust, discussed below.

Although both express and implied trusts are equitable devices, usually an implied trust does not involve the same kind of duties of management of the trust property over time as does an express trust. Rather, the primary duty of the trustee is to convey the property to the settlor (or to another) on demand. Because implied trusts arise by operation of law, they are not subject to the requirement of a writing under the Statute of Frauds.

Example 12.10:   Emma's will leaves her villa to Rodolphe, in trust for
Charles for his lifetime. Rodolphe is instructed to keep the villa in
good repair, to lease it to reliable tenants, and to pay the income to
Charles monthly. Emma neglects, however, to name a remainderman
following Charles's life estate. Upon Charles's death, Rodolphe will
hold the villa on a "resulting trust" in favor of Emma's successors,
with the duty merely to convey it to them. The original trust in favor
of Charles is an express trust; the resulting trust for the successors is
an implied trust.

The most common form of **resulting trust** arises, by operation of law,
when an express trust fails. The failure may be for almost any reason, such
as the lack of an ascertainable or competent beneficiary or the impossibility
of the purpose of a charitable trust where the doctrine of cy pres cannot be
applied (see Chapter 16). A resulting trust also may arise after only a partial
failure of an express trust, such as when the interest of only one of several
beneficiaries lapses or, as in Example 12.10 above, the settlor creates a trust
naming a life beneficiary but no remainderman. In these instances, it can
be presumed (in the absence of evidence to the contrary) that the settlor
did not wish the trustee to take the beneficial interest, and the only usual
alternative is to return the property to the settlor if alive or, if not, to the
settlor's successors (residuary legatees or heirs). In other words, a court imposes a resulting trust in an attempt to carry out what the settlor presumably
intended or would have intended had the circumstances been anticipated.

The **purchase money resulting trust** arises in a very narrow circumstance: The consideration for the purchase of property is paid by one person,
but title is taken in the name of another.

Example 12.11:   Emma purchases a villa but takes title in Rodolphe's
name. Unless there is a family relationship that warrants a presumption of a gift, it is presumed that the payor (Emma) intended that
the transferee (Rodolphe) hold the property in trust for her benefit.
This presumption depends on certain (sometimes complex) conditions, and it is rebuttable by evidence of a contrary intent of the
payor.

A **constructive trust** is an equitable device used to avoid unjust enrichment of a person who receives property from another under circumstances that would make retention unconscionable. (Thus it is not, like the
resulting trust, theoretically based on any presumed intent of the transferor.)
It usually is imposed on a person who has committed some wrong in ob-
taining the property, but in most jurisdictions it also may be imposed on an
innocent person who, without personal fault, receives property as a result of
a wrong of another.

Example 12.12:   Emma is preparing to execute a will leaving her estate
to Rodolphe. Charles, one of her heirs, physically prevents her from
executing the will, with the result that her estate passes by intestacy
to her heirs, including Charles. A constructive trust in favor of Rodolphe would likely be imposed not just on Charles but also on the
innocent heirs, who did not participate in preventing the will's execution, to avoid their unjust (that is, unfair from Rodolphe's point
of view) enrichment.

Although in theory the constructive trust can be imposed wherever
necessary to avoid unjust enrichment in the acquisition or retention of property, it is most commonly employed in certain circumstances. For example,
a constructive trust will be imposed on one who: obtains property from
another, by deed or will, through fraud, duress (as in Example 12.12), or
undue influence (or, in some cases, mistake); wrongfully kills another to
obtain a benefit from the decedent's estate (usually where a "slayer's statute"
is not in effect); promises to hold a bequest in trust for another, the promise
being oral and thus not enforceable under the Statute of Wills (a "secret
trust"); or acquires property in breach of the fiduciary duties of a trustee.

The constructive trust will be imposed in favor of (that is, the beneficiary entitled to a conveyance from the constructive trustee will be) either
the original transferor or another person who would have retained or received the property but for the wrongful act in question.

A constructive trust may also be called a **trust ex maleficio** (the third
syllable rhyming with "fish"; the phrase often refers to a wrongful acquisition
by the trustee) or **ex delicto** (also "ex delictu," a trust created for an unlawful
purpose), a trust **de son tort** (created because of one's own wrong; the second
word rhyming with "lone"), a **trust in invitum** ("against one's will or consent," rhyming with "invite 'em"), and an **involuntary trust**. (There is a
corresponding *trustee* ex maleficio, ex delicto, and so on). All these terms
suggest the trustee's (or another's) wrongdoing or the imposition of the trust
against the trustee's will, and they are sometimes used interchangeably. It is
probably more accurate to say that each of these is a particular form of the
generic constructive trust.

E.   LIMITED TRANSFER OF TRUST INTERESTS

Ordinarily, the beneficial interests in trusts may be transferred freely, like
any other type of property interest. Subject to the usual restrictions that
apply to all forms of property, they may be bought, sold, or encumbered by
an owner/beneficiary, and they may be attached or seized by creditors. In
certain types of trusts, however, the transfer (or alienation) of such interests
is more limited. These are discussed in this section.

Spendthrift Trust

A trust that includes a provision — a disabling restraint — prohibiting voluntary or involuntary alienation of the beneficial interests. The name derives from the use of such trusts by the wealthy to pass large fortunes to "spendthrift" offspring who were likely to squander it foolishly or run up large debts and have it seized by creditors. Partly because of this and partly because of its inherent unfairness in permitting enjoyment of property without the risk of exposure to legitimate debts, the spendthrift trust has been a controversial — but popular — device.

To create a spendthrift trust, the settlor would insert a clause stating, in effect, that one or more of the beneficial interests could not be transferred by the beneficiary and was not subject to payment of the beneficiary's debts. (One such provision can be included without the other, although the latter usually would not be permitted without the former.) In some states, however, even if no such language is included, all or certain trusts are statutorily presumed to be "spendthrift" in nature with respect to voluntary or involuntary transfers or both.

Example 12.13: Emma wishes to give the income from her villa to Charles, her irresponsible husband. She transfers the villa to Rodolphe, in trust for Charles for his lifetime, remainder to charity. Emma is afraid, however, that even though Charles will not own the legal interest in the villa and cannot transfer it, he might be induced to transfer away his beneficial (equitable) interest in the income, perhaps to pay off a gambling debt, or perhaps one of Charles's many creditors may decide to attach his interest. Since Emma does not intend the transfer to benefit Charles's creditors, she puts into the trust the following clause:

> V. The interest of Charles in this trust shall not be subject to the claims of his creditors or others, or to any legal process, and it may not be transferred by him or otherwise voluntarily or involuntarily alienated or encumbered.

It is not necessary that a spendthrift restraint be as express as that in Example 12.13. Sometimes the very presence of trustee discretion to withhold income (a discretionary trust) or a direction to use income only for the beneficiary's support (a support trust) will be interpreted as a general intention to prohibit alienation and to create a spendthrift trust.

Spendthrift trusts are permitted in most American jurisdictions. The only beneficiary for whom one cannot establish a spendthrift trust is oneself; and in most jurisdictions classes of creditors, such as spouses and children seeking support, can reach a spendthrift trust interest even if other creditors cannot.

Spendthrift trusts are not enforceable in some states and in England. Even where they are prohibited, however, insulation of a beneficial interest can be achieved (with some of the same limitations just indicated) by use of a support trust, a discretionary trust, or a protective trust, all of which are explained below.

It should be noted that whatever the law respecting the validity of spendthrift provisions, their protection can extend to the trust property only until it is paid to the beneficiary. Upon payment the beneficiary holds a legal interest, which cannot be subjected to a disabling restraint.

Discretionary Trust

A trust that leaves to the trustee's discretion whether, and in what amounts, to pay income or principal (or both) to the beneficiaries. (Of course, other aspects of the trustee's duties may also be discretionary, but the term "discretionary trust" generally is reserved for discretion over the payment or withholding of income, or income and principal.) If the trust is not discretionary, it is **mandatory**.

Some disagreement exists as to the effect of a trust clause that purports to give the trustee "absolute" (or similarly unbridled) discretion. Given the nature of a trust and the separation of legal and equitable interests, all courts will assume that the trustee must act in good faith and for proper purposes (and not, for example, for personal benefit at the expense of the beneficiaries). All agree as well that the trustee must actually exercise discretion to act or not and cannot "decide not to decide." However, while most courts will further impose an objective standard of reasonableness on the trustee's exercise of even "absolute" discretion, some will not unless this is spelled out in the trust instrument. Whatever the standard, if the trustee acts within it, a court generally will not interfere.

One of the principal characteristics of a discretionary trust is its ability to prevent alienation of a beneficiary's interest. A beneficiary cannot assign that interest, nor can a creditor reach it by attachment if the trustee chooses not to pay. In other words, neither the beneficiary nor a creditor can compel the exercise of discretion in favor of either the beneficiary or another. Generally, however, the trustee may be prevented by a creditor's attachment from paying the beneficiary before paying the creditor, so that in effect both the creditor and the beneficiary are denied any payment. In this way, the discretionary trust, like the similar support trust (discussed below), is an alternative — if an imperfect one — to a spendthrift trust.

Example 12.14: As in Example 12.13 (see *Spendthrift Trust*), Emma wishes to establish a trust giving income to Charles but protecting him from squandering it. Even if the jurisdiction does not recognize spendthrift trusts, Emma still can protect the trust interest of irresponsible Charles by giving trustee Rodolphe broad discretion to pay the income to Charles or to withhold it. Unlike the true spendthrift trust, however, a creditor's attachment might prevent Charles from being paid the income unless his creditors are also paid. (Emma probably can avoid this stalemate by giving Rodolphe the right to pay third parties for the benefit of Charles: Courts have held that if no payment is made to Charles, none need be made to the creditors.)

Support Trust

A trust that directs the trustee to use income (and/or principal) as needed for the support of the beneficiary. Often the language used is "support, maintenance, and education" or the like, but the import is similar.

A trust directing the trustee to pay to the beneficiary all the income (rather than only the amount needed for support) or a fixed sum (whether or not needed or sufficient for support), with the stated intent that the funds be used for the beneficiary's support, is not technically a support trust because it is not limited to that purpose. Whether a true support trust exists can have significant implications, including certain tax consequences. Under the Claflin doctrine, for example, the beneficiary of a support trust may be unable to terminate the trust because support is generally considered a material purpose of the settlor. Perhaps the most important limitation, however, is that a beneficiary cannot assign an interest that is limited to support nor can the interest be reached by the beneficiary's creditors (except by those creditors furnishing necessities, and except where the beneficiary is also the trustor); in other words, the beneficiary's interest is not alienable voluntarily or involuntarily. This makes the support trust, like the discretionary trust, an alternative to a spendthrift trust.

Because a support trust generally can be reached by creditors that furnish necessities to the beneficiary, a state agency providing services (such as hospital care) to the beneficiary of such a trust may be able to reach the beneficiary interest for reimbursement. If, however, it is within the trustee's discretion whether to provide support (a discretionary trust), the state generally cannot force the trustee to pay. If the trust has both support and discretionary language (sometimes called a **hybrid trust**), such as "for Charles's maintenance and support as determined in the trustee's sole discretion," it will be a matter of interpretation in light of surrounding circumstances whether the discretionary language will prevail and the claim be denied. Obviously, this is a place where careful drafting and a clear expression of intent are especially important.

Blended Trust

A trust, the beneficiaries of which are described as a group (such as "all of Charles's children") and are intended to benefit as a group, not as individuals. Any benefits must be applied to the advantage of the entire group. The beneficiaries of such a trust do not own interests that can be individually transferred or reached by their individual creditors. (See *Spendthrift Trust.*)

Protective Trust

An ordinary express trust that automatically converts to a type of discretionary trust if the beneficiary should attempt to alienate it or creditors attempt to reach the beneficiary's interest. This prevents ("protects against") alienation, at least to the extent that discretionary trusts do so. It is used primarily in England, where it takes the place of and accomplishes much the same purpose as a spendthrift trust, which English courts do not recognize.

13

Alteration and Termination

A. INTRODUCTION AND OVERVIEW OF CHAPTER

This chapter briefly discusses alteration or termination of a trust, including attempts to deviate from the terms of a trust or to terminate a trust before the time it would normally terminate by its own terms.

B. ALTERATION OF TRUSTS

Administrative Deviation

The power of a court of equity to permit some change in the method of administration of a trust from that which the trust instrument directs. This is to be distinguished from a change in the dispositive provisions (who receives how much from the trust), which courts seldom permit, except in the case of charitable trusts (discussed in Chapter 16). Of course, if the settlor has reserved the power to amend the trust (or has given that power to another person), alteration of the trust according to those terms creates no difficulty.

Example 13.1: Camille establishes a trust for his wife, Julie, and his infant son Lucien, Julie to have a life estate and Lucien the remainder. He directs Claude, the trustee, to invest the trust funds in government bonds and similar safe investments, but to retain in the trust certain paintings and sell them at a rate of one per year, adding the proceeds to the trust principal. At Julie's death Lucien is to receive the remaining principal, including whatever paintings have not been sold. The trust makes no provision for invading the principal.

After Camille has died, an unanticipated event occurs: Julie needs more money for an emergency operation than the trust income produces. The trustee, Claude, wishes to invade the principal to pay for Julie's operation. The request probably will be denied, as it would require an alteration in the shares of the trust allocated to the two beneficiaries.

Note that in Example 13.1, if Lucien is of age and agrees to the invasion of principal, or if the court is willing to appoint a guardian ad litem to consent for Lucien (which is unlikely), the court might agree to the dispositive deviation.

Example 13.2:   Assume the same facts as in Example 13.1. Although Camille had assumed the fine art market would be fairly stable (or rising) for the foreseeable future, there is a sudden (though probably temporary) collapse of the market. Claude wishes to delay selling any paintings until the market has become more stable. This request, seeking only a change in the method by which the trust is administered, probably will be granted. The court will examine Camille's purposes in setting up the trust; if it finds that those purposes would be seriously endangered by a strict adherence to the administrative terms of the trust, it will permit the administrative deviation. Here it is likely that Camille intended to increase the trust's liquid assets over time by sale of the paintings, but to do so gradually and preserve as many as possible for Lucien. To require a hasty sale under temporarily adverse conditions would serve neither purpose and result in a net loss for both beneficiaries.

Had the trustee in Example 13.2 wished to depart from the trust terms and sell all the paintings immediately, merely because there was a temporary rise in the fine art market or the trustee knew of better forms of investment, the court would decline. The doctrine of administrative deviation is a means of relief from serious erosion of the settlor's purposes as a result of unanticipated circumstances; it is not a license to substitute the court's or the trustee's preferred methods of administration for those established by the settlor.

C. TERMINATION OF TRUSTS

Although termination of a trust is generally a simple and straightforward process, there are many ways in which, and certain restrictions on when, this can occur. This section discusses both conventional and unconventional trust termination and the principal restrictions on both.

Termination

Bringing a trust to an end in one of several ways. A trust may terminate "naturally," or by its terms, because the settlor has so directed in the trust instrument, because all trust purposes have been accomplished, or because those purposes have become illegal or impossible to accomplish. The settlor also may have reserved a power to revoke the trust at will or under specified conditions. Or under some circumstances the beneficiaries may be able to terminate the trust earlier than directed by the trust terms.

Generally a settlor who is not the sole beneficiary has no power to terminate a trust unless that power has been specifically reserved. In other words, trusts are generally presumed to be irrevocable, although in a few states by statute trusts are presumed revocable unless otherwise stated. Nor can the trust beneficiaries usually terminate the trust earlier than the terms direct. (See *Claflin Doctrine*.) The settlor and the beneficiaries together can agree to terminate the trust at any time; this often is impossible, however, because at least some of the beneficiaries are still unborn, unascertained, incompetent, or just plain unwilling.

Claflin Doctrine

A rule prohibiting termination of a trust by the beneficiaries in advance of the time for termination under its terms if such termination would defeat a material purpose of the settlor.

Example 13.3: Camille has established a testamentary trust under which his wife, Julie, has a life estate and his son Lucien has a remainder. Claude, the trustee, is directed to use so much of the trust income as is necessary to support Julie and, upon Julie's death, to continue the trust and use the income as necessary to support Lucien until he reaches the age of 35, at which time he is to receive the principal and accumulated income in fee. Julie and Lucien both agree that they would prefer to terminate the trust immediately and divide the proceeds in a fair manner between them. As Camille is dead, he of course cannot agree to this change, so the two beneficiaries ask the court to order Claude, the trustee, to divide the trust property as they have agreed. The court, if it follows the Claflin doctrine, will not terminate the trust, because a material purpose of Camille — Claude's management of the principal and its preservation for the beneficiary's support until Lucien is 35 — would be defeated by such premature termination.

Such provisions as restriction to support or an age limitation, as well as a spendthrift clause, will almost always be considered a material purpose that would be defeated by termination.

England and some American states do not follow the Claflin doctrine. In these jurisdictions if all the beneficiaries agree, they can terminate without the consent of the settlor and regardless of the existence of an unfulfilled material purpose of the trust.

In some instances a dispute over the validity or construction of the trust may lead to litigation and a **compromise settlement** by the parties. Such a settlement often will require modification or termination of the trust, contrary to its terms and to the result that would be reached under rules such as the Claflin doctrine. In at least some jurisdictions, if the court is convinced that the dispute is bona fide and the settlement is fair to all concerned, it will accept the proposed change despite the usual rules against alteration or termination.

Although the duration of a trust is not directly limited by the Rule Against Perpetuities, generally a trust cannot remain indestructible (the settlor cannot prevent termination and the Claflin doctrine will not apply) beyond the perpetuities period.

Merger

The combining of the legal and equitable, or all the equitable, interests in a trust into one interest held by one person. The result generally is termination of the trust. Thus if the trustee acquires the interests of all beneficiaries and therefore holds full legal and equitable title, no purpose is served in continuing the trust: It no longer has divided ownership and no one can enforce it. The effect is the same as would follow at the outset of the trust if the sole beneficiary were also the sole trustee: The trust would then fail at its creation for want of a beneficiary to enforce it. (See *Trustee.*) If, however, a beneficiary remains who is not the trustee, a court may order the trust to continue. If the court considers a purpose of the settlor to be unfulfilled and capable of fulfillment despite the change in ownership, it will not declare a merger.

One way in which a trustee may acquire the beneficiary's interest is by **surrender** of that interest to the trustee. The trustee also may simply purchase the interest from the beneficiary or receive it by gift.

C. Termination of Trusts

Example 13.4: Camille establishes a trust for his wife, Julie, and son Lucien, with Claude as trustee. After Camille's death, Julie surrenders her life interest to Claude, and Lucien dies, bequeathing to Claude his remainder interest. As Claude now owns both the legal and equitable interests in the trust, the interests will merge and the trust will be terminated.

Example 13.5: In the trust described in Example 13.4, assume that Lucien dies and bequeaths his interest to Julie. Julie now owns both of the equitable interests, which can merge into one. If, however, the court is convinced that Camille would have desired the trust to continue, perhaps to give Julie the protection of the trustee's management during her lifetime, it will not terminate the trust. (See also *Claflin Doctrine.*)

14

Powers of Appointment

A. INTRODUCTION AND OVERVIEW OF CHAPTER

This chapter discusses the nature and function of powers of appointment, a common way to postpone decisions as to the ultimate disposition of trust assets. It begins with the definition and principal characters involved in the creation and exercise of a power, it distinguishes the various types (and subtypes) of power, and it concludes with several doctrines that apply to attempts, successful or not, to exercise a power.

B. DEFINITION AND ELEMENTS OF A POWER OF APPOINTMENT

In this section a power of appointment is defined and its general uses explained. The various persons who play a role in the creation or exercise of a power are described, together with the function of each in the process.

Power of Appointment

The right ("power") to select ("appoint"), within prescribed limits, who shall receive an interest in property or how various interests in the property shall be allocated. Its primary function is to permit a person to dispose of property while postponing or giving to another the authority to decide the precise manner of disposition. This makes the power of appointment an important estate planning device, especially when a trust contemplates successive enjoyment of the trust property by persons who are as yet unborn or whose status may change before enjoyment of the property passes to them.

Example 14.1:   George wishes to leave his house in the city of Zenith in trust for the benefit of his wife, Myra, for life, should she survive him, and at her death to the one or more of his three children (Ted, Katherine, and Verona) who then need(s) it most. The problem is that George does not know now (and he may not know even at the time of his death) which child or children will be most in need at the time of Myra's death, so he cannot now direct precisely the house's eventual disposition. Nor does he want to leave the property outright to Myra, as she might remarry and leave the house to her second husband. He does, however, feel comfortable in leaving to Myra the decision on the selection among their children, and in postponing that selection until her death. He thus executes a will that gives Myra "my house in Zenith for her lifetime, with the power to direct in her will how the house should be divided among our children after her death." (Technically, this is a special testamentary power of appointment.) In the event Myra neglects or declines to make such a selection, George directs that the property pass to his son Ted, who George believes is most likely to need it.

Let us break down the above example into its component parts. George, who created the power of appointment in his will, is considered the **donor** of the power; not surprisingly, Myra is called the **donee.** (This use of the terminology of gifts can be confusing; terms such as "creator" and "holder" would seem much more logical. In fact, an alternative term for donee, used by the Restatement of Property, is "powerholder.") Ted, Katherine, and Verona are the **objects of the power,** otherwise known as the **beneficiaries** or the **permissible appointees.** (Therefore anyone else is a "nonobject" of the power.) The house itself is referred to as the **appointive property** (or "appointive assets"). Ted, who takes the house if Myra fails to appoint, is the **taker in default** (of appointment). Finally, if Myra does appoint among the children in her will (if she **exercises** her power), those whom she designates to receive the property become the **appointees.** To these common usages the Restatement adds the terms "appointive interests," the sum of all the interests created by the power in the appointive assets (here a fee), and "owned interests," the beneficial interests a donee might have in the appointive property other than as an object of the power (here Myra's life estate).

Note that, as in the case of a trust, it is possible for a single person to occupy more than one role in this cast of characters. Thus Ted is both an object of the power and the taker in default; Myra could easily have been given a power exercisable during her lifetime and made one of the permissible appointees as well as the donee (which would have created in her a general power of appointment). And George, the donor, could have created the power during his lifetime, made himself both the donee and a permissible appointee, and then appointed to himself. Furthermore, more than one person can fill a single role: Myra and Ted could be made joint donees of the power, and all the children could be takers in default.

Myra's power is not, strictly speaking, a property interest; but it has some of the characteristics of one, and for certain purposes some powers of appointment (particularly general powers) may be treated as the donee's property. For other purposes, however, the donee is considered to be dealing with property owned by the donor. (See *Relation Back Doctrine.* The power also is personal to Myra: She cannot convey it or delegate its exercise to another.

Powers of appointment generally do not involve a fiduciary relationship between the donee and the objects of the power. This most clearly separates the power relationship from that of trustee and trust beneficiary. (However, a trustee of a discretionary trust may be considered to hold a power of appointment over the trust property, and of course the trustee is a fiduciary with respect to the trust assets.) Just as the term "power" implies, the donee

(Myra in our example) has the right and ability, but not the duty, to act in the objects' favor; she is not required to do so, and if she wishes she can decline to act at all. Nor does she have any ongoing fiduciary duties with respect to the appointive property, such as a trustee would have with respect to trust property. For these reasons a power need not be created with definite beneficiaries who can enforce its terms, a primary requirement of a valid private trust. In these and other ways, the power and the trust should be carefully distinguished.

Another relationship that sometimes is confused with a power of appointment is the "power of attorney." While both may, in certain circumstances, give the holder of the power the right to make decisions with respect to property owned by another, they actually serve very different functions. Unlike a power of appointment, a power of attorney creates an agency relationship that enables one person to act on behalf of another (the principal), either for some limited purpose, such as signing a particular contract, or more generally, perhaps because the principal is temporarily disabled. The power of attorney is conferred by the principal, and it ends with the principal's death or (except in the case of a so-called durable power of attorney) incompetency. This aspect alone prevents its serving one of the most important functions of a power of appointment, that of postponing exercise of the power until after the death of its creator.

Special rules apply to analysis of powers of appointment under the Rule Against Perpetuities. (See *Second-Look Doctrine*.)

C. TYPES OF POWERS OF APPOINTMENT

Powers of appointment can be classified in many ways, such as according to how they are created, who holds them, in whose favor they operate, or how they are to be exercised. Of course, these categories overlap such that any given power falls into several categories. This section describes those categories and explains some of the similarities and distinctions among them.

In the following chart, the various alternative types of powers are set out as opposing choices: Every power can be described as having one (and only one) of the two or three alternative characteristics in each horizontal line (either general or special, testamentary or inter vivos, and so on). (As with the Chinese restaurant menu, you choose one from row 1, one from row 2, and so forth.) All are discussed in detail in this section, except for the last, which is discussed in Section D.

General	Special (or Nongeneral)
Testamentary	Inter Vivos (Presently Exercisable)
Discretionary	Imperative (Mandatory, Power in Trust)

176

C. Types of Powers of Appointment

Collateral	Power Appendant	Power in Gross
Exclusive	Nonexclusive	

Note that these choices are largely "mix and match": A general power, for example, may be testamentary or inter vivos, and a discretionary power may be collateral, appendant, or in gross. However, the choices exclusive/nonexclusive are relevant only to special powers.

General Power of Appointment

A power of appointment that permits the donee to appoint to (that includes among its objects) the donee or the donee's creditors, estate, or estate's creditors. (This is also the definition used for federal tax purposes.)

Example 14.2:   George creates a power of appointment in his wife, Myra, under which she can appoint to "anyone she chooses." The power is general because Myra, the donee, can appoint to herself or her estate.

The alternative to a general power — one that cannot be exercised in favor of the donee's self, creditors, estate, or estate's creditors — is a special power of appointment.

It should be noted here that this is an area in which there is not complete agreement on the use of terms. Thus if Myra's power were restricted to persons related to the donor by blood or marriage, while by our definition this also is a general power (because it permits Myra to appoint to herself), some would call it a "particular" power because it limits the class of objects. A power restricted to persons designated in the creating instrument is also sometimes called a "limited power." Furthermore, some definitions of "general power" refer only to inclusion of the donee, or the donee and the donee's estate, without reference to the donee's or the estate's creditors (thus departing from the federal tax definition). Nevertheless, the definitions and usages given here are those most often encountered in the study of powers of appointment.

Because the donee of a general power — and especially one that permits a donee like Myra to appoint to herself — can become the outright owner of the appointive property merely by exercising the power in her own favor, such a donee may be considered the effective owner for purposes such as income taxation, creditors' rights, or the Rule Against Perpetuities. (See *Second-Look Doctrine.*)

Special Power of Appointment

A power of appointment limited to a group or class of permissible appointees that does not include the donee or the donee's creditors, estate, or estate's creditors.

Example 14.3:   George creates a power in his wife, Myra, to appoint their house in Zenith among one or more of their three children (and no one else). George has created a special power of appointment.

If George had permitted Myra to appoint to herself (or her creditors, etc.), the power would have been general.

As indicated elsewhere (see *General Power of Appointment*), there is not complete agreement on definitions in this area, and those given here are the most commonly encountered. One distinction is worth specially noting. Usually the class of objects is quite limited (for example, George and Myra's three children). In theory, however, the above definition would include a power given Myra to appoint to "anyone in the world except Myra, her creditors, her estate, or her estate's creditors." There is some disagreement whether the latter should be classified as a special power, since it is not general (excluding Myra, her creditors, and so on) but otherwise is nearly unlimited in scope. The Restatement of Property and the Uniform Probate Code simply classify all powers that are not general as **"nongeneral" powers**. (See, *e.g.*, UPC 2-901(c).) Others avoid the issue by leaving unclassified powers that are unlimited except as to the donee. (The first Restatement of Property had added still another term, "hybrid power," to describe those that were neither general nor special, but the second Restatement dropped both this term and the term "special power.")

For most purposes and the least confusion, it is safest to divide all powers between "general" and "special," based only on whether appointment is permitted to the donee's self, creditors, and so forth, but with a caveat as to the possible "grey area" between the two in the case of unlimited special powers.

Testamentary Power of Appointment

A power of appointment that is exercisable only through the will of the donee.

Example 14.4:   George creates in his wife, Myra, a power "to appoint in her will" their house in Zenith. He has created a testamentary power.

Note carefully that the fact that George creates the power in *his* will does not make it "testamentary" if Myra can exercise it during her lifetime, as the terminology refers only to the manner of exercise, not that of creation. (Admittedly this can be confusing, especially in light of the fact that a "testamentary trust" refers to a trust created by the settlor's will.)

A power that can be exercised during the donee's lifetime is called an **inter vivos power,** or a **presently exercisable power**. (Technically, a power may be made exercisable inter vivos but not "presently" — that is, exercise may be delayed but not until death; this is unusual, however, and it still might be called a "presently exercisable" power. An alternative term is "life-time power.")

Another common way to refer to powers is according to how, rather than when, they are exercisable: A power is exercisable "by deed," "by will," or "by deed or will"; the first and third of these are inter vivos powers, the second testamentary.

Example 14.5: George creates in his wife, Myra, a power to appoint their house in Zenith "by deed or will." Myra has an inter vivos power: Although she can exercise it by will, she also may exercise it during her lifetime. "By deed or will" is something of a term of art, frequently employed in this context. A power exercisable "during her lifetime," "at or before her death," or of similar effect would also create an inter vivos power.

Power in Trust

A special power of appointment that the donee has a duty to exercise. Also called an **imperative power** (as distinguished from a **discretionary power**), a power in trust assumes that the donor intended that the appointive property be distributed to the class of permissible appointees (objects) even if the donee failed to appoint.

A power in trust is not an actual trust, but it does have some trust characteristics. The principal importance of the designation is that if a donee of a power in trust (imperative power) fails to exercise it, the court will do so in the donee's stead by dividing the appointive property equally among the permissible appointees. (Division will be equal even if the power was exclusive and would have permitted the donee to select among the objects.) Because of the requirement that the court be able to divide the property among the objects, a power in trust — like a trust and unlike other powers — must have ascertainable beneficiaries. Note that, unlike with a real trust, the court will not compel the "trustee" (donee) to act, but it must itself act upon the donee's failure.

It is not easy to determine when a power in trust has been created, the question being one of a donor's intent that is seldom expressed. Probably the most common test is whether the donor named any takers in default: If not, it may be assumed that the donor intended that in all events the donee (and, if necessary, the court) appoint to the objects, as no one else was intended to take the property. There is, however, an alternative theory for distributing the property among the objects when no taker in default is named: The power is still discretionary, but if it is not exercised there is an **implied gift in default** to the objects. The latter theory has the advantage of reaching the same result while avoiding the somewhat confusing concept of a trust/power hybrid.

Collateral Power of Appointment

A power of appointment held by a donee who has no other interest in the appointive property.

Example 14.6:   George leaves his house to his wife, Myra, but he gives his son Ted a power to appoint to anyone upon Myra's death. Ted, having no property interest in the house, is the donee of a collateral power of appointment.

A common instance of a collateral power is one held by a trustee of a discretionary trust. As the trustee has no (equitable) interest in the trust property, the power to allocate the trust property among the beneficiaries is, in effect, a (special) collateral power of appointment.

Power Appendant

A power of appointment held by a donee who also has an ownership interest in the appointive property that is affected by exercise of the power.

Example 14.7:   George conveys his house in Zenith to his wife, Myra, in fee simple and also gives her a power to appoint the property in fee simple among their children. Myra has a power to appoint property that she also owns outright and thus has an "appendant" power (traditionally and somewhat archaically called a "power appendant").

The problem with a power appendant is that it is redundant. If Myra has a fee simple, she can convey to whomever she pleases, without — and despite the limitations of — the purported "power." In technical terms, the power and the fee "merge" and the power disappears. (If Myra was given only a life estate, the power still would be redundant to that extent.) For these reasons, and because the historical (basically feudal) justification for it has now disappeared, American jurisdictions do not recognize the power appendant; any attempt to create one is void. (English law, however, does recognize such a power.) Thus in the above example, Myra has a fee simple, and the power appendant is void.

Power in Gross

A power of appointment held by a donee who has some other interest in the appointive property that is not affected by the power. (This is in contrast with the power appendant, which does affect the donee's interest.)

Example 14.8:   George conveys to his wife, Myra, a life estate in his house, with a power to appoint it in fee in her will (a testamentary power). Myra has a power in gross. She owns a life estate, but her power relates only to the remainder in which she has no interest. Although she can appoint a greater interest than her own (a fee), because her life estate would end before (or, more accurately, at the same time as) she could exercise the power, it would not be affected by that exercise.

Subpower

A power of appointment created by the donee of another power of appointment in the exercise of the latter power.

Example 14.9:   George creates in his wife, Myra, a power to appoint his house to anyone she chooses, and Myra exercises the power by appointing a life estate to her daughter Katherine and giving Katherine a power to appoint the property in fee simple at her (Katherine's) death. Myra has created a subpower in Katherine.

The donee of a general power may appoint by creating subpowers, and the donee of a special power may create in an object of the power a general subpower or even a special subpower whose objects are also objects of the original power. However, creation of a special subpower whose objects are not also objects of the original power would be void as an improper indirect appointment to a nonobject. Thus in Example 14.9 Myra could appoint the house as indicated; if, however, she had been given a special power to appoint only among her children, and she attempted to appoint to her son Ted a life estate and the power at his death to appoint further among his (Ted's) children, who are not objects of the original power, Ted's subpower would be void.

D.   DOCTRINES RELATING TO EXERCISE OF A POWER OF APPOINTMENT

All or most of the concepts discussed above, with respect to the elements and types of powers of appointment, are concerned as well with the matter of exercise of a power. For example, the type of power and the nature of the objects of the power will control such matters as who can be an appointee and what can be appointed. This section concerns a few special doctrines that are addressed to the nature or particular aspects of the process of exercise, including those that might apply when an attempted exercise fails.

Exclusive Power of Appointment

A special power of appointment that permits the donee to appoint to one or more of the objects of the power, and not necessarily to all of them.

Example 14.10: George gives to his wife, Myra, the power to appoint among "one or more of our children." Myra has an exclusive power: She may "exclude" one or more of the children from appointment.

A **nonexclusive power**, in contrast, does not permit exclusion of any of the objects, as where the donee may appoint "among all of our children, each to receive a share but the amount to be determined by [the donee]." Often, however, a power to appoint in terms such as "among our children" is unclear as to whether it is meant to be exclusive or nonexclusive. Many courts will presume the power is exclusive in the absence of a contrary indication, and a few states make all special powers exclusive by statute.

The existence of nonexclusive powers raises the possibility that the donee may make only a token appointment to one or more of the objects, keeping within the letter of the power's terms but violating its intent. Some courts will consider such an **illusory appointment** to be the equivalent of no appointment at all and void; others deem any amount to be a valid appointment.

A few terms, seldom used, further describe the choices of a donee. A "distributive" power permits appointment among all the objects. (Thus an exclusive power may be distributive or nondistributive.) And property subject to a "mixed" power can be distributed to one or more objects, but the shares of each appointee must be equal.

Relation Back Doctrine

The theory that the exercise of a power of appointment is an extension of the transaction that created the power ("relates back" to the creation of the power) so that the appointee takes title from the donor and not the donee. This concept of the donee as an agent merely completing a transaction affecting the donor's property most clearly distinguishes a power of appointment from actual ownership of the appointive property.

Example 14.11: George's will leaves "my house in Zenith to my wife, Myra, for life, with a power to appoint the remainder among our children." If Myra appoints to their daughter Verona, technically Verona takes title from George, not from Myra. It is as if George's will had read: "my house in Zenith to my wife, Myra, for life, with the remainder to our daughter Verona." (In fact, sometimes it is said that the donee is merely "filling in the blanks" in the donor's creating instrument.)

While the relation back doctrine is a useful and generally accurate description of the operation and underlying theory of a power of appointment, it is not a strict rule that explains every circumstance relating to powers. Courts have declined to follow the doctrine when they have considered the result of its application unjust or otherwise unacceptable. Thus in applying the Rule Against Perpetuities to the validity or exercise of a power, the relation back doctrine is recognized with respect to special and general testamentary powers; but with respect to general inter vivos powers, which in many ways are the equivalent of ownership by the donee, the property is treated as if it were the donee's, and the period of the Rule runs from the date of exercise, not the date of creation, of the power. (See also *Second-Look Doctrine*.) Other areas in which the relation back doctrine might not apply (especially to general powers) include computation of estate taxes or succession duties and availability of the appointive property to creditors of the donee.

Fraud on a Power

An appointment by the donee of a special power of appointment to an object of the power, with the intention to benefit a nonobject. The result is a void (or, in some jurisdictions, voidable) appointment. This is to be distinguished from an outright appointment to a nonobject, which is void on its face. Usually an appointment to an object that is intended to benefit both that person and a nonobject is void as to both.

Fraud on a power does not require a showing of actual fraud so long as an intent is found to benefit a nonobject.

Example 14.12:   George creates a special power in his wife, Myra, to appoint the proceeds of his house in Zenith among their three children. Myra appoints to their son Ted on the understanding that Ted will give half of the proceeds back to Myra, who is not an object of the power. The appointment is in fraud of the power and void. A similar result ensues if Myra appoints to Ted in trust for Ted's children or even (as happened in one actual case) if she appoints to Ted because he was terminally ill and likely to die soon and she would be his heir.

Blending Clause

A clause in a will that purports to treat as one fund for disposition the property owned by the decedent and that over which the decedent holds a power of appointment. A typical blending clause in the will of the donee of a general power of appointment might state: "I give my estate, including all interests in property which I may own and any property over which I have a power of appointment, as follows: . . ." In other words, the decedent has "blended" owned and appointive property.

The concept of a blending clause is especially useful in applying the doctrines of capture and marshaling (discussed below), both of which assume that a decedent intended to treat appointive property as, or at least interchangeably with, owned property.

Capture

An implied appointment to the donee's estate in the event of the failure of an attempted exercise of a general power of appointment.

Example 14.13:   Myra, the donee of a general power, has included in her will a blending clause that treats as a single unit both owned and appointive property. If an attempted appointment fails (for example, because the appointee predeceases Myra), it will be assumed that Myra intended to "capture" the appointive property for her own estate in the event of such failure.

Note that if the property is not captured, it will pass either to the takers in default or, if there are none, to the donor or the donor's successors.

The capture doctrine also may be applied when the donee expressly appoints the property in trust and the trust fails. Even in the absence of a blending clause, many courts will consider the appointive property "captured," and the trustee will hold it on a resulting trust for the donee's estate.

Marshaling

The allocation of owned and appointive property among the dispositions by a donee of a power of appointment to give maximum effectiveness to the dispositive instrument. Also known as the doctrine of **allocation**, marshaling assumes that the donee's dispositions would have been valid had the beneficiary of owned property been given the appointive assets and the appointee been given instead the owned property.

A common example of marshaling concerns the Rule Against Perpetuities. Sometimes the exercise of a power of appointment in favor of certain beneficiaries violates the Rule, although it would be valid if in favor of other beneficiaries or if it were a gift of owned property. (This latter possibility has to do with the "relation back doctrine," under which the Rule's period is measured for appointive property from the date of creation of the power by the donor, whereas for owned property the period runs from the date it is given. See *Relation Back Doctrine*.) If the instrument contains a blending clause that treats owned and appointive property as one fund, it is possible to allocate owned property to the purported appointee and appointive property to another beneficiary to whom an appointment could be made without violating the Rule. The result is the same as the donee intended but by a somewhat different route. In other words, if a "switch" of owned and appointive dispositions among beneficiaries will better carry out the transferor's intent, and if a blending clause makes such a switch possible, a court applying the doctrine of marshaling will effect such a reallocation.

Example 14.14:   George gives to his wife, Myra, a life interest in a fund worth $100,000 and the power to appoint the remainder by will among her children (a special testamentary power of appointment). Myra's will contains a blending clause that treats her own property and that subject to the power as a single unit. It then leaves $100,000 to Myra's friend Zelda and the residue to Myra's children. Myra's estate consists of cash and jewelry that she owns worth $100,000 and the $100,000 fund over which she has the power to appoint. Under the blending clause, the owned and appointive assets usually would be allocated ratably between the two gifts, in this case 50 percent ($50,000) from each fund. Because Zelda is a non-object of the special power, however, none of the appointive assets can be allocated to her, and this would ordinarily result in a failure of half of the disposition to Zelda. The children, however, are objects of the power and could take all the appointive property with no difficulty, whereas there is no restriction on Zelda's taking property owned outright by Myra. This is where marshaling steps in: Because Myra has blended her own and appointive property, a court can treat the two sources of the total of $200,000 as interchangeable and simply allocate the owned $100,000 to Zelda and the appointive $100,000 to the children. The result is essentially the same as Myra intended, and the court has prevented a partial failure of her plan.

Example 14.15:   George dies survived by his wife, Myra, and their daughter Katherine. His will creates a general testamentary power of appointment in Myra. Myra remarries and has another child, Ted. At her death, Myra leaves $10,000 in trust "to my son Ted for life, remainder to his children." She gives the residue to Katherine. Her owned property is worth $5,000, the appointive property $10,000. Myra's will also contains a blending clause stating that she is bequeathing "her own property and any over which she has a power of appointment."

Because of the relation back doctrine, the perpetuities period for an appointment to Ted's children begins at the date the power was created. Ted was not, of course, alive at the time of George's death, when the power was created; thus an appointment to Ted's children is invalid. However, had Myra used her own property to create Ted's life estate and his children's remainder, the gift would have been perfectly valid; and had she directed the appointive property outright to Katherine, that gift too would have been valid. Presumably Myra was concerned with the result itself, not with what property would be used to achieve it. Applying the doctrine of marshaling, a court can allocate the gifts so that Ted and his children receive Myra's own property and Katherine receives the appointive property. Unfortunately, only $5,000 is available to allocate to Ted's children, so the gift can be only partially saved. Nevertheless, to the extent possible, Myra's intention has been carried out.

15

The Rule Against Perpetuities

A. INTRODUCTION AND OVERVIEW OF CHAPTER

In this chapter the principal aspects of the Rule Against Perpetuities are discussed. After a general overview of the nature of the doctrine and several examples illustrating its operation, the elements of the Rule are defined and interrelated. The next section treats doctrines that apply to specific circumstances and that are especially likely to create unexpected difficulty, such as the "unborn widow" and the "fertile octogenarian." The final section covers the means by which a drafter can avoid inadvertent violations of the Rule and by which various jurisdictions have "reformed" the Rule to make such violations less likely or to mitigate them should they occur.

Explanation of illustrations: Several examples in this chapter are accompanied by time lines (set out as "Figure 1," "Figure 2," and so on) to help you keep the sometimes complex series of events in order. Note that each illustration has one long horizontal line representing the passage of time and shorter horizontal lines representing the lives of each of the persons in the example. On the time line are indicated significant events such as births, deaths, and marriages. In addition, the starting of the perpetuities period and the vesting of the interest in question are indicated by broken vertical lines labeled "P" and "V," respectively. This allows you to see the critical points in the perpetuities analysis as they relate to the lives and events in the problem. Finally, if there is a life that can be used as a validating life (life in being), it is set out in bold type. As will become clear, *only a life line that extends at least from one vertical line (P) to the other (V), or to within 21 years of the second line, can qualify as a validating life.* The time lines are not drawn to scale.

B. GENERAL DISCUSSION AND EXAMPLES OF OPERATION

This section defines the Rule Against Perpetuities and offers several examples of its operation. More detailed discussion of the various concepts contained within the language of the Rule is left for the following section.

Rule Against Perpetuities

A rule of law that prohibits the creation of future interests that possibly may vest beyond the period of those lives in being at the date of its creation plus 21 years. Put another way, the classic statement of the Rule (as formulated by John Chipman Gray in 1886) declares that to be valid, an interest "must vest, if at all, not later than twenty-one years after some life in being at the creation of the interest." (This span of time is known as the perpetuities period.) While nearly all the words and phrases in the above definition merit detailed analysis, our purpose here is only to clarify the general meaning of the Rule and its application. (Note the capitalization of "Rule": while this is not a universal practice, it is common and reflects the Rule's status as more than just another legal doctrine. It is *the* Rule, more feared, criticized, misunderstood, and, ironically, ruthlessly applied, than any other in the law of property.)

The Rule Against Perpetuities is actually misnamed in that it really limits only the time between the creation of a future interest and its vesting (that is, becoming a fixed right subject to no contingencies); it does not, at least directly, limit the duration of a trust or of an interest in property, although that often will be its indirect effect. Thus it has been suggested that a better name would be the "Rule Against Remoteness of Vesting." However, it is far too late in the game to make any such change; courts will continue to apply the Rule as a means to prevent creation of a **perpetuity**, a perpetual interest, even if it may in fact do no such thing.

A few simple illustrations will demonstrate how the Rule works in a typical, straightforward case, even if they belie the inordinate complexity of many of its applications. Note that the Rule applies to both legal and equitable interests and to those created either inter vivos or by will. (The following examples and discussion assume application of the traditional, common-law Rule without any of the mitigating "reforms" that many jurisdictions have adopted. Because most such reforms operate only to save or adjust interests that violate the common-law Rule, however, its operation is still relevant to modern transactions.)

Example 15.1:   Henry's will leaves his manor house at Whitehall in trust "to Catherine for her life, remainder to Catherine's first child Mary." Catherine and Mary are alive at Henry's death. Henry's will does not violate the Rule. Catherine's life estate is vested in that it is given to a living and ascertained person, is subject to no contingency, and takes effect immediately on its creation, which in this case occurs when Henry dies and his will becomes effective. Mary's remainder interest also is vested, created in an existing person, subject to no contingency, and taking effect immediately on the expiration of Catherine's life estate (which is not considered a "contingency" for these purposes).

It often is helpful to draw a time line that sets out the relationship of the important events in applying the Rule. The time line for this example (Fig. 1) on page 190 is quite simple. (See the Chapter Introduction for an explanation of how to interpret the time line.)

Note that the perpetuities period (P) and the vesting of the interests (V) occur at the same time, making everyone a "life in being."

Example 15.2:   Suppose the remainder in Example 15.1 was to "Catherine's first child," Catherine having as yet no children at Henry's death. The child's interest will vest in the child as soon as it is born;

Figure 1

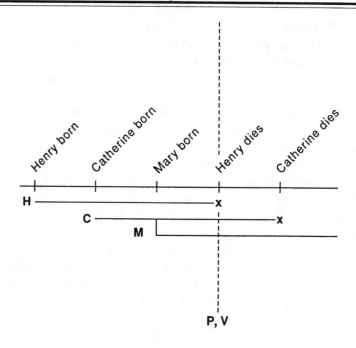

but an interest cannot vest in an unborn person, so until the first child is born, its interest is not vested. We then must ask whether it might "possibly vest beyond the period of a life or lives in being plus 21 years." Since Catherine does not have a child at the time of Henry's death and may not have one even within 21 years of his death, Henry cannot be the life that validates the child's interest: The child may "possibly" be born and its interest vest "beyond [Henry's] life in being plus 21 years." Because, however, Catherine herself was alive at the time of the remainder's creation (at Henry's death), and because by necessity her first child will be born within her own lifetime (ipso facto within 21 years of her death), Catherine can be the "life in being" (plus 21 years) beyond which the child's interest cannot possibly vest. See Fig. 2 on page 191.

In Fig. 2 Catherine's lifetime is shown in bold because it extends from (and before) the beginning of the perpetuities period (P) to (and beyond) the date of vesting and so is a validating life.

Example 15.3:   Now let us assume the gift is to "Catherine's first child if and when that child reaches 25 years of age," Catherine still having as yet no children. While it still is true that any child of Catherine, though born after Henry's death, will be born within her (Cath-

Figure 2

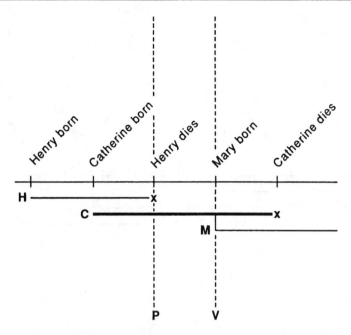

erine's) lifetime, the gift will not vest in that child unless and until it reaches 25 years of age; an age contingency must be satisfied before the child may take the interest. It is *possible* that Catherine will have her first child after Henry's death and then die (along with everyone else who was alive at Henry's death) before her child is 4 years old, or more than 21 years before the child reaches the age of 25. Therefore it is *possible* that the child's gift will not vest, if it vests at all, until more than 21 years after the death of Catherine, the only available "life in being." Thus the child's interest is void. See Fig. 3 on page 192.

Note that in Fig. 3 Catherine's life line begins before "P" but ends more than 21 years before "V," whereas Mary's life line runs beyond "V" but begins after "P." Thus neither can be a validating life.

Example 15.4: Finally, assume that the gift is to "Catherine if and when lightning strikes the big tree in her garden," an event that possibly could happen tomorrow or in 200 years or never. Here Catherine could be the life in being if the interest is contingent on lightning striking the tree *within Catherine's lifetime.* However, the usual interpretation of this type of contingent interest is that it is "transmissible" to future generations, not contingent on Catherine's survival until the event occurs. (See *Life in Being.*) In light of this interpretation, Catherine might pass the interest down to her

Figure 3

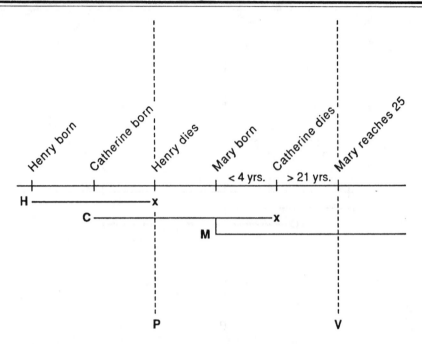

first child, who might in turn do the same, and so forth. If lightning finally struck the tree more than 21 years after Catherine's death, thus vesting the interest in its then-current holder, the Rule would be violated; therefore the interest is void. See Fig. 4 on page 193.

The examples above illustrate several important things about the Rule Against Perpetuities:

(1) The taker of the interest in question need not actually obtain possession (or, as it is commonly phrased, "possession and enjoyment") of the property within the perpetuities period, or ever, so long as the unconditional (noncontingent) right to do so is established within the perpetuities period. If in Example 15.1 Henry had given Catherine a life estate and Mary a vested remainder *for life*, and Mary died before Catherine, Mary would never possess Whitehall, although she had a vested interest in it. In the language of the Rule, the interest must vest in interest, but it need not vest in possession. (See *Vest*.)

(2) The interest need not *ever* vest, in interest or otherwise, in the taker. The only question asked is whether, *if it ever does vest*, it will do so within the perpetuities period. If in Examples 15.2 and 15.3 Catherine never has children, the interest in potential little Mary will fail for want of a person in whom to vest; but *if Catherine did have a child and the interest did vest*, it would *necessarily* do so in Example 15.3.

Figure 4

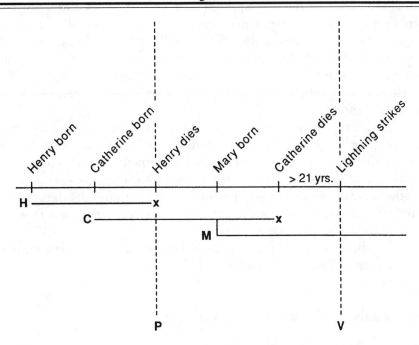

(3) The Rule is not limited to what *will* happen, what is *likely* to happen, or even what will *quite possibly* happen, but is interested as well in what *by some far-fetched stretch of the imagination might conceivably* happen. Even the most remote contingency that would place vesting beyond the perpetuities period will invalidate the interest. In Example 15.3 above, it is quite possible that Catherine will die during the first four years of her child's life. But even if the event on which the interest of the child depends were so remote as to be practically impossible, so long as it is theoretically possible it will invalidate the interest. Thus if the gift of the remainder were to "Catherine upon there falling any rain in the city of Seattle," the *only* contingency on which it could vest beyond the Rule being a lack of rain in Seattle for more than 21 years, the interest still would fail. (For other remote-but-fatal contingencies, see the *Fertile Octogenarian* and *Unborn Widow* rules, discussed separately.)

(4) While anyone (and everyone) in the world theoretically can be the measuring life who validates a gift under the Rule, it is useful only to consider persons whose lives have some connection with the vesting of the interest in question. In Example 15.2, for instance, Catherine's first child will necessarily be born within Catherine's lifetime. It is true that the child also *probably* will be born within the lifetimes (or 21 years of the lifetimes) of a good many other persons alive at Henry's death — probably many millions of others worldwide. But apart from the practical difficulty of ascertaining that this is true for all such persons, it is irrelevant: *In theory*, everyone in

193

the world who was alive at Henry's death could die before Catherine's first child is born; everyone, that is, *except Catherine*. Therefore Catherine is the only person whose existence makes it certain that the child's interest will vest "in time." If, however, the gift were to "Catherine's first child 20 years after the death of the last surviving person of *A, B, C,* and *D*" (four names taken at random from the local telephone directory), these four would become relevant to the vesting of the interest and so would become the validating lives.

(5) Finally, if the interest in question possibly may vest too late and so possibly may violate the Rule, the interest is void ab initio, that is, from the outset. Only if a jurisdiction has adopted a reform measure that allows us to "wait and see" whether the interest in fact vests too late (whether in fact Catherine dies before Mary is 4 years old, or lightning hits the tree more than 21 years after Catherine's death) do we permit the interest to survive its potential to violate the Rule.

For the operation of the Rule in the context of powers of appointment, see *Perpetuities Period* and *Relation Back Doctrine*.

C.   PRINCIPAL ELEMENTS AND CONCEPTS

One of the most difficult aspects of the Rule Against Perpetuities is its use of somewhat arcane concepts and terminology. This section defines and discusses in detail some of those concepts that are contained within, and are crucial to, the application of the Rule.

Perpetuities Period

The period of time, commencing with the creation of an interest in property, during which the interest must be certain to vest or fail in order to satisfy the Rule Against Perpetuities. (The perpetuities period also is used to measure such related matters as the time during which trust income may be accumulated or a trust can remain indestructible.)

The common-law perpetuities period was, and is, "lives in being plus 21 years" (plus the gestation period for a person conceived but not yet born). The 21 years must follow, not precede, the "lives in being." Some modern reform statutes have changed the period, such as to 90 years in gross. (See *Wait-and-See* doctrine.) The primary difficulty lies not in the theoretical length of the period but in determining when the period begins and when it ends. The period generally begins at — and so the possibility of vesting beyond the period is viewed from — the date of creation of an interest, which is when the creating instrument takes effect (for a will, when the testator dies; for a deed, upon its delivery; and so on). If, however, there is a power to terminate the interest and vest it in one person absolutely, the perpetuities period runs from the time that such power ends. Thus if the interest is created by a revocable trust, the period begins when the power to revoke ceases (which probably will be at the trustor's death).

Special mention should be made of the perpetuities period as it relates to powers of appointment. Two issues arise in this context: whether a power is valid, and whether its exercise is valid, under the Rule. Concerning both issues, the rule for general inter vivos powers differs from that for special and testamentary powers. The issue of exercise of a power is discussed under the *Second-Look Doctrine*; suffice it to say here that for general inter vivos powers the period begins at the time of *exercise* of the power and for special and testamentary powers it begins at the date of *creation* of the power.

As for the validity *ab initio* of the power itself, the test is fairly simple: General inter vivos powers are valid if they become exercisable — if they *can*, for certain, be exercised within the perpetuities period (even if they could also be exercised beyond the period); special and testamentary powers are valid only if they not only can but absolutely *must* be exercised, if at all, within the period (that is, if they *cannot* be exercised beyond it).

Example 15.5:   Henry leaves Whitehall to Anne for life, "remainder as Anne's then-oldest child appoints by deed or will, at any time after Anne's death" (a general inter vivos power). The power is valid; although it could conceivably be exercised beyond the perpetuities period (the then-oldest child could be one born after Henry's death and could exercise the power more than 21 years after Henry and Anne die), it also can be exercised within the period, just after the death of Anne, a life in being. If, however, the power had been limited to appointment by will (a general testamentary power) or to appointment to Anne's descendants (a special power), the possibility of exercise beyond the perpetuities period would have rendered the power invalid.

Contrast the above with Example 15.6:

Example 15.6:   Henry leaves Whitehall to Anne for life, "remainder as Anne's first child to graduate from college appoints by deed or will" (a general inter vivos power). Anne is alive at Henry's death. Unless at Henry's death Anne has a child who already has graduated from college, the first child to do so might be an afterborn child who does not graduate until more than 21 years after the death of Anne and all others alive at Henry's death. Since it is not certain that the power will become exercisable (that the donee will be known) within the perpetuities period, the power is void at its inception as violating the Rule Against Perpetuities. Of course, it would be invalid as well if it were a general testamentary or special power: If it is not certain even

195

to become exercisable within the perpetuities period, it can hardly be certain to be exercised within that period.

Life in Being

A person who was alive at the time of the creation of a contingent future interest and within whose lifetime or within 21 years of whose death that interest must either vest or fail. A "life (or lives) in being plus 21 years" (plus any period of gestation) measures the perpetuities period under the Rule Against Perpetuities. Thus traditionally the life in being is called the **measuring life**. The term does not refer to just anyone who was alive at the time of the interest's creation; rather it refers only to one whose life can be used to demonstrate that the interest will not violate the Rule. For this reason, the term **validating life** has also come into use to express more precisely the fact that the life in question is that by which the interest is validated.

Example 15.7: Henry has created a trust by will that gives a life interest to Anne and a remainder to Anne's first child, she being childless at Henry's death. Anne is the "life in being" (measuring life, validating life) who validates the remainder interest and within whose lifetime (plus 21 years, were it required) the remainder must vest, if it is to vest at all. Either Anne will have a child during her lifetime, or she will not: If she does, the remainder vests in the child at that time; if she does not, it fails.

The life in being need not be someone who takes an interest or who even is mentioned in the gift. If in Example 15.7 Henry's bequest were to Anne for life, remainder to Henry's first-born nephew, Henry then having none, the measuring lives would be those of Henry's sisters and brothers, within whose lifetimes any nephew must be born. (They could, however, serve as lives in being — could validate the gift — only if Henry's parents were not still alive at Henry's death; otherwise Henry could have more brothers and sisters, born too late to be measuring lives.)

Using Figs. 5 and 6 you can see that only in the first time line is there a person (Henry's sister) whose life line extends from the beginning of the perpetuities period (Henry's death) to the vesting of the first nephew's interest (the nephew's birth). (Note that in this context, it is not a problem that Anne, the life tenant, has died before the remainderman (Henry's nephew) was determined.)

One common but often confusing situation is illustrated in Example 15.8.

Example 15.8: Henry makes a testamentary gift "to Anne, but if it ever rains in Seattle, to Elizabeth." Both Anne and Elizabeth are alive at

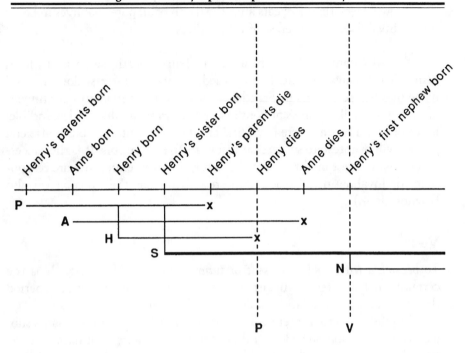

Figure 5. Henry's parents predecease Henry:

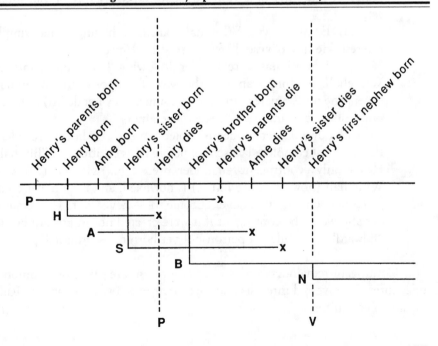

Figure 6. Henry's parents survive Henry:

Henry's death. The remote possibility that it will not rain in Seattle until more than 21 years after the death of all potential lives in being invalidates the interest of Elizabeth.

But why cannot Elizabeth, alive at Henry's death, serve as a life in being? It is because, as usually construed, Elizabeth's interest does not end if she dies before it rains in Seattle. In other words, Elizabeth's contingent future interest (like Anne's present interest) is **transmissible**, or descendible: it not only can be transferred by Elizabeth during her lifetime but it also can pass by will or intestate succession to Elizabeth's successors. It is the successors whose interest might vest too remotely and, therefore, who are responsible for invalidating Elizabeth's interest as well as their own. (See also Example 15.4.)

Vest

To become a fixed right of present or future enjoyment of property. It is the certainty that an interest will either vest or fail within the perpetuities period that prevents its invalidation under the Rule Against Perpetuities.

In effect, a vested interest is one that is not contingent — that is subject to no condition precedent (other than the necessary termination of any preceding estate) — and that is created in an ascertained (or immediately ascertainable) person.

Example 15.9: Edward has an interest in Whitehall, the family estate. Whether that interest is vested depends on the nature of that interest:

(a) Edward owns Whitehall outright, having a fee simple interest. He has a "vested" fee interest in Whitehall.

(b) Edward has a remainder following Jane's life estate in Whitehall. Nothing stands in the way of his possessing Whitehall except the necessary termination (presumably by her death) of Jane's prior estate. Edward has a "vested" remainder.

(c) Edward's remainder is subject to the condition precedent that he must complete law school before he is entitled to Whitehall. He has only a contingent remainder interest; his right ever to possess Whitehall (now or in the future) is not fixed, and if he never completes law school it will never become so — never vest. The remainder also would be contingent if it were created not in Edward but in "Edward's first child," a person not yet born or ascertained.

Contingent remainders and executory interests are the most commonly encountered nonvested interests and those that most often violate the Rule Against Perpetuities.

Whitehall is **vested in interest** if Edward has a present right to future enjoyment (use) of it (*e.g.*, Edward's remainder following Jane's life estate, Example 15.9(b)). It is also **vested in possession** if he has a present right to *present* enjoyment of it (Edward's fee simple, Example 15.9(a)). To be valid under the Rule Against Perpetuities, an interest need only vest in interest (or fail), not vest in possession, within the perpetuities period.

As indicated elsewhere (see *Vested and Contingent Interests*), an interest is vested subject to divestment (or "defeasible") if it is subject to no condition precedent, but there is a condition subsequent under which it may be taken away.

Example 15.10:   Edward has a (vested) fee interest in Whitehall, "but if Edward should ever be disbarred, Whitehall shall pass to Jane." Edward's interest is vested subject to being divested upon future disbarment.

If there is no condition subsequent, the interest is indefeasibly vested. An interest that is defeasibly vested still satisfies the Rule Against Perpetuities. If, however, an interest is vested subject to open (a class gift still open to admit further members), it is not "vested" for purposes of the Rule.

Over the years many rules have arisen that govern whether an interest should be considered vested or contingent, from the very general ("a interest is presumed vested") to the very particular (*e.g.*, the Rules in Clobberie's Case). Usually if an interest is "vested" under any of these rules, it is considered vested for Perpetuities purposes, regardless of whether the policies behind the former are consistent with those behind the latter.

D.   DOCTRINES RELATING TO SPECIFIC CIRCUMSTANCES

Even when one has mastered the general principles of the Rule Against Perpetuities and its difficult terminology, other doctrines applicable to certain circumstances must be learned. They are not necessarily "exceptions" to the Rule, as they do follow from its premises; however, they often defy logical or scientific probability, seem to have no basis in policy, and so can easily lead to inadvertent violations of the Rule. This section discusses several of these doctrines.

Unborn Widow

The name given to those cases in which the Rule Against Perpetuities invalidates an interest because of the remote possibility that one's spouse at the time of one's death might turn out to be someone who was not alive when the interest was created and who thus cannot be a life in being. This is easier to illustrate than to explain:

Example 15.11:   Henry's will leaves Whitehall "to my son Edward for life, remainder to my son's widow for life, remainder to Edward's surviving children." At Henry's death, which begins the running of the perpetuities period, Edward is 50 years old and married (for the past 30 years) to Margaret, who is 49; they have several children. The remainder to the surviving children violates the Rule Against Perpetuities.

In the above example, the surviving children's interests will vest when Edward's widow dies and it is determined who survives her. All that is required, therefore, to validate a child's remainder is that Edward's widow be a person who was alive at the time of Henry's death. Unfortunately, however, "widow" is traditionally construed to mean the person who is Edward's wife at the time of his death, regardless of whether she is his wife at present. It is considered possible (and indeed it is quite possible, in theory) that Edward will divorce Margaret or outlive her; that he will marry another woman (say, Jane) who was not alive at the time of Henry's death; that after Henry's death Edward will have at least one more child, Anne (despite his age: see *Fertile Octogenarian*); that he will still be married to his second wife, Jane, at the time of his death and she therefore will become his widow; that she will live at least another 21 years after Edward's death (and the death of his other children and all others who were alive at Henry's death); that therefore the remainder will not vest (the survivors will not be ascertained) until more than 21 years after the death of all potential lives in being; and the remainder thus violates the Rule Against Perpetuities. (Note that the widow's interest itself is valid. Her identity will be known, and her interest will vest, at the death of Edward, a life in being.) See Fig. 7. (The Chapter Introduction explains how to interpret the time line.)

This result is not, of course, mitigated by the fact that Jane would have to be more than 50 years younger than Edward at the time of their marriage: If Edward married Jane when he was 51 years old, Jane would have to be less than one year old at the time. Nor is it affected by the fact that the widow would also have to outlive by 21 years all of Edward's children who were alive at Henry's death, but be survived by one who was not. That is why the "unborn widow" is second only to the "fertile octogenarian" in illustrating to most observers both the strictness and the possible absurdity of the common-law Rule.

Some jurisdictions have specifically addressed the matter. They may deem a person described as the spouse of a person in being to be also a life in being for purposes of the Rule, or they simply may construe the term "widow" to mean the person's spouse at the time of creation of the interest.

Figure 7

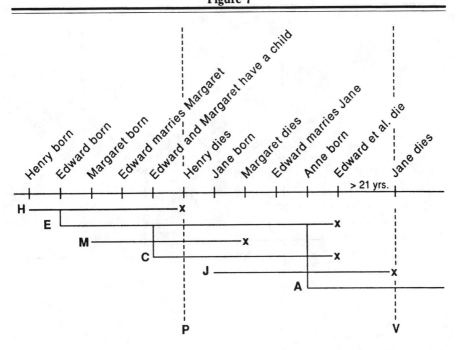

Fertile Octogenarian

A somewhat irreverent designation for the rule that, for purposes of the Rule Against Perpetuities, a person is conclusively presumed to be capable of bearing children until death and regardless of age. It is best exemplified by the famous English case of *Jee v. Audley* (1787), in which a gift was struck down because, inter alia, it was deemed possible that Mr. and Mrs. Jee, although 70 years old, might still have another child. (The expression applies even though Mrs. Jee was a mere septuagenarian.) Physiological "bright lines" being difficult to draw, none was drawn at all. (Note that the possibility of adoption had no bearing on this rule because adoption was unknown to early English law. Its presence in modern law, however, does add some logical force to the idea of "perpetual fertility.")

In simplest form, the fertile octogenarian rule operates as follows:

Example 15.12:   Henry leaves Whitehall to Anne for life, remainder in fee to the first child of Anne who graduates from college. At Henry's death, Anne is a 94-year-old widow and has one child, Mary, who is in college. The remainder violates the Rule Against Perpetuities.

Because Mary in Example 15.12 is alive at Henry's death, and because the contingent remainder necessarily will vest or fail before or upon the

Figure 8

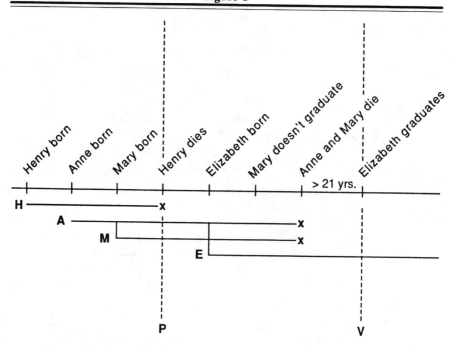

death of Anne's last surviving child, the only theoretical way in which that remainder could violate the Rule Against Perpetuities would be for Anne to have another child. Events would have to proceed somewhat as follows: After Henry's death, Anne has another child, Elizabeth, who would not be a life in being; Mary fails college and becomes a plumber instead; Anne and Mary both die; and, finally, Elizabeth enrolls in college and, more than 21 years after the death of everyone alive at Henry's death, Elizabeth graduates and takes the remainder. Of course this is just what the law would presume, despite the fact that history records no woman of Anne's age — no "fertile nonagenarian" — ever bearing a child (at least since Biblical times). See Fig. 8. (The Chapter Introduction explains how to interpret the time line.)

As in the case of the "unborn widow," some modern legislation has specifically abolished the fertile octogenarian rule by either eliminating the presumption altogether, changing it to a presumption of infertility after a given age such as 55, or permitting introduction of evidence of inability to bear children. Some statutes also deem the possibility of adoption irrelevant for perpetuities purposes.

Infectious Invalidity

A doctrine allowing a court to declare invalid not only the part of a disposition that violates the Rule Against Perpetuities but also other provisions that do not violate the Rule when invalidation of the former alone would gravely distort the transferor's overall plan.

Ordinarily, if an interest violates the Rule, it is stricken from the disposition and any remaining interests that do not violate the Rule are left to stand. Thus if a remainder following a life estate is stricken, the life estate stands and the interest reverts to the transferor (or the transferor's successors) following the life estate. Under the infectious invalidity doctrine, however, the life estate as well could be deemed invalid.

Example 15.13:   Henry, a widower, leaves half of his estate to his son Edward for life, remainder to Edward's issue, and half to his daughter Mary for life, remainder to her issue. Because of some condition attached to the gift to Edward's issue (but not to the gift to Mary's), it violates the Rule and is stricken. Under intestacy laws, the invalid interest (remainder in half the estate) would be divided equally between Edward and Mary. This would result in Mary's side of the family receiving a total of three-quarters of the estate (less Edward's life estate in a quarter) and Edward's side only one quarter (plus the life estate). If this result is deemed contrary to Henry's probable intention, the court might declare the entire gift invalid, thus passing the entire estate to Edward and Mary equally through intestacy. The gift of Mary's part of the estate has become "invalid" through the "infectious" effect of the part that violated the Rule.

All-or-Nothing Rule

The requirement that an interest transferred to a class vest or fail within the perpetuities period with respect to all members of the class in order to avoid violation of the Rule Against Perpetuities. Even if the interest has already vested in all present class members, if it is vested subject to open, so that others still might enter the class, it is not vested in any member for purposes of the Rule. Thus the requirement for validity of a class gift is that (1) the class must close, and (2) all conditions precedent to vesting for all members of the class must be satisfied, if they are to be satisfied at all, within the perpetuities period.

Example 15.14:   Henry leaves a fund of $50,000 in trust "to pay the income to Anne for life, then to Anne's children for their lives, and then on the death of the last surviving child to pay the principal to Anne's grandchildren." At Henry's death, Anne is alive and has one child, Elizabeth, and one grandchild, Charles. Because the interest of an afterborn grandchild could vest too remotely, the interests of all the grandchildren, including that of Charles, violate the Rule Against Perpetuities.

Figure 9

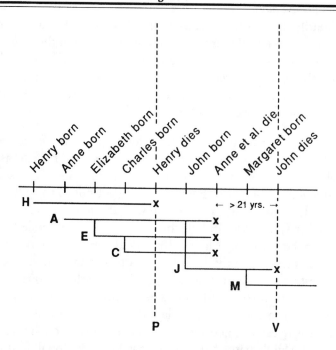

Both Elizabeth and Charles in Example 15.14 have interests that are vested, but vested subject to open, since both classes (children and grandchildren) are still open to admit future members. As for the children, their class will close and their interests vest indefeasibly within the perpetuities period — at the death of Anne, a life in being. Thus Elizabeth's interest is valid, as is that of any child born after Henry's death. But their children (Anne's grandchildren) might be born too remotely: Anne could have another child, John, after Henry's death. Anne, Elizabeth, and all other persons alive at Henry's death then could die, leaving John as Anne's "last surviving child." John then might have his own child, Margaret, whose interest would vest, but still subject to open. John could die more than 21 years after all those living at Henry's death, beyond the perpetuities period. Only then, upon the death of John, who is not a life in being, would the class of grandchildren close and their interests (including that of Margaret, who also is not a life in being) vest indefeasibly. Because the interest of at least one class member, Margaret (in fact, of all potential children of subsequently born children of Anne) is invalid, under the all-or-nothing rule the interests of all grandchildren fail, including that of Charles. See Fig. 9. (The Chapter Introduction explains how to interpret the time line.)

An age contingency also might trigger the all-or-nothing rule:

Example 15.15:   Henry leaves the fund of $50,000 "to the children of Anne who reach age 22." Anne is alive at the time of the gift. The gift is void in its entirety, even if Anne already has children (under age 22 — see text below) at Henry's death, since an afterborn child could reach 22 more than 21 years after the death of all alive at Henry's death.

Note that anything that causes the class to close sufficiently early that no member's interest can vest (and no condition precedent can still be unfulfilled) beyond the perpetuities period will save the class gift from invalidity. In Example 15.14, if Anne were already deceased at the time of Henry's death, the class of children would be physiologically closed; Anne could have no more children; the class of children's issue would close at the death of Elizabeth, Anne's only child and a life in being; and, therefore, the entire gift would be valid. In the case of the age contingency in Example 15.15, the gift would be invalid as to all children if none was yet 22 at Henry's death, but valid as to all if at least one was then 22, since that one would be ready to take, the class would immediately close under the rule of convenience, and no afterborn children would be allowed in.

There are two principal exceptions to the all-or-nothing rule. Both depend on the amount of a share being fixed within the perpetuities period. First, if the gift is per capita, that is, of a stated amount to each member of the class, each member's gift will be analyzed separately for validity.

Example 15.16:   Henry leaves a gift of "$1,000 to each child of Anne, whenever born, who reaches age 22." This gift would be analyzed separately as to those children alive at Henry's death (valid) and those as yet unborn (void). (The phrase "whenever born" is necessary to avoid the special class closing rule for per capita gifts — see *Closing of a Class.*)

The second exception is for a gift to so-called **subclasses**.

Example 15.17:   Henry leaves a gift of $50,000, "income to Anne for life, then the income to Anne's children for their lives, and on the death of each child to pay the percentage of principal equal to that child's share of income to his or her issue in fee." The gift to the issue is actually several separate class gifts. Each child's issue represents a class (or "subclass") independent of the others and is analyzed separately for violation of the Rule Against Perpetuities.

Unlike the situation in which the entire fund is distributed among all the children's issue at the death of the last surviving child, in Example 15.17 each child's share of principal is a separate fund to be divided upon the death of each among the "subclass" of his or her issue. The number and size of the subclasses' shares would be fixed at the death of Anne — not at the death of the last surviving child, who might not have been alive at Henry's death. Therefore each subclass is considered separately for purposes of the Rule Against Perpetuities: Gifts to issue of children alive at Henry's death would be valid; gifts to issue of afterborn children would be void.

As indicated, in both the per capita and the subclass exceptions the shares of some persons will vest indefeasibly within the perpetuities period, even if the shares of others will not. We do not have to await an event (such as the birth of another grandchild) that may occur beyond the period in order to know the shares of the entire class. This is what justifies, in theory, the exceptional treatment of these two cases.

Splitting Contingencies

Expressly conditioning a gift on two alternative events, one being valid under the Rule Against Perpetuities and the other being invalid. The valid condition will be enforced. (These are sometimes called **alternative gifts**.)

Example 15.18: Henry leaves Whitehall "to Elizabeth, but if she has no children, or if no child of hers ever graduates from college, to Mary." Elizabeth is alive at Henry's death. Mary's gift is good under the first condition (as it will be fulfilled or not by Elizabeth's death), but not under the second (as Elizabeth, after Henry's death, could have a child who graduates more than 21 years after Elizabeth's death). If Elizabeth dies without children, Mary will take; the second condition will be stricken as violating the Rule.

If, however, the contingencies are not expressly split but are stated together, under this rule they both will be invalid. Suppose the gift in Example 15.18 were worded "to Elizabeth, but if no child of hers graduates from college, then to Mary." The effect of the wording is really the same; but because Henry did not himself split the contingencies, traditionally a court will not do so for him and Mary's interest will fail, whether Elizabeth dies with or without children.

Second-Look Doctrine

A rule permitting the consideration of circumstances existing at the time of the exercise of a power of appointment for purposes of the Rule Against Perpetuities, although the transfer is presumed to have occurred and the perpetuities period to have begun at the time of the power's creation.

When considering whether exercise of a power of appointment violates the Rule Against Perpetuities, general inter vivos powers are treated differently from general testamentary and all special powers. For general inter vivos powers, the period of the Rule is deemed to begin at the time of

Figure 10

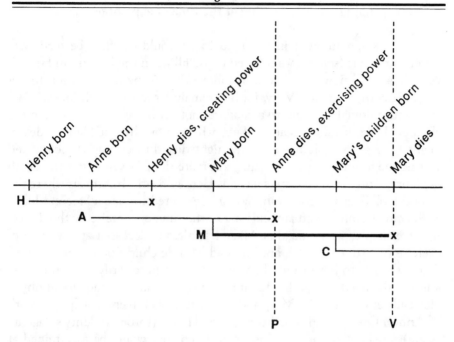

exercise, largely following the theory that such powers are the equivalent for most purposes of outright ownership by the donee. For general testamentary and all special powers, the perpetuities period begins upon creation of the power, as if the donee were merely acting as an agent of the donor. (See *Perpetuities Period; Relation Back Doctrine*.)

Example 15.19: Henry by will creates a life estate and a *general inter vivos* power in Anne, and she then exercises it by will, appointing "to my daughter Mary for life, remainder to her children who survive me or are born after my death." The interest in the children is valid even if we assume that Mary survives Anne by more than 21 years but was not yet alive at the death of Henry. The perpetuities period begins at the time of exercise (Anne's death), when Mary was already alive, and all of Mary's children will be born within Mary's lifetime. See Fig. 10. (The Chapter Introduction explains how to interpret the time line.)

Example 15.20: Henry by will creates a life estate and a *special* (or *testamentary*, whether general or special) power in Anne, and she then exercises it by will, appointing "to my daughter, Mary, for life, remainder to her children who survive me or are born after my death." The period would begin at the death of the donor Henry, when the interest was created. The appointment might be valid or invalid, depending on facts existing at the time of appointment.

Anne's appointment in Example 15.20 would in effect be read back into Henry's gift (sometimes referred to as "filling in the blanks" in Henry's will). That will now would read as follows: "to Anne for life, then to her [as yet unborn] daughter, Mary, for life, remainder to Mary's children." (We ignore the anomaly of a gift to a daughter not yet born.) The interest in the children looks invalid because Mary, who is not alive at Henry's death, might have a child, John, and she might die, thus closing the class and vesting the interest indefeasibly in John more than 21 years after the death of Henry, Anne, and all others alive at Henry's death. But this is where the second-look doctrine comes in: We are permitted to take a "second look" at the circumstances actually existing at the time of exercise by the donee. If, for example, we found that Mary was already deceased at the time of exercise (at Anne's death), and she had left one child, John, who survived Anne, the gift to John would be valid. It would necessarily vest on its creation at the death of the life tenant, Anne (the class having closed physiologically at the death of Mary and by the rule of convenience at the death of Anne). On "second look" the gift by Henry (through Henry's "agent" Anne) turns out to be to a class of children that would be ascertained at the death of a life in being, Anne. Figs. 11 and 12 illustrate how the gift that was invalid because of hypothetical events becomes valid after a second look at actual events.

Note that in Fig. 12 Anne's life line extends from the beginning of the perpetuities period (Henry's death) to the vesting of the interest (Anne's death), making Anne a validating life.

E.   AVOIDANCE AND REFORM

A drafter can avoid violating the Rule Against Perpetuities in two ways: (1) by drafting only provisions that comply with the Rule, or (2) by including an extra provision (a "saving clause") to take care of any accidental failures to do so. In fact, in most instances a drafter should employ *both* methods, learning the Rule well enough to avoid its prohibitions but including a saving clause because, after all, "nobody's perfect." Even if a drafter has taken neither step, however, many states have adopted legislation intended to decrease or eliminate the possibility of a violation of the Rule or, at least, to mitigate the consequences of a violation. These "reform" statutes range from outright abolition of the Rule, to "waiting to see" whether there is in fact a violation, to granting courts the power to change the provisions of a gift so as to eliminate the offending portion. This section discusses all these alternatives, most of which can, and do, coexist.

Figure 11. Invalid (hypothetical events):

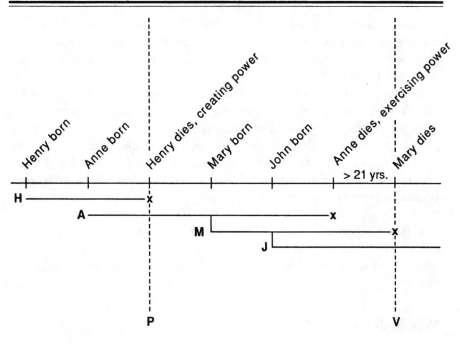

Figure 12. Valid (actual events on "second look"):

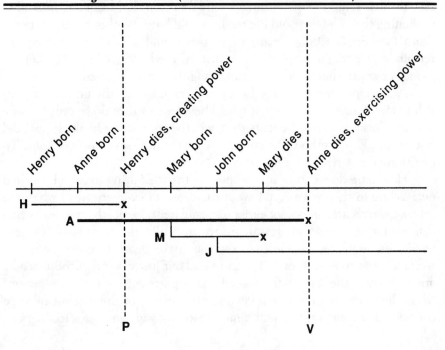

Perpetuities Saving Clause

A clause (sometimes called a "savings clause") in a trust or other document of transfer, operative only if some part of the disposition violates the Rule Against Perpetuities, that directs the disposition of the offending interest in such a manner as to prevent such violation. Typically it directs that if the trust has not yet terminated 21 years after the death of some person alive at the trust's effective date (a named person or perhaps any surviving beneficiary who was then alive), the trust shall then terminate and be distributed in some appropriate fashion (perhaps to the then-income beneficiaries in proportion to their shares of income). Such a clause often is considered a standard "boilerplate" item in any well-drafted document that creates future interests because it prevents inadvertent invalidation of the transferor's intended disposition.

Absent such a clause, a disposition that violates the Rule either will fail or will be subject to whatever "reform" measure the jurisdiction has adopted, which may not be the alternative that the transferor would have preferred.

Wait-and-See Doctrine

One of the principal modes (together with cy pres) of reform of the Rule Against Perpetuities. Under wait-and-see, it is not presumed (as it is under the common-law Rule) that anything that possibly could happen to cause an interest to vest outside of the perpetuities period will happen. Instead, we "wait and see" if those remote possibilities actually do occur. For example, instead of presuming that a 94-year-old life tenant could have another child before her death (see *Fertile Octogenarian*) when this would invalidate a subsequent remainder, we might simply "wait" until she died, to "see" that she did not in fact have another child, thus validating the future interest.

Adoption of wait-and-see by a jurisdiction avoids the unnecessary invalidation of many interests that would have been struck down only because of some possible series of events that, whether remote or likely, in fact did not occur. This method of reform, however, raises several objections. To mention (if not resolve) a few:

How long do we wait, and whose are the measuring lives to be waited out? While in theory we could await the death of everyone alive when the interest was created, it is a lot easier to postulate those deaths en masse when demonstrating why an interest might theoretically violate the Rule (for example: "Y might have a child 22 years after the death of everyone in the world alive at the death of X") than to find out just who all of those people are and when the last of them died. As a practical matter, only persons whose lives are in some way related to the vesting of the interest need be considered at common law, and some versions of wait-and-see select persons from this group as the measuring lives. Other versions (such as the Restatement of Property) utilize some group of persons related to the subject property but not necessarily to vesting. Some statutes do not mention the measuring lives, leaving this problem to the courts. The **Uniform Statutory Rule Against Perpetuities,** adopted by several states and the Uniform Probate Code, establishes a 90-year waiting period "in gross" and dependent on no lives at all: Every interest has 90 years from its creation in which to vest and be valid or terminate. See UPC 2-901.

Another criticism of wait-and-see is that it delays a decision on the validity of the interest until the end of the chosen waiting period, 90 years in the case of the Uniform Act. Unlike cy pres, if there is a theoretical violation, the matter cannot be definitively resolved at the time of the initial transfer.

Many wait-and-see statutes, including the Uniform Act and the Restatement, combine the theory with a "delayed" version of cy pres. If, at the end of the waiting period, it is seen that the interest would indeed violate the common-law Rule, cy pres is applied and the gift is reformed to the closest possible alternative that does not violate the Rule. Thus the Uniform Act first seeks to validate an interest under the common-law Rule or the 90-year waiting period; it then mandates reformation of any interests that still require it. See UPC 2-903.

Cy Pres

A reform of the Rule Against Perpetuities under which a court modifies ("reforms") provisions in a transfer that, left unmodified, would violate the Rule. The doctrine, usually pronounced to rhyme with "see pray" (or sometimes "sigh pray"), literally means "as near as," and that is what the court is enjoined to achieve: a modification that comes as near as possible to the original intent of the transferor but still avoids violation of the Rule.

Many jurisdictions that have adopted the "wait-and-see" version of reform of the Rule also have adopted a delayed version of cy pres: If, having waited, we see that the contingency that would violate the Rule has indeed come to pass, the court will at that time modify the gift to avoid violation. See, *e.g.,* UPC 2-903. Other jurisdictions employ cy pres immediately, without "waiting."

Example 15.21:   Henry leaves Whitehall in trust "to Catherine for life, remainder to her first child to reach age 30." At Henry's death Catherine is alive and has two children, neither yet 30 years old. Because Catherine could have more children, and Catherine and the two older children could die more than 21 years before an afterborn child reaches 30, the remainder is void at common law. A court that applies cy pres, however, will reform the gift to comply with the Rule.

It could, for example, change the language to "the first child of Catherine, living at the death of Henry, to reach age 30"; however, this would unnecessarily narrow the class of possible takers. The court could instead lower the age requirement to 21, assuring that Catherine could be a life in being. Or it could do what the drafter should have done: insert a saving clause that would terminate the trust if and when (and only if) the perpetuities limit was reached. This would have the advantage of not disrupting Henry's plan unless it actually turned out to last beyond the perpetuities period.

Cy pres often is said to have an advantage over wait-and-see because it can be applied immediately to make the interests in question clearly valid from the outset. No waiting is necessary. It has a concomitant disadvantage, however, especially if applied by changing the original gift instead of simply adding a saving clause: By not waiting, the court may reform some (perhaps most) transfers that, left alone to await actual events, would not in fact have violated the Rule. Thus the court interferes in, and to some degree violates the intent behind, more transfers than under wait-and-see.

16

Charitable Trusts

A. INTRODUCTION AND OVERVIEW OF CHAPTER

Charitable trusts share most of the characteristics of noncharitable, "private" trusts. However, charitable trusts differ from their private counterparts in important ways, particularly in their purposes and in the consequences of those purposes. This chapter discusses those differences, setting out the elements and operation of charitable trusts and contrasting parallel aspects of noncharitable trusts.

B. DEFINITION AND CHARACTERISTICS OF A CHARITABLE TRUST

A few characteristics of charitable trusts set them apart from noncharitable trusts. These generally follow from the different purposes that a charitable trust serves. In this section those purposes are defined, the unique characteristics of charitable trusts are explained, and their noncharitable equivalents are contrasted.

Charitable Trust

A trust whose purpose primarily benefits the general public or a segment of the public (and thus is a charitable purpose). A charitable trust also may be called a **public trust**. It is in contrast to a **private trust**, the primary purpose of which is to benefit specific persons. Of course, in the process of benefiting the public, a charitable trust may (and probably will) aid and benefit certain individuals; and by providing benefits to individuals, a private trust may indirectly serve the public good, as by keeping people off welfare. Nevertheless, courts endeavor to draw a distinct line between "charitable" and "noncharitable" purposes, and this line can have important implications for the validity and operation of the trust.

Not every benevolent purpose is classified as charitable. (In fact, use of terms such as "benevolent" to describe a trust's purposes may result in its being declared noncharitable.) The usually accepted categories are the relief of poverty, the advancement of education or religion, and the promotion of health or of some governmental purpose. A catchall category encompasses other purposes "beneficial to the community"; its scope largely depends on a particular court's view of the importance and wisdom of the stated purpose. Of course, these categories may well overlap in a given trust.

One general advantage of charitable trusts over private trusts is that they are favored by the law, and courts will go out of their way to uphold them. But the three most important differences are that a valid charitable trust can (and usually must) have indefinite beneficiaries, can have an indefinite duration, and under some circumstances can vest in a charity beyond the period of the Rule Against Perpetuities. (See *Rule Against Perpetuities* later in this chapter.)

It is important to remember that a trust that purports to be "charitable" but fails to satisfy the criteria for such a trust does not automatically fail. It simply is considered — and must meet the usual criteria for — a private trust.

Indefinite Beneficiaries

Beneficiaries of a trust who are not specifically identified or identifiable as those to whom the benefits of the trust must pass. Although it is common to speak of a charitable trust as permitting (or even requiring) "indefinite beneficiaries," this is misleading in that the true ultimate beneficiary of such a trust is the public. In fact, it is for this reason that individual beneficiaries need not be definite: A private trust will fail for lack of definite beneficiaries primarily because no one could enforce it by claiming a right to the benefits (see *Beneficiary (Trust)*); however, since the public is the ultimate beneficiary of a charitable trust, the attorney general of a state can enforce it. Thus a trust for the benefit of "my friends," or even "my friends who are deserving," usually would be too indefinite for anyone to enforce as the beneficiary of a private trust; yet a trust simply "for the poor," with no mention at all of any particular or even class of poor people, would be upheld as a charitable trust, with the trustee free to select the means of relieving poverty, a proper charitable purpose.

A charitable trust not only need not have definite (individual) beneficiaries, but ordinarily it cannot. If a trust is for a specific person or limited group of persons (such as "Peter Piper," or "the Piper family," or even "impoverished members of the Piper family"), a court ordinarily will find that the trust is not charitable because it lacks a sufficient benefit to the general public. Generally, definite charitable beneficiaries are permitted only when, for example, they constitute a large class defined by their need ("to aid the victims of the earthquake of 1906"), they are chosen from a broad class according to criteria that are charitable ("to reward the student with the best paper in estates and trusts each year"), or they are merely among a series of persons who, over time, constitute an indefinite class and whose duties render a public benefit ("to pay the salary of whoever is the Dean of the law school from time to time").

Mixed Trust

A trust whose purposes are both charitable and noncharitable. If such a trust has been or by implication can be separated into distinct parts, one devoted to charitable and the other to noncharitable purposes, a court will determine its validity separately according to the respective rules for the two types of trust. If the trust cannot be so separated (for example, a trust "to be devoted to those charitable and beneficial purposes selected by the trustee," where "beneficial" is construed to include noncharitable purposes), it may fail altogether if it cannot meet the requirements for a private trust.

C. DOCTRINES PARTICULARLY APPLICABLE TO CHARITABLE TRUSTS

Charitable trusts not only have unique characteristics, such as indefinite beneficiaries, but they also are subject to some specific doctrines that do not apply to noncharitable trusts. These doctrines are primarily intended to facilitate the creation and perpetuation of charitable trusts and their beneficial purposes; however, at least one such doctrine, discussed first, is based on the perception that the beneficent nature of a charity can pose a threat to free testation.

Mortmain Statutes

Statutes prohibiting testamentary gifts to charity (including charitable trusts) that exceed a certain percentage of the testator's estate or that are executed within a certain period before the testator's death. First adopted in early England and continuing in only a few states today, these statutes were intended to protect the testator — or, more precisely, the testator's successors — against the possible undue influence of the church and other charitable institutions at a time when the testator might be most susceptible to their pleas. They also were meant to prevent an excessive amount of property from falling into the hands (literally, "dead hand") of such institutions.

A mortmain statute typically nullifies any gift to charity that is made within a certain period (such as 90 days) prior to the testator's death and/ or exceeds a certain fraction (perhaps one-third) of the estate. It also may limit its protection to certain successors of the testator, such as spouse and issue, providing that only they have standing to challenge a gift that violates the statute. Usually the remaining, noncharitable part of an offending will remains valid; where the charitable gift exceeds the maximum allowable percentage, it may be valid up to that amount, with the invalid portion passing to residuary or intestate takers of the estate.

Note that the execution of a codicil within the prohibited period, even if it does otherwise republish the will, does not invalidate a charitable gift if the republished will was originally executed prior to that period.

Rule Against Perpetuities

[For a definition and discussion of the common-law Rule see Chapter 15.]
The Rule Against Perpetuities operates on charitable trusts in the same manner as it does on private trusts, with one significant exception: So long as the interest in question has vested in some charitable beneficiary within the perpetuities period, the fact that it might later be transferred to and vest in some other charitable beneficiary at a time beyond the period does not invalidate the second charity's interest.

Example 16.1: Hyacinth leaves $50,000 in trust for the benefit of the Red Cross (a charitable organization), "but if the Red Cross should ever cease to operate in this state, then to the Sierra Club" (another charitable organization). The contingent interest of the Sierra Club is valid although it may vest beyond lives in being plus 21 years. So long as the gift has vested in some charity (the Red Cross) in time, the law is not concerned that the identity of the charity (or the charitable purpose) might change along the way.

Compare, however, the above example with Example 16.2:

Example 16.2: Hyacinth leaves $50,000 in trust to General Motors Corporation, a noncharitable organization, "but if GM should ever cease to operate, then to the Sierra Club." The gift might possibly vest in charity for the first time beyond the perpetuities period, and thus the Sierra Club's interest would be invalid.

The gift in Example 16.2 would likewise violate the Rule Against Perpetuities if it were made to the Red Cross, with a gift over to GM. The fact that the charity's gift vested in time would not save the contingent interest of GM if it violated the Rule. In other words, the property must vest in time in charity, and once the perpetuities period has passed it must stay vested in charity.

Two related rules are not generally applied to charitable trusts: the rule against the suspension of the power of alienation, and the limitation on the duration of an indestructible trust (see *Claflin Doctrine*).

Cy Pres

The power of a court to vary the dispositive terms of a charitable trust to prevent the trust's failure. A court will apply cy pres (pronounced "see pray," or sometimes "sigh pray") if it finds that the original charitable purpose of the trust has become impossible or impracticable and that behind the narrow specific purpose the settlor had a more general charitable intent.

Although courts vary in how broadly they interpret the requirement of impossibility or impracticability, it is not sufficient that the trust fund could be put to better or more efficient uses than originally contemplated by the settlor.

Example 16.3: Hyacinth makes a charitable gift in trust to State University for the use of its medical school. The school's administration believes (correctly) that the State U. law school is in far greater need of the money and that its use for the law school would be of greater benefit to the community. A court will not apply cy pres to transfer the benefits to the law school. But if the medical school ceases to exist, and if the court finds that the settlor's broader purpose was to benefit professional education at State U., and not just to benefit its medical school, the court has the power to make that transfer.

Note that "cy pres" means "as near as," and the court must attempt to transfer the benefits to a purpose as near to the settlor's original intent as possible. Thus if, in Example 16.3, the settlor's more general purpose was to benefit medical education, the more appropriate transfer of benefits would be to another medical school; if Hyacinth really wished to benefit only the State U. medical school, her alma mater, the court should decline to apply cy pres and should allow the trust to terminate. Because courts tend to favor charitable trusts, however, they often will make every effort to find a general charitable purpose behind the original more particular one.

A mistake often made is to believe that cy pres is a "cure" for an attempt to create a charitable trust that fails for lack of the necessary charitable purpose; in fact, it applies only to *otherwise valid* charitable trusts whose valid charitable purposes cannot be further carried out.

Example 16.4:   Hyacinth makes a gift in trust to educate her son Sheridan at State U. medical school (a private, noncharitable trust). Sheridan then dies (or decides to attend drama school instead) and this renders the trust's stated purpose impossible. The court cannot apply cy pres to transform the trust into a charitable trust for the general benefit of the medical school. And because cy pres does not apply to private trusts at all, the court also generally would not vary the now-impossible terms to benefit some other person or accomplish some other private purpose.

Finally, cy pres should be distinguished from administrative deviation, the process of varying the administrative directives of a trust because of changes in circumstances, which is available for both private and charitable trusts.

17

Fiduciary Administration

A. INTRODUCTION AND OVERVIEW OF CHAPTER

As indicated by its title and its place in Part 2, this chapter concerns fiduciary administration in general, and more particularly administration of a trust by a trustee. Most of what is said applies equally to fiduciaries other than trustees and to relationships other than that of trustee and beneficiary. The discussion is largely in the context of a trust, but where practical any distinction between trust and other fiduciary administration (such as administration of a decedent's estate by a personal representative) has been noted.

After a general discussion of the institution of trust administration, there is extensive coverage of the two complementary concepts of a fiduciary's powers and duties, together with the many doctrines that limit them. In the process can be seen the relationships between powers and duties in general, and the interactions among the various powers and duties themselves.

B. DEFINITION AND CHARACTERISTICS OF ADMINISTRATION

Administration of a Trust

Conservation and management of trust assets by the trustee over the period of the existence of the trust. Generally included are such functions as: taking control of the trust property; taking steps for its preservation and protection; investing it and making it productive; paying expenses and attributing those payments to the various beneficiaries' interests; allocating receipts among and making other payments to the beneficiaries from principal or income; and rendering periodic and final accountings to the beneficiaries and, if required, to the court.

Unlike the personal representative's administration of a decedent's estate, which is intended primarily to collect the estate's assets and distribute them to the beneficiaries of the estate after payment of taxes and creditors' claims, a trustee's administration is a continuing process of preservation, management, and distribution. However, although the purposes of the two offices differ, many of the principles of fiduciary administration apply to both. The personal representative and the trustee both are fiduciaries, and as such they owe similar duties of good faith, loyalty, and due care to their beneficiaries. Therefore, although this chapter focuses on the trustee's office, to the extent that a personal representative performs similar functions most of the discussion will apply to both. (See generally *Administration (Decedent's Estate)*.)

C. POWERS OF THE TRUSTEE

Powers of the Trustee

The functions that a trustee is permitted and enabled to perform, as distinguished from trust duties, which are functions that the trustee must *perform.* Whereas a personal representative has many inherent powers, such as to collect the estate's assets and to pay creditors' claims, a trustee is said to have no powers that are not expressly granted by the settlor, the legislature, or the court, or necessarily implied from the circumstances.

If a power is **mandatory** (or **imperative**), as opposed to merely **discretionary**, it is both a power and a duty. Sometimes the general requirement to perform a function (such as to distribute income periodically) is mandatory, but the manner of its performance (such as to whom to distribute the income) is left to the trustee's discretion. Although a power is discretionary, the trustee not only must exercise that discretion — that is, make a decision whether to act — but must do so in a proper manner. (This is, in effect, a duty not to act in excess of one's powers.) While courts differ somewhat as to the leeway they will allow a trustee who has been given wide discretion, even trust language purporting to grant **absolute discretion** usually will not insulate the trustee against a lack of good faith or a failure to consider — and act in the best interests of — the trust's purposes. If a court finds an **abuse of discretion**, it can order correction of the error, surcharge the trustee, or even remove the trustee from office, just as it could for any other breach of duty.

As indicated, a trustee's powers may be **express** or **implied**. An express power is specifically enumerated in the trust instrument, a court order, or a statute. A power is implied when its existence is necessary or highly desirable for the proper functioning of the trust, and it thus can be inferred that the settlor intended the trustee to exercise it. (Of course, a specific prohibition in the trust instrument would negate any such intent.)

Most trust powers are incidental to, or "attached to," the office of trustee so that they may be exercised by whatever trustee holds the office. Occasionally, however, a power is deemed **personal** to the original trustee and cannot be exercised by a successor, perhaps because of the special relationship or expertise of the named trustee. Courts usually will not consider a power to be personal in the absence of specific language in the trust instrument to that effect.

A trustee generally will be given expressly whatever powers are clearly required to carry out the purposes of the trust, and probably many that are not required but are included "just in case." The list can be quite extensive; typically (but not always) included are powers to buy, mortgage, and sell property, borrow money, pay or settle claims, vote corporate securities, and so forth. As indicated, those not expressly granted may be implied. Statutes like the Uniform Trustees' Powers Act may further extend or elaborate the powers of the trustee and obviate the need to list specific powers in the trust instrument (unless the settlor wishes the trustee to have different or additional powers).

A failure — inadvertent or through lack of foresight — to include a power can tie the trustee's hands in the face of changed circumstances. For example, the trust instrument may neglect or expressly decline to provide for **invasion of corpus** (dipping into the trust's principal to supplement the share of the income beneficiary) or **accumulation of income** (withholding income and adding it to principal). If conditions make either appear necessary, a court might not permit the trustee to deviate from the trust's terms. (See *Administrative Deviation*.) Note that some states limit the power to accumulate income, at least if it is mandatory, to a given period, such as the perpetuities period, or to benefit only certain beneficiaries, such as minors.

Co-trustees of a private trust generally must exercise their powers — must act — unanimously, whereas trustees of a charitable trust may act by majority vote. Trustees may **delegate** some powers but have no power to delegate — that is, they have a duty not to delegate — other powers. Sometimes the distinction is drawn between so-called ministerial acts (such as painting a building), which may be delegated, and discretionary acts (such as deciding whether to purchase or sell the building), which may not. Usually the distinction is not so clear, in which case the trustee may delegate such powers as would a reasonably prudent person in dealing with similar property for the purposes established by the trust. Recent legislation, including the Uniform Trustees' Powers Act, greatly expands the power of a trustee to delegate even clearly discretionary functions.

D.   DUTIES AND LIABILITIES OF THE TRUSTEE

Previous sections have illustrated the scope and power of the trustee's (or other fiduciary's) office. This section examines the other side of that coin, the trustee's duties and responsibilities — or the beneficiaries' rights — as well as potential liability for breach of those duties. Also discussed are the rights and liabilities of certain third parties, such as trust creditors and bona fide purchasers.

Duties of the Trustee (In General)

The functions of a trustee that are mandatory (rather than merely discretionary) and that the trustee must carry out. Failure to perform a duty is a breach of trust. The various duties of a trustee can be extensive and, like trust powers, are subject to enumeration in the trust instrument, a statute, or a court order. (Certain trusts and trustees are subject to special statutes, such as **Regulation 9** of the Comptroller of the Currency, governing national banks, and the Employment Retirement Security Act of 1974 (**ERISA**), controlling qualified retirement plans.) No attempt will be made here to examine all such possibilities. Certain duties, however, are either expressly or implicitly attached to almost every trustee's office by the very nature of trusteeship; these are discussed briefly in the following entries.

Most trust duties are judged according to the same standard of reasonable prudence applied to other aspects of the trustee's office. Almost any of them can be altered or eliminated by direction in the trust instrument. However, **exculpatory** (or "exoneration" or "immunity") **clauses** that purport to relieve a trustee of fundamental duties, such as the duty of loyalty, are generally construed narrowly and upheld only to the extent considered consistent with public policy.

Duties of Loyalty and Impartiality

The duty to act for, and only for, the good of the trust and its beneficiaries and not in the trustee's own personal interest or that of any third person. The duty of loyalty is the overriding duty that informs nearly all other aspects of trusteeship. The duty of loyalty is owed to all the beneficiaries, whose interests often are in conflict; the trustee thus has a duty of impartiality and must avoid actions that favor one beneficiary over another.

Example 17.1:   Patience has transferred both real and personal property to her friend Jane as trustee, income payable to Archibald for life, remainder to Reginald. Once Jane has accepted the office, she has taken upon herself the duties of loyalty and impartiality toward the beneficiaries. She cannot, for example, purchase trust property for her own account (see below) or favor Archibald's life interest over Reginald's remainder by investing only in high income, high risk securities (see *Duty to Make Trust Property Productive; Duty to Diversify Trust Investments; Duty to Allocate Trust Receipts*) unless, of course, the settlor has expressly or implicitly authorized or required her to do so.

Inherent in a trustee's duty of loyalty is a prohibition against **self-dealing** and other forms of **conflict of interest**. A conflict of interest exists whenever the trustee has reason to favor some party other than the beneficiaries; self-dealing exists when the party favored is the trustee.

Example 17.2:   Assume that the trust assets in Example 17.1 include a Coca-Cola bottling plant, which Jane as trustee is empowered to operate, but she already sits on the Board of Directors of rival Pepsi-Cola. Jane has a conflict of interest. If, on the other hand, she purchases the plant from the trust for her own account, she is guilty of self-dealing.

The distinction between self-dealing and other conflicts of interest can be crucial: A transaction in which the trustee has a general conflict of interest is usually justified if it is fair to the beneficiaries and the trustee acted in good faith; if there is also self-dealing, however, under the **no-further-inquiry rule** the trustee is liable for any losses that occur, *regardless of good faith or objective fairness.* Only consent by the beneficiaries after full disclosure of the facts will protect a trustee engaged in self-dealing, and then only if the transaction is also fair and reasonable. Clearly the intent of the law is to remove from the trustee even the temptation of a breach of loyalty. The line between self-dealing and other conflicts of interest is usually clear; sometimes, however, the trustee's conflicting interests are not so clearly personal, and the line is drawn more on the basis of the seriousness of the conflict. Some conflicts of interest that are considered beneficial to the efficient management of the trust, such as a corporate trustee's deposit of trust assets in its own institution, are permitted by modern statutes.

Duty to Take Possession of and Protect Trust Property

The initial duty of a trustee to secure the trust property, whether from the settlor, the settlor's executor, a predecessor trustee, or a third party. This duty, like most of those other than loyalty, pertains to the mechanics of trust management. It may entail a simple assumption of physical possession or some formal transfer of title. Thus Jane, the trustee in Example 17.1, must assure herself that she receives from Patience what she is supposed to, in terms of quantity, value, and so on. She also must take steps to protect and preserve the property; such steps may include keeping the property in repair, insuring it, or putting it in a safe place.

The Uniform Probate Code provides for **registration of trusts**, a new and somewhat controversial procedure that has yet to gain acceptance. See UPC 7-101-105. The trustee files a simple statement concerning the trust with a court in the state of the trust's principal place of administration (which might differ from where the trust was created). Registration is mandatory and gives the court jurisdiction over the trustee and beneficiaries for purposes of administering the trust. It does not increase the court's role in supervising the trust, but it provides a forum should an interested person wish to bring a proceeding relating to trust affairs.

Duty to Segregate and Earmark

*Keeping trust property separate from the trustee's own property (segregation) and labeling it clearly (**earmarking** it) as belonging to the trust (or the equivalent in terms of title or other records), where either is practicable.* This helps to avoid **commingling** (mixing together) of trust and personal assets, either inadvertently or intentionally blurring the lines of ownership. The trustee holds legal title to the trust property but is not the beneficial (equitable) owner; therefore in the trustee's hands the property remains, in effect, "someone else's." Thus if Jane, the trustee in Example 17.1, were in debt and had commingled personal and trust assets, her creditors might attach property that appears to be hers but that actually belongs to the trust.

Example 17.3:   Your mother has entrusted two one-dollar bills to you, one for your use and the other for your little brother. (See *Trusts* and

Example 12.1.) She tells you to keep the dollar bills and any change you get from spending them in different pockets so that when you return with, say, 78 cents, it is clear how much is change from your money (and therefore you can keep) and how much is change from your brother's. If you simply had a pocket full of loose change, it would be too easy for you — purposely or not — to lose track of the "accounts."

Failure to earmark or segregate traditionally rendered the trustee liable for any losses to the funds, regardless of whether such losses were caused by that failure, as a means of penalizing the trustee; more modern rules generally limit liability to losses caused by the breach of duty. (There are a few exceptions to the requirement of segregation, such as for corporate trustees using **common trust funds**, into which are put the assets of more than one trust to gain the benefits of investing larger sums and the economy of reduced investment expenses.)

Duty to Make Trust Property Productive

The duty to manage the trust property in such a way as to produce a reasonable return in the form of income, appreciation of principal, or both. The primary function of most trustees is that of managing trust property for another's benefit, and this entails the duty to deal with the property so as to produce such a benefit.

The basic guideline for trust investment is the **prudent investor** ("prudent man," "prudent person") **rule**, which in effect requires the trustee to invest as would a reasonably prudent investor in the (nonspeculative) management of the investor's own property or, as the standard is more commonly described today, in the management and safeguarding of the property of others. This is an objective standard, with the "reasonable investor" against whom the trustee is judged acting either for personal benefit or for the benefit of others — that is, as a reasonable trustee. Clearly the latter — the investor acting for the benefit of others, which is found in UPC 7-302 — is the more conservative standard, at least if we assume that one generally is (or should be) more careful with others' money than with one's own. In 1991 the Restatement (Third) of Trusts adopted a new standard that avoids the distinction between personal and trust investment, requiring the trustee to act as a prudent investor would, "in light of the purposes, terms, distribution requirements, and other circumstances of the trust." It remains to be seen whether this flexible standard will produce any substantial change in what is considered prudent trust investment.

An earlier standard for investment, which still exists in various forms in many states, is the **legal (or statutory) list**. A legal list sets out certain types of investments (such as obligations of the United States or municipalities) that are either mandatory, in which case only those investments on the list are permitted, or permissive, meaning a trustee may depart from the list but has the burden of justifying that departure. Even if the trustee stays within the list, however, there remains a duty to act prudently in making particular investments. Although early legal lists were quite narrow and conservative in the types of investments they permitted, in recent times most have been expanded to include almost anything a contemporary investor would consider prudent, such as common and preferred stocks; as a result, little practical difference remains between these and more modern "prudent investor" standards.

Duty to Diversify Trust Investments

The duty to invest in more than one, or several, different entities or types of asset, subject to different market forces. It generally would be imprudent to "put all the trust's eggs into one basket" by investing in only one enterprise or one category of asset, and some states impose a specific duty to diversify investments. With the greater breadth permitted by modern rules and statutes, investments can become very diverse indeed. This means, however, that some investments may perform considerably better or worse than others, leading to problems in judging the trustee's overall performance, at least under traditional standards.

In judging the prudence of investments by trustees, the traditional approach has been to evaluate each separate investment on its own merits and according to its individual performance, divorced from the context of the trustee's overall investment strategy. A loss from one investment will not be balanced against a gain from another (sometimes called the **antinetting rule**). It has been argued, however, that because prudent investors diversify their holdings and attempt to balance their portfolios to take into account various market conditions, what may appear "speculative" or otherwise imprudent in isolation may actually provide a proper balance to other and different investments the trustee has made; what seems to be an imprudent "risk" that turned out badly may have been justified by its potential return and an integral part of a prudent overall investment strategy; and the degree of risk may be less important than the degree of **covariance** of portfolio investments — the degree to which the risk of individual investments depends on the same external factors. Recently it has become more common for courts and statutes to consider specific investments in context, and some modern statutes expressly sanction a **total asset management** approach to investment evaluation. The 1991 Restatement (Third) of Trusts explicitly recognizes this need to view investments "not in isolation but in the context of the trust portfolio" and of the overall investment strategy, taking into account suitable degrees of risk. An investment under this standard will be judged not merely by its degree of risk and how well it turned out but by

227

whether its inclusion in the overall trust portfolio was appropriate in the first place.

An important issue that has arisen in recent years and has yet to be resolved is the propriety of so-called **social investment** policies, particularly **disinvestment**, the process of ridding the trust (and avoiding the purchase) of investments in entities that follow policies or practices considered to be socially undesirable (such as companies that manufacture environmentally harmful products). At issue, of course, is whether the standard of a "prudent investor" permits considerations of "values" other than the highest or safest monetary return on investments; and, if it does, which or whose social values a trustee can or must consider in making "social investment" decisions. If taking into account social factors does not interfere with (or even enhances) economic return, the few decisions suggest that no difficulty should arise; but if such considerations are seen as significantly diminishing investment income or safety, they are unlikely to be considered prudent.

Duty to Allocate Trust Receipts

A duty to divide trust receipts in a fair and reasonable manner among the various beneficial interests. This primarily involves determining whether particular receipts should be treated as **principal** or **income**. In general, a trust's principal is simply the original trust res — that which passed to the trustee from the settlor or the settlor's estate — together with any property which replaces or is received in exchange for it (such as cash, corporate bonds, an apartment house, or cash and bonds received in exchange for a trust-owned apartment house). Income is property received for the use of trust principal (such as interest on a bank deposit or a bond, or apartment house rents). Unfortunately, a number of categories of receipts are not so easily allocated to the principal or income accounts.

Allocation is a very complex subject, greatly aided by widespread adoption of the **Uniform Principal and Income Act** (and its Revised version). The Act answers most of the common questions as to allocation, sometimes differently than did case law. An example is a bond bought at a **premium** (more than face value) or **discount** (less than face value). Purchase at a premium favors the income beneficiary because on maturity the trust receives back less than was originally paid, thus diminishing the principal. Purchase at a discount favors the remainderman for the opposite reason: More is received on maturity of the bond than was originally paid for it. Case law generally required allocation to the remainderman of some of the income of a bond bought at a premium to make up for the diminution of principal, but (with seeming illogic) it did not require a similar allocation to the income beneficiary of part of the proceeds on maturity of a discount bond. Under the Uniform Acts, however, no allocation is made in either case, apparently on the theory that over time the two types of investment balance out.

Another common allocation problem concerns corporate dividends. Ordinary cash dividends are clearly income, and most modern statutes (including the Uniform Acts) follow the **Massachusetts rule** that **stock dividends** in the distributing corporation's own stock are allocated to principal. **Stock splits** also are allocated to principal, being only an increase in the number of shares that represent a given ownership interest in the corporation (one who held 10 shares of Coca-Cola worth $100 per share now holds 20 shares worth $50 per share).

Probate (or **administration) income**, earned on the corpus of a testamentary trust during the period of estate administration and before transfer of the corpus to the trustee, generally is allocated to the income beneficiary, even if it is earned in part on residuary funds that ultimately are used to pay administration expenses and so do not become part of the corpus.

The trustee must be sure to avoid (and change if received) any **underproductive investments**. On one hand, if an investment such as a fine painting earns no or too little income as compared with the current market, then the income beneficiary is prejudiced. Even if the painting is certain to appreciate in value over time, such an increase only benefits the remainderman at the life tenant's expense, which is a breach of the trustee's duty of impartiality. On the other hand, **wasting assets** such as patent royalties or mineral rights (also called property subject to **depletion**) can produce relatively high income but in the process constantly deplete the principal, thereby benefitting the life tenant at the expense of the remainderman. Barring express or implied authorization to hold such investments, the trustee may be required to dispose of underproductive property and pay **delayed income** to the income beneficiary out of the receipts, and to dispose of wasting assets or at least apportion their receipts so as to make up for the imbalance between the beneficiaries. (Standard apportionment rules and formulas are set out by statute.)

Finally, mention should be made of the common-law **open mine doctrine** (which has nothing to do with tort liability for falls into exposed mine shafts). Under this doctrine, the income beneficiary of a trust would be entitled to all the receipts of a wasting asset (such as a gold mine) so long as the settlor had begun exploitation of those rights (had "opened the mine") prior to creation of the trust. Usually all receipts would be allocated to principal if exploitation had not yet begun. Statute or case law may abrogate this doctrine in favor of a pro rata apportionment.

Duty to Provide Information and Accountings

The duty to keep the beneficiaries informed of pertinent facts relating to the management and condition of the trust. At the termination of the trust, as well as periodically during its existence, the trustee has a duty to render an account of trust transactions. This may range from a formal accounting submitted to the court after notice and a hearing (usually required only for testamentary trusts) to a very informal accounting directly to the beneficiaries (more common for inter vivos trusts). Generally intermediate accounts are required to be filed periodically, and a final account is required upon termination of the trust. While statutes usually control the timing, method, and content of accountings, trustees often will submit periodic accounts voluntarily to gain approval of actions performed to date. Beneficiaries also can petition the court to order an accounting if one has not otherwise been forthcoming. The Uniform Probate Code requires a trustee to "keep the beneficiaries of the trust reasonably informed" about it. More specifically, it requires an initial written communication to beneficiaries and then the furnishing of information and of annual and final accountings to those beneficiaries who request them. UPC 7-303.

Not only does the accounting inform the beneficiaries of the status of the trust assets and the actions of the trustee respecting them, but in most circumstances it protects the trustee from liability for any actions fairly disclosed in the account to which the beneficiaries have not objected. See UPC 7-307.

Liabilities of the Trustee

A trustee's responsibility to the beneficiaries for any **breach of trust,** *that is, any violation of a trust duty.* To assure payment in the event of breach, the trustee may be required to give a security bond, which obligates a third party (the "bondsman") to pay the trustee's damages. Possible remedies include not only damages or a **surcharge** of the trustee for a loss to the trust but also specific performance of the duty owed, a constructive trust of wrongfully withheld assets, the tracing and recovery of assets improperly transferred, and for some breaches of trust denial of compensation for services or removal from office.

Beneficiaries can be precluded from holding the trustee liable by prior consent to, or subsequent ratification or affirmance of, the transaction or by a formal release of liability. They must, however, have been *sui juris* and aware of all relevant facts and of their legal rights in the transaction. They also will be precluded from suit by the equitable doctrine of laches if they wait an unreasonable time to pursue their remedy.

A trustee may have either **personal liability** to third parties or only **representative liability**.

Example 17.4: Trustee Jane signs a contract with Arthur, a third party, for services to be rendered to the trust. Traditionally she would be personally (individually) liable for any breach of contract, even if the contract terms identify her as a trustee, unless the terms expressly relieve her of personal liability. Likewise she would be personally liable for torts committed against Arthur by her or her agents in the course of her trusteeship. Arthur would proceed against her as if the trust did not exist.

If the contract in Example 17.4 was properly entered into, or if Jane was not personally at fault for the tort, she would be entitled to **indemnification** from the trust assets to the extent they were sufficient to repay her. (Usually Arthur would have to sue Jane personally even if she were entitled to indemnification.)

Under modern statutes such as the Uniform Probate Code, Jane would be personally liable only if the contract were improper or the tort her personal fault; if not, Arthur would sue her in her representative capacity only and collect directly from the trust. See UPC 7-306.

Even at common law, under certain circumstances (seldom clearly defined but generally involving some difficulty in suing a trustee who had a clear right of indemnification) a creditor might be given a **derivative right** to proceed against the trust directly, in effect enforcing the trustee's right of indemnification.

Tracing

A remedy for breach of trust that permits a beneficiary to follow trust assets or their "product" (substituted property) into the hands of the trustee, a successor trustee, or a third person to recover them from the holder. This is also known as the **trust pursuit rule**. The traced assets (or their product) remain the property of the beneficiary, although they have changed form or possession; unless the holder is a bona fide purchaser for value and without notice of the breach of trust, the beneficiary is entitled to their return. (See *Bona Fide Purchaser Rule*.) A beneficiary must elect whether to pursue the traced assets or to sue for damages instead.

If the trustee has used trust assets to pay personal creditors and then has died or become insolvent, it would appear that the trustee's estate has received no net benefit (it now owes the beneficiary instead of the creditor), and there is no trust property or product that can be traced to the trustee's estate. The beneficiary merely has a creditor's claim against the estate. Under the so-called **swollen assets doctrine**, however, some courts have held that the trustee's estate does indeed gain by retaining property that otherwise would have been used to pay the creditor, and recovery is permitted as with traced trust assets.

Where the trustee's payment of a personal or a third party's debt does not permit tracing, the beneficiary is entitled to be **subrogated** to the rights of the creditor so paid; that is, the beneficiary stands in the shoes of the former creditor, with the same remedies as that creditor would have had.

Bona Fide Purchaser Rule

A doctrine that protects one into whose hands trust assets have been transferred in breach of trust, provided that person has purchased the property for value and without notice of the breach. Unless the transferee is such a bona fide purchaser, the beneficiary can recover the assets as a remedy for the breach of trust.

What constitutes "value" is subject to some very complex rules, especially where the consideration given is not a conventional payment of money (for example, the satisfaction of an antecedent debt). Suffice it to say that the term may be much less expansive than those definitions of "value" or "consideration" that apply to general contract law.

Whereas "value" may be defined somewhat narrowly, "notice" often can be defined quite broadly for purposes of this rule. It includes both actual and constructive notice. Any knowledge of facts that would lead a reasonable person to inquire into and then discover the existence of a trust, or the possibility of a breach of trust, will put the transferee on constructive notice of that which such inquiry would have revealed, including the legal effect of the trust's terms.

Some recent legislation greatly lessens the duty of inquiry owed by a person dealing with a trustee, in effect protecting third parties unless they have actual knowledge of a breach of duty.

Master Word List

Uniform Probate Code (1969)

Uniform Probate Code Table